The Ethics of Interrogation

The Ethics of Interrogation

Professional Responsibility in
an Age of Terror

Paul Lauritzen

Thomas
978 281 6430

Georgetown University Press
WASHINGTON, DC

Library of Congress Cataloging-in-Publication Data

Lauritzen, Paul.
    The ethics of interrogation : professional responsibility in an age of terror / Paul Lauritzen.
        p.   cm.
    Includes bibliographical references and index.
    ISBN 978-1-58901-972-0 (pbk. : alk. paper)
    1. Torture—Moral and ethical aspects. 2. Terrorism—Prevention. I. Title.
    HV8593.L383 2013
    174'.9363254—dc23

                                                                 2012037546

15 14 13   9 8 7 6 5 4 3 2   First printing
Printed in the United States of America

For John P. Reeder Jr.,
Mentor and Friend

Contents

Acknowledgments

This book was initially conceived as a project for the Brady Program in Ethics and Civic Life at Northwestern University. I am deeply indebted to the Brady Program and its director, Laurie Zoloth, for the invitation to spend a year at Northwestern working with the students in the Brady Program and conducting research for this volume. I found the Brady students inspiring, and the faculty at Northwestern could not have been more supportive. Special thanks to Debby and Larry Brady for their generosity and vision in establishing a program designed to foster moral leadership for the future. The Brady students were not merely inspiring in a general way; they pushed me to think much more carefully about the meaning of professionalism. The book has the structure it does largely because of the questions posed by students in the course of one memorable class on professional responsibility.

Although the book was conceived in relation to the Brady Program, the foundation for the volume was laid in a seminar that Barney Twiss and I organized, which brought together nine faculty members from the United States and Canada to discuss issues related to the theme, atrocities, humanities, and human rights. I am grateful to the participants in that seminar for the sustained conversation about atrocities and human rights. The participants were Diana Fritz Cates, Simeon Ilesanmi, Travis Kroeker, Hugh LaFollette, June O'Connor, William O'Neill, SJ, John P. Reeder Jr., and Sumner B. Twiss.

I am also grateful to John Carroll University for granting the leave that freed me to work with the Brady Program. John Carroll also supported an additional semester's leave, which allowed me to finish writing the volume. I am especially indebted to Lauren Bowen, Jeanne Colleran, and John Day for supporting the research leave that made the completion of this volume possible.

The list of friends, colleagues, and students who supported this project is long, and at the risk of missing some names, let me publicly thank the following: Jay and Sue Apple, Kathleen Arbuckle, Don Cozzens, Bryan Evans, Amos Guiora, Gillian Halusker, John Kelsay, Andrew Koppelman, John and Deanne Lentz, Susan Long, Jimmy Menkhaus, Kathy Merhar, Phil Metres, Brad Olson, David Ozar, Lieutenant Colonel (ret.) Eric Patterson, Mary Jane Ponyik, Jock Reeder, Tom Schubeck, Jurell Sison, John Spencer, Frank Summers, and Cristie Traina.

I am also extraordinarily fortunate to have a supportive and loving family. My sister-in-law, Diane Hayford, and her husband, Don Hayford, have been like a sister and brother to me. My children, Sam and Julia, are a source of great joy in my life. They are now old enough not just to tell me I'm wrong, but also to tell me why I am wrong. Having to explain and defend the views set out here has made this a much better book. Given my generally sunny disposition, my spouse, Lisa deFilippis, could not have been thrilled when I started a book on interrogation and torture. Fortunately, she really is an optimistic person. Happily for me, she is also my partner of thirty-three years.

Versions of chapters 4 and 9 have been published previously. I am grateful to the *Journal of Religious Ethics* and the journal *Soundings* for permission to use some of that material here.

Introduction

The ethical inheritance of American democracy consists, first of all, in a way of thinking and talking about ethical topics that is implicit in the behavior of ordinary people. Secondly, it also consists in the activity of intellectuals who attempt to make sense of that way of thinking and talking from a reflective, critical point of view.

—Jeffrey Stout, *Democracy and Tradition*, 7

A society entrusts professionals organizationally to pass judgment on their own, which includes the negative tasks of self-regulation and self-discipline and the positive tasks of education, research, and continuing education.

—William F. May, *Beleaguered Rulers*, 13

Toward the end of his book *Democracy and Tradition*, Jeffrey Stout argues that the virtues necessary to sustain traditions of democratic practice in the United States will be sorely tested in the coming years by the struggle against terrorism. Fear and resentment are the enemy of critical self-reflection, and democracy cannot flourish where self-reflection and the virtues that sustain such scrutiny are absent. Yet terrorism is designed precisely to induce fear, and fear can paralyze thought. I agree with Stout on this point, as well as with his contention that we had better be prepared to demand from our leaders and our fellow citizens reasons for actions taken in the "war" against terror, if we are to have any hope of prevailing in this struggle.[1] Fear not only paralyzes thought; it breeds violence and division.

This volume takes seriously Stout's argument that democracy is a tradition in which asking for and being prepared to give ethical reasons for our own and each other's actions is central. You may know a prophet by his fruits, but you will know a democrat by how he reasons in addition to how he behaves. How, then, are Americans doing in critically engaging terrorism with the resources of democracy? In raising this question, I am not asking how the US military is faring in Iraq or Afghanistan. Nor am I questioning how, say, the Department of Homeland Security is doing in preparing to deal with terrorist attacks. Instead, I am asking about something more amorphous, but no less important. How are citizens thinking and reasoning about the struggle against terrorism, and how is this reasoning manifest in their actions?

To make this question more concrete, I will focus on the way the attacks on the United States on September 11, 2001, forced policymakers and others to weigh the competing interests of national security and civil liberties. More specifically still, I will focus on how the question of striking the proper balance was debated when the issue was whether and how detainees could be interrogated. The question of what kind of interrogation was defensible was an issue that engaged a number of professional groups. While there is no easy way to answer the question of how Americans are reasoning about the war on terror, examining the role various professionals (and their organizations) have played in the war on terror provides one bit of evidence. Doctors, lawyers, psychologists, military officers, and other professionals have all been called on to support the war on terror. How they have responded, both as individuals and as groups, is fascinating and merits sustained attention. How they have responded to the question of the limits of appropriate interrogation provides a focus for such attention.

The subtitle of William May's book, *Beleaguered Rulers*, is *The Public Obligation of the Professional*. May argues compellingly that one of the marks of any profession is its moral nature; professionals are public servants who should serve the public good. Because, as May also correctly points out, professionals are expected to pass judgment on their own in relation to norms of professional responsibility, they must reason together in deciding what professional responsibility demands. The professions thus provide a locus for the ethical inheritance of which Stout speaks, and professionals are among the intellectuals who are responsible for maintaining that inheritance through critical self-reflection.

Such a view of the professions has not been much in vogue of late. Instead of this "social-trustee" model of professionalism, one that makes public responsibility an essential feature of professional life, a view of the professions that understands them largely as centers of neutral expertise has come to dominate sociological thinking about professionals. I do not dispute that many professionals have begun to see themselves as "hired guns," whose job it is to do the bidding of those who pay them. But to acknowledge a reality is not to accept that it cannot or should not be otherwise. I believe that professionals should be expected to serve the public good, however difficult it may be to reach agreement about what serves that good.

One of the more interesting insights that emerges from a careful examination of several professions and their activities in the war on terror is that professions may serve to shape character in important ways. This is significant, because in addition to finding Stout's vision of democracy as a tradition that requires the practice of asking for and giving reasons compelling, I think he is right to stress the importance within democracies of inculcating particular dispositions, virtues, and habits of thought that sustain democratic practices. I hope to show that the professions are one place where democratic character traits may take root and that we need to nurture a view of professionals as servants of the common good.[2] As we examine codes of professional conduct in relation to the role of professionals in the war on terror, we will see arguments about the values that professionals ought to embrace in their professional lives as well as about how promotion of the common good requires certain sorts of commitments. These kinds of arguments are crucial to the moral health of democracy, even if they have been largely neglected by social scientists in recent years.

Though this work is not a treatise on professionalism or professional ethics, we nevertheless need some working account of the professions to bring to the chapters that follow. In sketching an account of the professions I have drawn heavily on a number of writers, especially Eliot Freidson and Steven Brint.[3] It may not be the most optimistic note on which to begin a study of professional responsibility in an age of terror, but I fear that Eliot Freidson is correct when he points out that professional responsibility requires attention to the ethical values that sustain the institutions within which professionals work and that Steven Brint is also right that most professionals today are unconcerned by the social ideals with which their professions were historically identified. A companion volume to this one might profitably explore the history that has led to this state of affairs, if such a state of affairs in fact exists. Yet the history of professionalism is not my concern here. Instead, we need to be aware of theoretical models of professionalism or shifts in the nature of professions over time only to the degree that they help us to understand the role of professionals in the war on terror.

There are many fine studies of professions and professionalism. While I have drawn heavily on the works of Freidson and Brint, the work of others, including Andrew Abbott and Magali Larson, has been helpful as well.[4] These authors do not agree with one another, but any full treatment of professionalism must wrestle with their work. Not only do social scientists disagree with one another about how best to understand professionals and their role in society, but social scientists tend to approach the topics very differently from philosophers and ethicists. Among the latter, I have found the work of Michael Davis, Justin Oakley and Dean Cocking, and William May particularly useful.[5]

I will draw on the work of these writers fairly promiscuously. That is, I will not try to reconcile the tensions or contradictions that exist among the various accounts on which I rely, but will instead simply use ideas pragmatically as they help advance the goals of this study. We will certainly encounter points where a fuller discussion of professionalism would be helpful, and these points may suggest a direction or directions for future studies. Still, I plan to engage the literature of professionalism only enough to provide a framework for thinking about the role of psychologists, lawyers, doctors, and military officers in the war on terror. For all the disagreement found in the literature of the professions, no serious theorist would dispute the claim that lawyers, doctors, and psychologists are professionals by any definition of the term. Some may dispute that military officers are professionals, but even limited familiarity with the officer corps in the United States suggests otherwise.

We can begin, then, by providing a working definition of a profession and a sketch of the history of professions in the United States. Any conceivable definition is likely to be contested, and one point of contention is sure to involve whether a profession necessarily incorporates some commitment to the common good. Ethicists tend to define professions in this way, whereas social scientists often demur on this point. Although Michael Davis's definition of a profession has a classical provenance, many social scientists would reject its explicitly moral character. "A profession," he writes, "is a number of individuals in the same occupation voluntarily organized to earn a living by openly serving a certain moral ideal in a morally-permissible way beyond what law, market, and morality would otherwise require."[6] As an ethicist writing about professional responsibility in an age of terror, I find Davis's explicit incorporation of moral ideals as a defining feature of a profession appealing. But there are social scientific accounts of professions that also include a moral component. Consider Eliot Freidson's ideal-typical definition of professionalism. Freidson offers several interdependent elements as constitutive of this ideal type, including a body of theoretically based knowledge, a sheltered position in the labor market, and a credentialing system that requires higher education. But one necessary feature, he writes, is "an ideology that asserts greater commitment to doing good work than to economic gain and to the quality rather than the economic efficiency of work."[7] The claim that professionalism requires a commitment to the common good would almost certainly be the most contested element of Freidson's definition, in part because how professions are conceptualized has changed dramatically in the last forty to fifty years. Steven Brint has captured the shift in paradigms of professionalism in terms of two models, one that dominated roughly from the end of the nineteenth century until the early 1960s, and one that emerged in the 1960s and has become ascendant today. The first he calls "social-trustee" professionalism; the latter, "expert" or "expertise" professionalism.

Brint quotes R. H. Tawney's characterization of professions as an example of social-trustee professionalism. "[Professions uphold] as the criterion of success the end for which the profession, whatever it may be, is carried on, and [subordinate] the inclinations, appetites, and ambitions of individuals to the rules of an organization which has as its object to promote the performance of function."[8] One can hold a social-trustee model of professionalism without embracing such a high-minded conception of self-sacrifice in service of a social good, but the contours of a social-trustee model are clear in the passage. Professions have a higher purpose than promoting the avaricious desires of individuals or market interests in efficiency and productivity. To be sure, under this model professions would display the other elements highlighted by Freidson. They would have special status in the labor force premised on mastery of a complex knowledge base recognized through a system of credentialing that is state sanctioned in collaboration with professional associations. Nevertheless, under the social-trustee model the technical expertise and control over labor markets are understood to be for the purpose of promoting the common good. However much reality departs from the ideal, the ideal is framed morally. This, alas, is not the case with expertise professionalism.

As Brint notes, the idea of professions as in some ways the guardians of the public good did not always sit easily with notions of populist democracy and business entrepreneurship, even when few questioned a social-trustee model. Yet it was not until the early 1960s that this model came under serious assault. Many reasons have been offered for why this was the case, everything from explosive growth in the number of professionals—which in turn fueled concern for individual interests—to the erosion of trust in ruling elites. For our purposes, the causes of this assault are less important than the consequences. The fundamental result was that professions came to be defined almost exclusively in terms of expertise. Brint puts the point this way: "Over the last thirty years, the idea of professions as a status category has become increasingly disconnected from functions perceived to be central to the public welfare and more exclusively connected to the idea of 'expert knowledge.'" Indeed, continues Brint, "powerful social and economic forces have brought the older idea of professionalism linking social purposes and knowledge-based authority close to an end."⁹

I do not dispute Brint's analysis that expertise professionalism has very nearly eclipsed social-trustee professionalism and that the consequence of this is that the professions have lost their souls, to borrow Eliot Freidson's characterization. Yet, as I suggested above, we do not have to accept reality as we find it. Freidson's sketch of the social consequences of expertise professionalism offers a compelling picture of why the complete ascendancy of expertise professionalism should be resisted. In his terms, as the credibility of the voices of professionals is eroded, the power of wealthy elites and the state is strengthened. The irony, of course, is that the charges of elitism and abuse of power have been wielded as a weapon to silence the moral voice of professionals. And there is no denying that professionals have abused their power. Freidson's own work on the medical profession demonstrates that clearly enough.

Nevertheless, something like the social-trustee model of professionalism is worth nurturing. I say "nurturing" and not "recovering" because although it is weakened, the model survives in various professions. As we will see in the chapters to follow, in struggling with the issue of what their role should be in the war on terror, many professionals implicitly embraced a social-trustee model. That is, they sought to reconcile what they were asked to do both with the codes of ethics articulated by their professional associations and with the moral ideals of the professions that stood behind those codes. As a whole, professionals did not just ask whether they were being appropriately compensated and whether they were violating any laws in helping with national security work; they asked whether the work they were called on to do violated values that were essential to their professions.

The distinction between codes of ethics and professional ideals is worth examining a bit more fully before we turn to the debates within particular professions about the role of their members in the war on terror, for we will see this distinction at work repeatedly in the chapters that follow. For example, the two chapters each on law and psychology could be read as divided between these approaches. Freidson has suggested a helpful way of thinking about this distinction by suggesting that one can focus either on "practice ethics" or on "institutional ethics." Although practice ethics are not quite equivalent to codes of professional ethics, such codes typically address the concrete issues that practitioners address in their everyday work lives. These concrete issues that often concern how a practice is financed, managed, and administered are the stuff of practice ethics. By contrast, institutional ethics "are concerned with the moral legitimacy of the policies and institutions that constrain the possibility to practice in a way that benefits others and serves the transcendent value of a discipline."[10]

Freidson suggests that the move toward expertise professionalism has especially hurt the commitment to professional ideals and has thus restricted the ability of professionals to offer a principled moral perspective both "in broad policy-making forums and in the communities where practice takes place."[11] To that claim, I say yes and no. To be sure, there has been erosion in the confidence placed in professionals to act morally, either individually or in groups. But, as we will see in the chapters to follow, many professionals and their associations think of their work in explicitly ethical terms. And those terms are not understood exclusively in relation to practice guidelines or narrow provisions found in codes of ethics.

I hope it will also become clear that we are better off as a society when professions provide a moral voice for assessing public policy in a language not restricted by a limited vocabulary of individual self-interest or market efficiency. As I will argue in chapter 8, the attempt to understand professional behavior narrowly in terms of self-interest is particularly distorting. That is not to say that either individuals or the professional societies that represent them always behaved admirably when asked by the US government to be involved in fighting the war on terror. But both democracy and professional responsibility are messy affairs, and the fact that the issues we will address are not always black-and-white should not lead us to conclude that professional responsibility is impossible in fighting the war on terror.

Debates about what the common good requires have characterized public discussion about how best to pursue the war on terror. Interestingly, those debates have often been most intense among professionals. For this reason, the debates that have erupted over the proper role of professionals in the war on terror tell us both about how professionals themselves understand their public responsibilities and how particular cohorts of our fellow citizens are reasoning (and behaving) in their engagement with terrorism.

The book is divided into two parts. In part I, I examine how two professions, psychology and law, approached the issue of harsh interrogation. By "harsh" interrogation I mean the use of techniques beyond those typically found in criminal-justice interrogations or those traditionally allowed under the relevant military codes. The enhanced interrogation techniques approved by lawyers at the Office of Legal Counsel at the Department of Justice (DOJ) and implemented at Guantánamo Bay, Cuba, are examples. In labeling these as harsh interrogations, I do not mean to suggest that all harsh interrogations are morally problematic. In this, I follow Amos Guiora, who draws a distinction between coercive interrogation and other, morally unacceptable, techniques.[12] In this volume, harsh interrogation will cover both coercive techniques that are acceptable and abusive techniques that are not.

To get a sense of how professionals have conducted debates regarding their responsibilities in the war on terror, I begin in chapters 1 and 2 with an examination of the controversy among psychologists about the role they should play in the interrogation of detainees. Specifically, I take up the intensive debate within the American Psychological Association (APA) over whether its members violated codes of professional conduct by participating in national security–related activities. In particular, there were grave concerns within the APA about psychologists' involvement with Behavioral Science Consultation Teams (so-called biscuit teams [BSCTs]) whose job was to help design interrogation plans that would exploit the psychological vulnerabilities of detainees at Guantánamo Bay. These concerns led the president of the APA to create a task force to examine "psychological ethics and national security." The report of the presidential task force, known as the PENS report, in turn, sparked an ongoing debate within the APA, which continues today.[13]

Chapter 1 examines the work of the task force and shows how both supporters and critics of the involvement of psychologists in national security–related interrogations sought to ground their views in the APA's own Code of Ethics. The report of the task force was very controversial and the critics of the report sought to have its recommendations either withdrawn or significantly revised. Because many of these efforts attempted to show that the task force either misinterpreted or misapplied the APA Code of Ethics, examining the criticism of the report helps us to see how professionals reason together morally. Chapter 1 focuses on the APA code, but it will become clear that the debates surrounding the report and about the role of the APA code do not merely regard what I characterized above as practice ethics. Practice ethics are at stake, but we will see that debates about the PENS report are also arguments regarding institutional ethics; namely, the ideals for which the profession of psychology should stand. Although I seek to be fair to both sides in the debate, in the end, I conclude that the participation of psychologists at Guantánamo Bay threatened core values of the profession of psychology.

Chapter 2 expands the examination of the institutional ethics of psychology to take up the larger question of whether psychologists should be involved in national security–related work at all. Many critics of the involvement of psychologists with BSCTs at Guantánamo Bay have made far more sweeping judgments than that this activity was a violation of professional responsibility. In effect, these critics argued that the values central to the field of psychology are wholly incompatible with the dirty work required by counterintelligence and counterterrorism. I examine the arguments on both sides of this debate. Here, however, I find that the supporters of psychologists' involvement with national security operations have the better arguments. Even if the opponents of the PENS report are right in concluding that psychologists should not be involved with abusive interrogations, it does not follow that psychologists violate the core values of their profession when they use their expertise to support the sometimes distasteful work of counterterrorism. A strong case can be made for the involvement of psychologists in work involving information gathering, intelligence analysis, resource deployment, and information integration, and much of this work is vital to protecting national security.

Although I draw normative conclusions in both of the first two chapters, I am more concerned in these chapters with tracking the arguments of professionals in the field of psychology than with defending my own positions on whether psychologists should be involved in national security–related work and, if so, whether that involvement includes participation in harsh interrogations. As word of psychologists' role at Guantánamo Bay and elsewhere came to light, citizens debated whether such a role was appropriate. These debates took place in bars, on talk shows, around dinner tables, and many other places besides. But they also took place among psychologists and within the associations that represent and regulate the profession of psychology. The fact that much of the debate among psychologists took place publicly is a good thing. The public nature of the debate allows us a window on how some of our fellow citizens are reasoning about the war on terror. It also allows us to acknowledge professions as an important site of moral discourse.

I pursue a further excavation of such a site in chapter 3, where I turn to examine the role of attorneys in harsh interrogations. The debate among psychologists might not have occurred at all had lawyers not determined that enhanced interrogation techniques (EITs) were legal. Thus, in chapter 3, I explore the role of attorneys in authorizing EITs. The outline of this story is probably familiar to most readers. Attorneys at the DOJ were asked by the White House and by the CIA to determine whether particular interrogation techniques violated US law. The memoranda prepared by the Office of Legal Counsel, the office within the DOJ responsible for such determinations, were eventually leaked to the press and dubbed the "torture memos."[14]

Chapter 3 examines these interrogation memoranda and the debates that erupted within the legal community when they were made public. Like the PENS report, the interrogation memoranda were enormously controversial. Many legal scholars condemned the legal reasoning found in these memoranda as shoddy, disingenuous, and unprofessional. For example, shortly after the memoranda were made public, over one hundred prominent attorneys sent a letter to President George W. Bush condemning the authors, John Yoo and Jay Bybee, for failing to meet their professional obligations.[15] And within several months of the public release of the memoranda, the Office of Professional Responsibility (OPR) in the DOJ opened an investigation into the work of Yoo and Bybee to determine whether they were guilty of professional misconduct.[16]

Examining the analysis of the OPR in reviewing the work of Yoo and Bybee, like examining the APA's review of the work of military psychologists, provides insight into how a profession approaches a conflict that pits competing professional values against one another. Attending to the response within the DOJ to the work of Yoo and Bybee thus gives us an additional look at mechanisms of professional accountability, in this case, at the level of an institutional review that incorporates both general norms of professional conduct and values specific to a particular institution.

The review of institutional-level assessment is supplemented in chapter 3 by an examination of a decidedly noninstitutional review, though one admittedly carried out within an institutional context. Perhaps the most striking individual response to the interrogation memoranda came from Alberto Mora, the general counsel of the navy during the time that the memoranda were being operationalized, and I examine Mora's reasoning in seeking to block the use of EITs after they had been authorized by the legal analysis of Yoo and Bybee.[17] Mora was doubtful that the conclusions of Yoo and Bybee that EITs are lawful could withstand careful scrutiny. Yet, even if a narrow justification can be found for EITs, an attorney who is acting responsibly in offering advice on the legality of EITs must, Mora argued, consider the broader implications of authorizing such techniques. He or she must ask whether the mistreatment of detainees that such EITs would allow is not "contrary to American values."

As we will see, the basic problem according to Mora is that even if one wanted to authorize harsh interrogations, to do so would profoundly alter the relationship between the law and the character of the military, because the law is a school for character. Military training inculcates virtues and respect for the rule of law, and the rule of law in turn shapes military values. To authorize the military to conduct abusive interrogations is to undermine military training. Mora thus helps us to see that the range of considerations to which we ought to attend in asking about the legality of harsh interrogations is much broader than we might originally imagine. Professional responsibility involves more than staying within a prescribed set of guidelines in the conduct of one's labors. In the case of the profession of law, professional responsibility means asking whether a legal professional can defend an interpretation of the law that appears profoundly at odds with the values the law is meant to serve.

In chapter 4, I turn to consider the broader debate to which Mora's reasoning directs us. Specifically, I examine some of the arguments in the legal literature about whether abusive interrogations are fundamentally incompatible with the rule of law. One of the best examples of a sustained argument on this issue is found in the work of Alan Dershowitz. Chapter 4 takes up Dershowitz's argument that the United States should develop a system for granting "torture warrants" in cases where known terrorists have information that—if available to the appropriate authorities—could save many innocent lives.[18] Dershowitz's proposal is fascinating, in part because he vigorously defends his proposal by appealing to core democratic values. According to Dershowitz, because leaders of democratic regimes have a strict obligation to safeguard their citizens' lives as well as to promote human rights, in a situation where these two commitments cannot be met simultaneously, they will confront a tragic choice. Dershowitz insists that this is precisely the situation confronting political leaders who face a "ticking bomb" scenario. In the face of a terrorist threat where they cannot both protect innocent life and uphold human rights commitments, Dershowitz argues that political leaders must safeguard innocent life. But they must do so transparently, in order to insure the accountability that is central to the sort of oversight that citizens of democratic societies must exercise. If human rights cannot always be fully upheld, that is simply the price of responding to extremism.

Dershowitz's defense of the idea of torture warrants has generated a substantial literature, some of which is taken up in chapter 4. What is perhaps most interesting about the best of the responses to Dershowitz is that they tend to draw a connection between the rule of law and the formation of character and the commitment to values Mora sought to highlight. Jeremy Waldron, for example, argues that there is "an enduring connection between the spirit of law and respect for human dignity" that is severed when torture is legalized. While force and coercion are intrinsic to the nature of law, a prohibition against torture symbolizes the recognition that law should not compel compliance by reducing human beings to "a quivering mass of 'bestial, desperate terror.'"[19]

Indeed, if Dershowitz's critics are united by a common conviction it is that the proper functioning of the rule of law is undermined when the core values embedded in the law, values like avoiding brutality, condemning tyranny, and rejecting arbitrary detention, are threatened by a practice that, by its nature, works brutally and tyrannically and is unlikely to be contained within neat legal categories. To explore the debate between Dershowitz and his critics is thus to attend to another contested site in the debate about professional responsibility in an age of terror.

If part I is largely descriptive in its examination of what precisely a select group of professionals did in relation to harsh interrogation and how other professionals evaluated their actions, part II takes a normative turn. Chapter 5, for example, examines another group of professionals—namely, physicians—but this examination is meant to facilitate an exploration of the relationship between professional roles and moral responsibility. Following Arthur Applbaum, I argue that we should adopt a view of professional responsibility that can be characterized as practice positivism.[20] I suggest that while there is no "essential" or metaphysical nature of doctoring, by adopting a code of ethics physicians can moralize their profession by aligning medical practice with moral commitments. Professional practice expectations and moral commitments do not have to align, which is one reason it is important continually to monitor professional practice. If practices are what they are and not necessarily what they ought to be, then professionals who value the moral commitments embedded in practice codes have good reason to enforce the codes as a means of maintaining professional identity and integrity.

Chapter 6 develops this point further by examining the system of licensing that regulates professional life in the United States. We discover there that, just as there are two primary views of professionalism, there are two main views of licensing, the public interest model and what is sometimes referred to as the "capture" model. Consistent with my emphasis on a social-trustee model of professionalism, I argue that a public interest model of licensing is the best for serving democratic ideals of transparency and accountability. Chapter 6 thus highlights efforts to hold professionals accountable for their actions in the war on terror. We examine, for example, the work that has been done to bring psychologists who participated in abusive interrogation before state disciplinary boards in the hope that they would be stripped of their licenses. We also attend to efforts to pass state law that would make it easier to discipline professionals who participated in abusive interrogations.

In some ways, chapters 1 through 6 focus primarily on what I earlier referred to as practice ethics, as opposed to institutional ethics, for in those chapters the focus is upon the codes that function to regulate professional practice in the fields of psychology, law, and medicine. In chapter 7, I turn to the goals and value commitments that constitute the realm of institutional ethics. In turning to examine the values that stand behind the codes of professional ethics, we explore the way professions and the codes they adopt shape habits of mind and heart in ways that explain why it is appropriate to speak of the virtuous professional. Chapter 7 thus explores the relationship between virtue theory and the professions. Drawing on the account of the virtues and professional roles developed by Justin Oakley and Dean Cocking, I argue that certain goods are centrally important to human flourishing, among them physical and mental health, justice, and the rule of law. Because society has a vested interest in securing these goods, it is appropriate for the state to recognize the professions whose regulative ideals serve these goods. Psychology, law, and medicine are three such professions, and the public's trust in these professions is, for that very reason, extremely important.

The notion of a regulative ideal of a profession is particularly helpful because it draws upon a conception of correctness or excellence that is internalized by professionals in such a way that they conform their motivations and conduct to that standard. Codes of ethics help delineate the standard of excellence and they reflect an effort to specify in practical terms what excellence might require, but they do not exhaust or trump the standard. Ideally, they help shape the character of the professional who seeks to embody a standard of excellence, but, in the end, the code is judged by whether it promotes the ends that a profession is expected to serve.

Professions once spent considerable effort to inculcate virtues that served the regulative ideals that practitioners sought to realize through professional activity. The effort to form character is much less common today in most professions. One profession where it is still central is the military. It is thus particularly interesting that the professional group that most vigorously and consistently opposed abusive interrogation was that of the military. Chapter 8 examines this opposition with an eye to why military professionals were so opposed to the use of EITs at Guantánamo Bay and elsewhere.

One explanation of this military resistance, offered by John Yoo, among others, is that the military found itself in a power struggle with civilian leaders and opposed EITs in an effort to consolidate rather than cede power to civilians. On this account, opposition to EITs is essentially a form of enlightened self-interest and is not grounded in traditional military values. I argue that while the narrative of a power struggle has some merit, it fundamentally misses the centrality of the law of war in the formation of military officers. In particular, I draw on Samuel Huntington's classic account of military professionalism in *The Soldier and the State* to suggest an alternative account of military opposition to EITs. I believe that Huntington's focus on the military professional's code of ethics rooted in custom, tradition, and the spirit of military service captures the motivation for military opposition to EITs far better than the theory of rational self-interest offered by Yoo and others.

In chapter 9, I return to the question of how the United States is doing in responding to terrorism. Drawing on the discussion of the use of interrogation techniques in the war on terror, I suggest that the answer can only be mixed. I draw this conclusion because many of the techniques used at Guantánamo Bay and elsewhere are, in my view, morally impermissible. To draw this conclusion requires stating which techniques are impermissible and why. I take up the issue of impermissibility in chapter 9 and argue that an autonomy-based account of dignity offers a standard by which to judge various interrogation techniques morally. If my claim that many of the techniques that were used at Guantánamo Bay are impermissible is correct, then there is reason to conclude that the professions (and professionals) that facilitated morally impermissible interrogation failed in their professional responsibility to the common good.

Finally, in chapter 10, I consider where arguments regarding counterterrorism stand more than a decade after the attacks of September 11, 2001. Although President Obama reversed course on the use of EITs, there is reason to believe that other questionable counterterrorism techniques have taken their place. Moreover, there are calls for reconsidering the use of EITs. For example, the former head of the National Clandestine Service, Jose Rodriguez, has argued that EITs were crucial in preventing terrorist attacks and should be available for use by the CIA when suspected terrorists are captured. Indeed, Rodriguez argues that repudiating EITs has led to the use of considerably more (morally) questionable counterterrorism practices, such as targeted killing. If you forswear effective interrogation techniques, he argues, killing becomes a more attractive option than capture.

Chapter 10 examines these defenses of EITs and suggests that they are best evaluated in relation to traditions of moral practices associated with the professions. While all of the professions examined in this volume can be useful in the ongoing evaluation of counterterrorism policies and practices, the military profession provides a model of how moral traditions can be brought to bear in assessing counterterrorism.

Although I argue that at least some of the EITs should not be used in the fight against terrorism, I do not think the issues involved are morally unambiguous. I acknowledge, for example, that most supporters of EITs sought to justify their use in terms of appeals to the higher good of national security. This may not provide much consolation to those who believe the rule of law was abandoned after the attacks of September 11, but it should give us grounds for hope. Indeed, I suggest throughout the volume that the response of professional organizations to abusive interrogations is not just a cautionary tale, but also a hopeful one.

Notes

1. I have serious reservations about describing counterterrorist activity as a "war." Ann Mongoven has provided a compelling argument about the danger of war metaphors both in medicine and in characterizing antiterrorist efforts. She writes: "Both the war against disease and the war on terror have proven ethically problematic in legitimating high rates of collateral damage, promoting overmobilization, fostering distorted resource allocation, and undermining democratic process." (See Mongoven, "War on Disease and the War on Terror," 410.) Nevertheless, antiterrorist efforts have been waged as a war, both metaphorically and literally. Thus, I will not hereafter use scare quotes in referring to the war on terror. For a different but equally trenchant critique of war language, see Guiora, *Constitutional Limits*.

2. For a related but very different view of the role of the professions in democracy, see Dzur, *Democratic Professionalism*. Dzur is highly critical of the social-trustee model of professionalism, but nevertheless wishes to adapt aspects of this model to promote participatory democratic practice.

3. Freidson, *Professionalism*; Brint, *In an Age of Experts*.

4. Abbott, *System of Professions*; Larson, *Rise of Professionalism*.

5. Davis, *Profession, Code, and Ethics*; Oakley and Cocking, *Virtue Ethics and Professional Roles*; May, *Beleaguered Rulers*.

6. Davis, *Profession, Code, and Ethics*, 3.

7. Freidson, *Professionalism*, 127.

8. Brint, *In an Age of Experts*, 7.

9. Ibid., 8, 17.

10. Freidson, *Professionalism*, 216.

11. Ibid., 217.

12. Guiora, *Constitutional Limits*, 2.

13. APA (American Psychological Association) Presidential Task Force, *Psychological Ethics and National Security*.

14. The *New York Times* has collected a number of the relevant documents and made them available at the following webpage: "A Guide to the Memos on Torture," *New York Times*, accessed August 15, 2011, www.nytimes.com/ref/international/24MEMO-GUIDE.html.

15. "Lawyers' Statement on Bush Administration's Torture Memos," Office of the City Attorney, City and County of San Francisco, accessed September 4, 2011, www.sfcityattorney.org/Modules/ShowDocument.aspx?documentid=507.

16. "Investigation into the Office of Legal Counsel's Memoranda Concerning Issues Relating to the Central Intelligence Agency's Use of 'Enhanced Interrogation Techniques' on Suspected Terrorists," Office of Professional Responsibility, July 29, 2009, http://judiciary.house.gov/hearings/pdf/OPRFinalReport090729.pdf.

17. Alberto Mora to inspector general, memorandum, Department of the Navy, July 7, 2004, available at the Center for Constitutional Rights website, www.ccrjus tice.org/files/Mora%20memo.pdf.

18. Dershowitz develops his argument in a series of essays: "Should the Ticking Bomb Terrorist Be Tortured?"; "Reply: Torture without Visibility and Accountability Is Worse Than with It"; "Torture Warrant"; and "Tortured Reasoning."

19. Waldron, "Torture and Positive Law," 1727; he is quoting Arendt, *Origins of Totalitarianism*, 441.

20. Applbaum, *Ethics for Adversaries*.

Part I

One

If You Can't Oppose Torture, What Can You Oppose?

Psychologists Confront Coercive Interrogations

Professional societies may indeed have narrow agendas in publishing their ethics. . . . Nonetheless, the public statement of a profession's ethics serves a far wider purpose than mere regulation of its membership. Such public statements establish a voice in the community, provide unification of purpose, recruit community support, and concentrate political power.

> —Philip J. Candilis, "Reply to Schafer: Ethics and State Extremism in Defense of Liberty," 453

If a professional society is unable to take a stand against torture, it is pretty much unable to take a stance against any immoral behavior.

> —Robert Jay Lifton, in Peltz, "Learning from History," 715

If there is an iconic image of the prison abuse scandal at Abu Ghraib, it is that of Satar Jabar standing on a wooden box, his arms extended out to his sides. He is clothed in what appears to be a tattered blanket with a hole cut in the middle so that it can be draped over him like a poncho. Electrodes are attached to fingers on both hands, which are turned outward toward the camera, almost in supplication. An electrode snakes under the blanket, apparently attached to his genitals. He is barefoot and his head is covered with a dark hood.

There are of course other images from Abu Ghraib that are haunting. The pictures of Pfc. Lynndie England dragging an Iraqi man by a leash, of dogs snarling at terrified prisoners, of a perverse pyramid of naked prisoners are chilling. But for a nation that has often identified itself in terms of Christian tradition, it was hard not to see the image of Satar Jabar, the man whose ordeal standing on the box was captured in a photographic still, as a Christ-like figure. It was not a crucifixion, but it resembled one and the searing image could not be ignored.

Indeed, the public revelation of the pictures from Abu Ghraib and the abuses of Iraqi prisoners by American soldiers they depicted were not ignored. The pictures led to investigations of the policies and procedures that facilitated those abuses. From 2004, when the story first broke, through 2012 there have been countless government investigations with reports that run to tens of thousands of pages. Add to this material the reports issued by groups like Human Rights Watch and Physicians for Human Rights, and the government documents that the American Civil Liberties Union obtained through requests filed under the Freedom of Information Act, and there is a small mountain of evidence documenting abuse. One of the common themes in these reports, documents, and investigations concerns the role played by professionals in justifying, participating in, and facilitating the abuse of detainees in the war on terror. Not only did human rights groups raise questions about abuses at Abu Ghraib, they also inquired about alleged abuses at Guantánamo Bay, detention camps in Afghanistan, CIA black sites, and elsewhere.[1] Physicians, psychologists, psychiatrists, nurses, and other health care workers were all implicated in alleged abuses. Lawyers were accused of providing the legal framework that enabled the abuses to occur. Concern about the role of professionals in these abuses in turn led professional associations of physicians, psychiatrists, psychologists, nurses, and others to reflect on the role of their guilds. The American Medical Association, the American Nurses Association, the American Psychiatric Association, and the American Psychological Association (APA) all took stands on whether their members should be involved with coercive interrogations. In addition, some of the most prominent academic lawyers in the country debated the role of attorneys in promoting administration policies that arguably transgressed human rights, and the DOJ launched an inquiry into the role of lawyers within the Office of Legal Counsel in facilitating abusive interrogation.

This chapter and the next focus on the role of the APA and individual psychologists in the war on terror. In examining the role of professionals in the war on terror, it is fitting to begin with psychologists, both because the role of several individual psychologists has been clearly documented and because the APA, one of the largest professional societies in the country, was very active in defending the involvement of psychologists in detention centers.

Indeed, the role of the APA has been enormously contentious among psychologists, and looking at the debates about the role of psychologists and the APA in the war on terror is a good place to begin a careful examination of the public responsibilities of professionals in an age of terror.

To get a sense of the sort of activity that divided the profession of psychology, we can look briefly at the controversy surrounding the work of one military psychologist, Col. Larry James, who was the chief psychologist at Guantánamo Bay, Cuba, in 2003. According to a complaint filed against James in 2010 with the Ohio Board of Psychology, he was responsible for formulating policy on interrogation as well as overseeing interrogation strategies for individual detainees.[2] Although James disputes the claim that he recommended or implemented abusive techniques, the fact that EITs were used is well documented. For example, the report of the Senate Armed Services Committee on the treatment of detainees at Guantánamo Bay quotes from a memo of the commanding officer at Guantánamo, Major General Geoffrey Miller, expressing concern that he was no longer permitted to use EITs that in his view were "essential to mission success." These included the use of isolation facilities, deprivation of light and auditory stimuli, twenty-hour-long interrogation sessions, and other techniques designed to break down the detainees psychologically.[3]

It is also clear that the techniques, apparently designed by psychologists to break down detainees, worked. Reports of detainees released from Guantánamo Bay, as well as records from the prison, suggest that detainees were acutely traumatized. For example, the British detainee Shafiq Rasul described being pressed by interrogators to admit that he was pictured in a video he was repeatedly shown:

> I said it wasn't me but she kept pressing that I should admit it. She was very adamant. She said to me "I've put detainees here in isolation for 12 months and eventually they've broken. You might as well admit it now so that you don't have to stay in isolation". Every time I tried to answer a question she insisted I was lying. She kept going on and on at me, pressuring me, telling me that I was lying, telling me that I should admit it. Eventually I just gave

in and said "okay, it's me". The reason I did this was because of the previous five or six weeks of being held in isolation and being taken to interrogation for hours on end, short shackled and being treated in that way. I was going out of my mind and didn't know what was going on. I was desperate for it to end and therefore eventually I just gave in and admitted to being in the video.[4]

Should psychologists help efforts to break down detainees? Should they help identify phobias that can be used against detainees? Should they use their knowledge about the effects of sleep deprivation or visual and auditory stimulation to construct interrogation plans? These are some of the questions that the profession of psychology confronted when the techniques used at Guantánamo Bay and elsewhere came to light. And, as the complaint against James indicates, many psychologists argued that participating in abusive interrogation techniques was a violation of the APA code of professional ethics. In the case of James, the complaint alleges violations of at least eighteen sections or subsections of the Ohio Revised Code (ORC), and most of those provisions can be directly mapped to sections of the APA Code of Ethics. And in case there is any doubt that the APA code is relevant, the ORC is clear. Section 4732.17(A)(4) states, "Ethics codes and standards for providers promulgated by the 'American Psychological Association,' the 'Canadian Psychological Association,' and other relevant professional groups shall be used as aids in resolving ambiguities that may arise in the interpretation of the rules of professional conduct, except that those rules of professional conduct shall prevail whenever any conflict exists between these rules and any professional association standard."[5] The APA clearly needed to get involved.

The PENS Report

Although there were rumors of psychologists being involved with abusive interrogation techniques prior to 2004, serious debate among psychologists did not emerge in earnest until 2005, when the president and board of directors of the APA established the Psychological Ethics and National Security (PENS) task force to explore the proper role of psychologists involved with interrogating prisoners at Guantánamo Bay and elsewhere. The charge to the committee was to "examine whether our current Ethics Code adequately addresses [the ethical dimensions of psychologists' involvement in national security-related activities], whether the APA provides adequate ethical guidance to psychologists involved in these endeavors, and whether APA should develop policy to address the role of psychologists and psychology in investigations related to national security."[6]

The task force report was issued in June 2005, and a superficial reading of the PENS report would not lead one to expect significant controversy. The task force endorsed both a 1985 joint resolution with the American Psychiatric Association and a 1986 APA resolution against torture. In addition, the report is clear that psychologists are bound by the APA ethics code, even when acting outside traditional health care relationships. Indeed, the first of twelve statements of ethical obligations for psychologists set out in the report is seemingly unequivocal: "Psychologists do not engage in, direct, support, facilitate, or offer training in torture or other cruel, inhuman, or degrading treatment."[7] Why, then, was the report so controversial?

To answer that question we must take a closer look at the report and the twelve statements of obligations it sets out. We must also note that the report not only sets out prohibited activities, but also acceptable ones. At several points, we will need to examine the text of the report in some detail, but we can begin with a thumbnail sketch of the twelve statements of obligations. The statements can be divided in a number of ways, but the following schema is, I think, helpful. According to the task force, psychologists working on national security–related matters either must or must not do the following.

Psychologists *must*

- report acts of torture that they witness
- clarify their professional identity and function where it may be ambiguous
- be mindful of special or unique ethical considerations that may attend their work as consultants to interrogations
- always remember that those being interrogated may not have done anything wrong or may not know the information the interrogator seeks

- make clear the limits of confidentiality
- recognize that they have obligations to those who are not their clients
- consult others when wrestling with ethical questions or dilemmas

Psychologists *must not*

- engage in torture or support, facilitate, or train those who do
- use health care information from medical records to the detriment of an individual's safety or well-being
- violate the laws of the United States
- engage in multiple relationships with detainees—for example, as both health care provider and consultant to an interrogation
- act beyond the scope of their competencies

Dividing the statements of ethical obligations in this way begins to give us a sense of why the PENS report was controversial. If we focus on the list of activities that psychologists must not do, we might well draw the conclusion that psychologists will have almost nothing to do with any sort of coercive interrogation. They must not torture or engage in cruel, inhuman, or degrading treatment; they must not act beyond their competencies, which presumably do not include interrogation for most psychologists; and they must not confuse their relationships with detainees. Psychologists cannot be both consultants to interrogators and clinicians concerned about the mental health needs of detainees.

By contrast, when we attend to the list of activities that psychologists must engage in, it is clear that the task force expects and applauds the involvement of psychologists with interrogations. As the overview of the report puts it, the task force believes "that it is consistent with the APA Ethics Code for psychologists to serve in consultative roles to interrogation and information-gathering processes for national security-related purposes."[8] In this division between what psychologists must not do, which suggests that involvement in interrogation will be minimal, and what psychologists must do, which presupposes extensive engagement that must be constrained morally, lies the explanation for much of the acrimonious debate that has gripped the profession of psychology in recent years.

Responses to the PENS Report

If language like "acrimony" seems strong, the reality is that it may not be strong enough, for critics of the PENS report have been blistering in their responses. Mary Pipher, a psychologist who received two APA Presidential Citations, condemned APA action as complicity in war crimes based on a "heinous policy"; one task force member called the report "platitudinous" and argued that it is just a form of "damage control"; Stephen Soldz, past president of Psychologists for Social Responsibility, accused the APA leadership of "manipulations, distortions and downright lies" in relation to the report.[9] The report and the APA leadership's handling of efforts to strengthen the report's restrictions led to organized protests against the APA, including a movement for members to withhold dues.[10]

What precisely are the objections of critics? One of the best articulations can be found in an essay by Brad Olson, Stephen Soldz, and Martha Davis, published in *Philosophy, Ethics, and Humanities in Medicine* in 2008.[11] On their account, criticisms can be divided roughly into two types: process or policy issues. In terms of process, the main complaint is that the APA leadership filled the committee with psychologists with extensive ties to the Department of Defense, which in turn led to a lack of transparency in task-force deliberations and a failure to address concretely what psychologists should or should not do when involved with detainee interrogations. Indeed, six of the nine voting members of the committee had either been involved with or consulted on detainee interrogations. Although the APA leadership argued that having psychologists with real-life experience with the issues was crucial to an informed and realistic assessment of the role of psychologists in coercive interrogations, critics complained that there was a conflict of interest that biased task-force deliberations.

To be sure, process issues are important—and I will say more about them below—but I want to focus on the substantive policy issues that Olson, Soldz, and Davis raise, for these take us to the core questions of professional responsibility found in the debate among psychologists over the PENS report. One reason this particular critique is so important is that the authors carefully tie their criticisms to the APA Code of Ethics and attempt to show that the task force misapplied or misinterpreted the code. For this reason, the critique illustrates in compelling ways how professionals may demand of their colleagues justifications for their actions in terms of agreed-upon standards of the profession.

The 2002 APA Code of Ethics is the controlling normative document in relation to which both the presidential task force and Olson, Soldz, and Davis make their case.[12] One contested section of the 2002 code is "Principle B: Fidelity and Responsibility." It reads:

> Psychologists establish relationships of trust with those with whom they work. They are aware of their professional and scientific responsibilities to society and to the specific communities in which they work. Psychologists uphold professional standards of conduct, clarify their professional roles and obligations, accept appropriate responsibility for their behavior, and seek to manage conflicts of interest that could lead to exploitation or harm. Psychologists consult with, refer to, or cooperate with other professionals and institutions to the extent needed to serve the best interests of those with whom they work. They are concerned about the ethical compliance of their colleagues' scientific and professional conduct. Psychologists strive to contribute a portion of their professional time for little or no compensation or personal advantage.[13]

According to Olson, Soldz, and Davis, the task force used this principle to ground its commitment to having psychologists participate in national security–related interrogations by emphasizing the statement that psychologists must be "aware of their professional and scientific responsibilities to society" and by understanding the primary responsibility in this context to be "gathering information that can be used in our nation's and other nations' defense."[14] The problem here is twofold: First, there are other responsibilities that psychologists have to society that are arguably more important, including not eroding society's trust in the discipline by allowing its use for narrow political ends. Second, principle B includes much more than this one clause, and the other parts of principle B appear to pull in the opposite direction from where the task force wants to go. For example, Olson, Soldz, and Davis argue that the provision that psychologists should "uphold professional standards of conduct, clarify their professional roles and obligations, accept appropriate responsibility for their behavior, and seek to manage conflicts of interest that could lead to exploitation or harm" directly relates to issues psychologists face when participating in coercive interrogations and would have been difficult to meet given the conditions at Guantánamo Bay.

Moreover, by making a societal responsibility to support national security the cornerstone of the PENS report, the task force reverses the priority given to individual welfare evident throughout the Code of Ethics. In addition, by focusing on a social responsibility to national security, the task force is led to a utilitarian argument that ranks the possibility of harm in the future higher than the actual and immediate harm that will be done to vulnerable detainees if coercive interrogations exploit psychological weaknesses identified by psychologists. The APA Code of Ethics just does not support this set of priorities, say Olson, Soldz, and Davis.

There are also issues with how the task force understands the section titled "Principle A: Beneficence and Nonmaleficence." In the 2002 code, this principle reads:

Psychologists strive to benefit those with whom they work and take care to do no harm. In their professional actions, psychologists seek to safeguard the welfare and rights of those with whom they interact professionally and other affected persons, and the welfare of animal subjects of research. When conflicts occur among psychologists' obligations or concerns, they attempt to resolve these conflicts in a responsible fashion that avoids or minimizes harm. Because psychologists' scientific and professional judgments and actions may affect the lives of others, they are alert to and guard against personal, financial, social, organizational, or political factors that might lead to misuse of their influence. Psychologists strive to be aware of the possible effect of their own physical and mental health on their ability to help those with whom they work.[15]

According to Olson, Soldz, and Davis, the task force focuses more attention on nonmaleficence than on beneficence, and when it does engage the principle of beneficence its discussion is skewed by focusing narrowly on the benefit of psychologists' work to the military or to the abstraction "national security" and not on the benefit (or harm) to the detainees with whom they will be interacting. But this focus is at odds with how the code has historically been applied. Traditionally, the code has been understood to promote the welfare of "the individual or group receiving the psychological service, research attention, or consultation." Thus to apply the code with the understanding that it should first and foremost protect the military or "national security" is "to make a radical shift in the focus of the ethics code, too radical to be considered a traditional or widely accepted interpretation."[16]

There is also a problem created by changes made to the APA Code of Ethics when the 1992 code was revised in 2002. Table 1.1 presents a side-by-side comparison of the controversial section. Arguably, the fact that the APA revised section 1.02 of the code is the heart of the substantive criticism that opponents of the PENS report have lodged against APA actions in response to claims of professional misconduct by psychologists working in national security–related settings. The argument is that by changing the code to allow psychologists to defer to "requirements of the law, regulations, or other governing legal authority," the Ethics Committee opened the door to abuse. It did so, according to this line of argument, because psychologists were no longer required to abide by the APA Code of Ethics; instead, they could violate the code and defend their actions by saying that they were "following orders." As Olson, Soldz, and Davis point out, elsewhere the code indicates that, in a situation of conflict between the law and the code, psychologists may follow the law, but only when doing so does not violate human rights. Specifically, the 2002 code indicates that if psychologists' moral responsibilities conflict with laws or regulations, they should seek to resolve the conflict. If they cannot resolve the conflict, "psychologists may adhere to the requirements of the law, regulations, or other governing authority in keeping with basic principles of human rights."[17]

The problem is that this last qualifying clause, "in keeping with basic principles of human rights," is not found in section 1.02, and section 1.02 is enforceable, whereas the section in which the human rights restriction is found, "Introduction and Applicability," is aspirational only. The upshot, say Olson, Soldz, and Davis, is that "the 2002 Code's enforceable [section] 1.02 condones placing military commands and priorities over the ethical responsibilities of the psychologist."[18]

Many critics of the PENS report believe that the substantive problems with the report are connected to the process issues. For example, the fact that the task force appeared to privilege the commitment to national security over the commitment to benefiting and refraining from harming vulnerable individuals may be related to the fact that the

Table 1.1 Comparison of APA Code of Ethics 1992 vs. 2002

APA Ethical Standards 1992	APA Ethical Standards 2002
1.02 Relationship of Ethics and Law. If psychologists' ethical responsibilities conflict with law, psychologists make known their commitment to the Ethics Code and take steps to resolve the conflict in a responsible manner.	*1.02 Conflicts Between* ~~Relationship of~~ Ethics and Law, *Regulations, or Other Governing Legal Authority.* If psychologists' ethical responsibilities conflict with law, *regulations, or other governing legal authority,* psychologists make known their commitment to the Ethics Code and take steps to resolve the conflict ~~in a responsible manner~~. *If the conflict is unresolvable via such means, psychologists may adhere to the requirements of the law, regulations, or other governing legal authority.*

Source: Adapted from "Redline Comparison of APA Ethical Principles of Psychologists and Code of Conduct, December 1992 and December 2002," APA, accessed January 9, 2013, www.apa.org/ethics/code/92-02codecompare.pdf.

majority of task-force members worked in national security–related positions.

The role and influence of the task-force members with military backgrounds can be seen by consulting the archive of task-force e-mail exchanges. Although the group worked largely in secret, the e-mail list that was created for the committee was recorded and later made public.[19] The printed e-mail correspondence among committee members runs to 219 pages and provides a window on the workings of the group. The e-mail exchanges are striking because the initial deliberations of the task force were framed by its military members, some of whom had actually been involved with interrogations at Guantánamo Bay. These two facts help explain both why the task force appears simply to have assumed from the start that psychologists should be involved and why, from the start, the central question taken up was what psychologists should do when US law conflicts with the APA code.

The e-mail exchange begins with the chair of the task force, Olivia Moorehead-Slaughter, asking Michael Gelles, a military psychologist with the Naval Criminal Investigative Service, to introduce an article he had coauthored on the need "to adapt and interpret the ethical guidelines to a changing role of psychology that was beyond the treatment room and the classroom."[20] The work of the task force thus begins with comments on Gelles's article. Although Gelles has been applauded for his efforts to stop abusive practices he observed at Guantánamo Bay, and although his introductory comments for the task force demonstrate a nuanced appreciation of some of the moral issues facing psychologists working in national security settings, it is nevertheless the case that in these comments Gelles simply assumes that psychologists should work in these settings and that the Code of Ethics may need to be adjusted to provide relevant oversight and guidance. There is no consideration of the possibility that the APA Code of Ethics may actually preclude psychologists from participating in national security–related interrogations or that the task force might at least want to discuss endorsing a ban on the participation of psychologists.

In effect, the starting point for task-force deliberations—set by the psychologists who had participated in interrogations—was not whether psychologists should be involved but how they should be involved and how their involvement could be made consistent with the APA Code of Ethics. It is a very short step from this starting point to the issue of how to negotiate apparent conflicts between psychologists' participation in interrogations and the APA code, and, indeed, it is a step that task-force members took almost immediately. Within a half-dozen e-mail exchanges of Gelles posing his framing statement, Colonel Morgan Banks, the director of the army's Psychological Applications Directorate and a task-force member, defines the central challenge facing the task force to be how to handle "behavior that is legal under U.S. law, but that may violate the APA ethical standards."[21] A few exchanges later, Gerald Koocher, the incoming APA president and an ex officio task-force member, affirms Banks's assessment of the central challenge. Koocher writes, "This is the crux of the matter!"[22]

In retrospect, it is not surprising that the section of the PENS report dealing with section 1.02 of the 2002 APA Code of Ethics was the focus of criticism of the report and of efforts to revise the APA code and, therefore, of the task force's findings. Here, then, the process and substance issues are joined. The fact that the members of the task force that the APA leadership selected were disproportionately psychologists with military backgrounds led to the assumption that psychologists should be involved in interrogations and that the central issue for consideration was negotiating any conflicts with the APA code that might arise from involvement by psychologists. This in turn resulted in section 1.02 of the APA code being perhaps the most important section of the code for task-force deliberations, for, as we saw above, this section addresses conflicts between the code and US law or military orders.

Statement number 4 of the PENS report may thus be the most important section of the document, though the text of the statement is unremarkable at first glance. It reads, "Psychologists do not engage in behaviors that violate the laws of the United States, although psychologists may refuse for ethical reasons to follow laws or orders that are unjust or that violate basic principles of human rights."[23] The problem that emerges upon closer inspection is the difference between the behaviors "psychologists do not engage in" and those that "psychologists may" or may not engage in. Psychologists do not break US law, but they may follow orders that are inconsistent with the APA Code of Ethics and violate basic principles of human rights.

The commentary following statement 4 clearly indicates that it is section 1.02 of the APA code that allows for this slippage between "do not" and "may":

Psychologists do not engage in behaviors that violate the laws of the United States, although psychologists may refuse for ethical reasons to follow laws or orders that are unjust or that violate basic principles of human rights. Psychologists involved in national security-related activities follow all applicable rules and regulations that govern their roles. Over the course of the recent United States military presence in locations such as Afghanistan, Iraq, and Cuba, such rules and regulations have been significantly developed and refined. Psychologists have an ethical responsibility to be informed of, familiar with, and follow the most recent applicable regulations and rules. The task force notes that certain rules and regulations incorporate texts that are fundamental to the treatment of individuals whose liberty has been curtailed, such as the United Nations Convention Against Torture and Other Cruel, Inhuman, or Degrading Treatment or Punishment and the Geneva Convention Relative to the Treatment of Prisoners of War.

The task force notes that psychologists sometimes encounter conflicts between ethics and law. When such conflicts arise, psychologists make known their commitment to the APA Ethics Code and attempt to resolve the conflict in a responsible manner. If the conflict cannot be resolved in this manner, psychologists may adhere to the requirements of the law.

(Ethical Standard 1.02) An ethical reason for psychologists to not follow the law is to act "in keeping with basic principles of human rights" (APA Ethics Code, Introduction and Applicability). The task force encourages psychologists working in this area to review essential human rights documents, such as the United Nations Convention Against Torture and Other Cruel, Inhuman, or Degrading Treatment or Punishment and the Geneva Convention Relative to the Treatment of Prisoners of War.[24]

This statement evinces an understandable concern for psychologists working in national security–related environments in which "rules and regulations have been significantly developed and refined" in ways that arguably pose a conflict between ethics and law. When this happens, the task force appears to say, psychologists, including the psychologists on the task force who have been confronted with just this dilemma, can follow the law and not the Code of Ethics. Why? Because section 1.02 of the code says they can.

The fact that section 1.02 appeared to provide room for psychologists to engage in coercive interrogations that violated at least the spirit of the APA Code of Ethics can be seen from the reaction of critics to the task-force report, as well as in the actions of the APA leadership in response to criticism. Negative reaction to the PENS report was almost immediate. The report was released on July 5, 2005, and the August 6, 2005, issue of the *Lancet* contained a condemnation of the APA position as "grossly unethical" and a "disgrace."[25] This kind of criticism appears to have come as a surprise to task-force members, and the APA leadership has repeatedly contested any interpretation of the report that suggests that the APA sanctions the involvement of psychologists in abusive interrogations.

Indeed, a review of the "Timeline of APA Policies and Actions Related to Detainee Welfare and Professional Ethics in the Context of Interrogation and National Security," a page maintained and regularly updated on the APA website, suggests that the APA has consistently sought to deny what a literal reading of the task-force report would appear to suggest; namely, that psychologists may be involved in coercive interrogations as long as they do not violate US law or the appropriate governing authority.[26]

For example, in approving the task-force report, the Council of Representatives, the APA's governing body, issued a statement at the end of August 2005 that repudiated the idea that psychologists could abuse detainees if they were ordered to do so. The press release issued by the APA at the time highlights this fact:

> Following the recommendations of the task force, the APA Council of Representatives reaffirmed an Association resolution against torture and other cruel, inhuman, or degrading treatment. The Task Force Report prohibits psychologists from any participation whatsoever in such abusive behaviors and places an ethical obligation on psychologists to be alert to and report abusive behaviors to the authorities. The Council of Representatives stated that there are no exceptional circumstances whatsoever, whether induced by a state of war or a threat of war, internal political instability or any other public emergency, that may be invoked as a justification for torture, including the invocation of laws, regulations, or orders.[27]

Given the text of the PENS report, however, critics did not find this statement satisfactory and sought further clarification of the APA position and a change to the Code of Ethics that eliminated the apparent loophole opened by the 2002 changes to section 1.02. The response of the APA leadership was a series of resolutions adopted by the Council of Representatives that progressively restricted any possibility of interpreting APA policy as allowing participation in abusive interrogations. In August 2006, the Council of Representatives passed a resolution acknowledging and affirming principle 2.2 of the UN Convention against Torture and Other Cruel, Inhuman, or Degrading Treatment (CAT), which states that there are no exceptional circumstances, including the invocation of laws, regulations, or orders, that justify torture. In August 2007, the council reaffirmed this commitment to the exceptionless character of the prohibition against torture and specified techniques that it categorically rejected, including "mock executions; water-boarding or any other form of simulated drowning or suffocation; sexual humiliation; rape; cultural or religious humiliation; exploitation of fears, phobias or psychopathology; induced hypothermia; the use of psychotropic drugs or mind-altering substances; hooding; forced nakedness; stress positions; the use of dogs to threaten or intimidate; physical assault including slapping or shaking; exposure to extreme heat or cold; threats of harm or death; isolation; sensory deprivation and over-stimulation; sleep deprivation; or the threatened use of any of the above techniques to an individual or to members of an individual's family."[28]

In addition, the Council of Representatives took a number of steps in the years from 2008 to 2010 to limit the involvement of psychologists in abusive interrogations. The council revised one of its antitorture resolutions to specify the international treaties and agreements applicable to APA policies. It responded to a petition drive from APA members to restrict the settings in which psychologists could be involved in national security–related work. Specifically, the petition prohibited psychologists from working in "settings where persons are held outside of, or in violation of, either International Law (e.g., the UN Convention Against Torture and the Geneva Conventions) or the US Constitution (where appropriate), unless they are working directly for the persons being detained or for an independent third party working to protect human rights."[29] The council moved to make this restriction APA policy in February 2009. Finally, in August 2009, the council directed the APA ethics committee to draft an amendment to section 1.02 to eliminate the so-called Nuremberg defense that allowed psychologists to defend their involvement in abusive interrogations by claiming that they were following orders. In February 2010 the APA ethics code was revised to eliminate the controversial language of section 1.02.

Competing Histories of the PENS Report

Not surprisingly, there are very different accounts of the history I have just sketched. The account offered by the APA leadership is that the various resolutions and clarifications documented on the "Timeline of APA Policies and Actions Related to Detainee Welfare and Professional Ethics in the Context of Interrogation and National Security" are essentially restatements of the policy set out in the PENS report. Among the items listed in this time line are APA responses to articles in the *Lancet*, *Washington Monthly*, and *Vanity Fair*, and a response to an op-ed by Amy Goodman, the host of *Democracy Now*.[30] In each case, the APA claims that critics have misunderstood the PENS report and that the association categorically condemns the involvement of psychologists in torture or cruel, inhuman, and degrading interrogation tactics. In addition, the APA leadership points to the letters it sent to government officials, which are listed on the time line. These include letters to Presidents George W. Bush and Barack Obama, Attorneys General Michael Mukasey and Eric Holder, CIA Directors Michael Hayden and Leon

Panetta, Secretary of Defense Robert Gates, the Senate Select Committee on Intelligence, both the House and Senate Armed Services Committees, the Senate Judiciary Committee, and other government bodies. The general message delivered in these letters is that the APA opposes the involvement of psychologists in abusive practices.

By contrast, the history offered by critics of the PENS report and APA actions in response to allegations of misconduct by psychologists is that the APA undertook a series of grudging concessions to the public outrage that greeted the PENS report and sought to portray APA actions in a positive light, while simultaneously providing cover for psychologists who continued to work with military interrogators at Guantánamo Bay and elsewhere. For example, the Coalition for an Ethical Psychology, a group formed in 2006 with the goal of ending the participation of psychologists in national security–related interrogations, has repeatedly accused the APA leadership of complicity with torture and cruel, inhuman, and degrading treatment of detainees in American custody. In a July 2010 statement, "Reclaiming Our Profession: Psychology Ten Years after 9/11," the coalition accused the APA leadership of casting aside core ethical norms of psychology and then resorting to intimidation to overcome any resistance to policy that allowed psychologists to participate in abusive interrogations.[31]

Similar accusations were made by the coalition in a letter to APA president Carol Goodheart in August 2010. The letter claims that the APA leadership has misrepresented its role "in furthering and protecting the government's 'enhanced interrogation' torture program." Despite the fact that the APA has issued a series of resolutions condemning torture, "it has, in practice, twisted the language of these resolutions and policies to align them with U.S. interrogation policy."[32]

This letter also includes a bill of particulars supporting these allegations. The list includes the following:

- Although a 2008 APA resolution prohibits psychologists from any involvement with interrogations at sites that are in violation of US or international law, the APA has refused to call for psychologists at Guantánamo Bay or Bagram in Afghanistan to be withdrawn, even though the International Committee of the Red Cross has determined that both facilities violate international law.

- Although in 2007 the Council of Representatives supported a resolution specifying techniques that were prohibited, the leadership changed the language of the resolution at the last minute so that prohibited treatment would not be banned outright but only if "used for the purposes of eliciting information in an interrogation process." Moreover, four techniques, "isolation, sensory deprivation and over-stimulation and/or sleep deprivation," were only prohibited if "used in a manner that represents significant pain or suffering or in a manner that a reasonable person would judge to cause lasting harm."

- Although the Council of Representatives passed a resolution condemning psychologists' involvement in "torture, cruel, inhuman, or degrading treatment or punishment," it defined torture and cruel, inhuman, or degrading treatment in terms consistent with the infamous torture memos and not with international law. That is, the definition was not based on CAT, but on the US reservations to CAT—the same source used by Yoo and Bybee in the torture memos to argue that the techniques used at Guantánamo and by the CIA were not torture, cruel, inhuman, or degrading treatment.

- Although the APA has strict conflict-of-interest policies, the APA leadership has continued to appoint psychologists "whose careers and income are beholden to military and/or intelligence agency contracts on every committee and task force responsible for APA ethics policy on interrogations and detention practices since PENS."[33]

What we see in these competing histories of APA action in the PENS report and its aftermath are two fundamentally different narratives of the role of the APA leadership in response to allegations of abuse by psychologists in the war on terror. The story consistently articulated by the Ethics Office of the APA is that, from the start, the association condemned both torture and cruel, inhuman, and degrading treatment of detainees and that psychologists worked to prevent abuse and thereby demonstrated why psychologists should be involved with detainee interrogation. The counternarrative of APA actions offered by the Coalition for an Ethical Psychology, Psychologists for Social Responsibility, and others is that the association's leadership sought to curry favor with the Department of Defense because the military was a source of funding, power, and prestige for the field of psychology. For that reason, the leadership publicly condemned the abuse of detainees but privately and through mechanisms internal to APA bureaucratic structures actually facilitated the abuse.

Although deciding which of the competing narratives is most compatible with the available evidence is important, it is enough now to note that the skirmishes around the PENS report and the actions taken in response to the report were focused on the definitions of torture and cruel, inhuman, or degrading treatment and on what to do if there is conflict between the APA Code of Ethics and US law or the orders given by commanding officers. I will turn to consider some of the issues associated with definitional matters in chapter 3. For the remainder of this chapter, however, I want to dwell a bit more on the matter of apparent departures from the code. It is worth reflecting on the significance of the fact that so much attention has been devoted to whether the code permits certain actions and how to negotiate conflicts with the code, if they arise. In the acrimony found in the competing narratives of APA actions, it is easy to miss the fact that both sides are united in the belief that the APA code is foundational for deciding how psychologists should act in national security–related settings.

In an epigraph to this chapter, I quoted Philip Candilis's observation that the "public statement of a profession's ethics serves a far wider purpose than mere regulation of its membership." The intensity of the debate over the public presentation of the APA's standards for the involvement of psychologists in the interrogation of detainees in the war on terror suggests that Candilis is correct. But it is also the case that the public statement of a profession's ethics serves to regulate the membership of the profession. As I indicated in the introduction, this social-trustee model of professional responsibility is sometimes thought to be quaint and outdated. Yet it is nearly impossible to make sense of the intensity of the debate about APA policy without taking seriously the idea that psychologists, as professionals, are expected to pass judgment on one another in relation to norms internal to the practice of psychology as a profession.

While some sociologists may favor a neutral "expertise-based" conception of professional life, it is clear that many professionals do not. And at least in the case of the profession of psychology, the law supports a social-trustee model. Indeed, one reason that psychologists on both sides of the debate about the PENS report have been so adamant in their interpretations of the APA code is precisely that the profession is regulated by laws that reflect or explicitly follow the APA code. We will see this clearly in chapter 6 when we turn to consider the complaints about military psychologists that have been filed with state boards of psychology that oversee professional licensure in the field.

Conclusion

There can be little question that the role of professionals in American society has undergone change during the past fifty years. As professional services have come to be understood largely in market terms, the social-trustee model of professional life has waned. Many professionals have come to think of themselves largely as hired guns serving only those who pay for their expertise. Yet the social-trustee model survives, at least in part, because the hired-gun model misconstrues how many professionals actually understand their professional responsibilities. Certainly the hired-gun model misconstrues how psychologists have thought about their responsibilities in pursuing the war on terror. The work of the APA presidential task force opened a deep fissure within the field of psychology. But it was not a divide between those who understood psychologists as shrinks for hire, whose only responsibility is to the client/customer, and those who rejected that model. Indeed, those on both sides of the divide believed that the Code of Ethics extended to the work of psychologists qua psychologists, whoever their client might be and whatever expertise psychologists brought to their work. To be sure, the competing interpretations of what the code allowed and prohibited were starkly different. Many within the APA leadership believed that psychologists should have a role in national security–related interrogations, that the code not only allows for such a role but essentially demands it. By contrast, the leadership of the Coalition for an Ethical Psychology and Psychologists for Social Responsibility insisted that the code is better interpreted as underwriting an absolute ban on the involvement of psychologists. It is to the arguments for these normative positions that I next turn. Nevertheless, I hope it is clear, even before turning to these arguments, that what unites supporters and critics of the PENS report may be more important than what divides them; namely, a conception of psychology as a profession that demands of its members adherence to a code of ethics that is binding wherever one works as a psychologist.

Notes

1. "Black sites" refer to secret prisons outside of US territory operated by US government agencies.

2. The complaint against Larry James can be found in Michael Reese, Trudy Bond, Colin Bossen, and Josephine Setzler to Ronald Ross, "Complaint Form— Larry C. James, License No. 6492," July 7, 2010, available on the Harvard Law School Human Rights Program website, www.law.harvard.edu/programs/hrp/documents/Larry_James_6492.pdf.

3. Committee on Armed Services, US Senate, *Inquiry into the Treatment of Detainees in U.S. Custody*, November 20, 2008, www.armed-services.senate.gov/Publications/Detainee%20Report%20Final_April%2022%202009.pdf, 113–14. In his book, *Fixing Hell*, James acknowledges that various abusive techniques were used but disputes that he engaged in them or supported a policy that included such techniques. We will return to the complaints lodged against James and others below. For now, it is enough simply to have a list of the activities in which psychologists may have been asked to engage.

4. "Detention in Afghanistan and Guantánamo Bay," statement of Shafiq Rasul, Asif Iqbal, and Rhuhel Ahmed, last modified July 26, 2004, available on the Center for Constitutional Rights website, http://ccrjustice.org/files/report_tiptonThree.pdf.

5. Ohio Revised Code, sec. 4732.01, "Psychologist Definitions," LAWriter Ohio Laws and Rules, last modified May 14, 2002, http://codes.ohio.gov/orc/4732.

6. APA Presidential Task Force, *Psychological Ethics and National Security* (hereafter, PENS report), 1; bracketed text in the original. Although the task force was established in response to contemporary reports of abuse of detainees by psychologists, this was not the first time the APA had addressed the issue of torture. In 1985, the APA had issued a joint resolution with the American Psychiatric Association condemning torture "wherever it occurs" because "torture victims often suffer from multiple, long-term psychological and physical problems" and because "psychologists are bound to 'respect the dignity and worth of the individual and strive for the preservation and protection of fundamental human rights.'" (The statement can be found on the APA website at www.apa.org/news/press/statements/joint-resolution-against-torture.pdf; accessed August 15, 2011.) Similarly, in 1986, the APA passed a resolution condemning torture and affirmed the UN Declaration and Convention against Torture and Other Cruel, Inhuman, or Degrading

Treatment or Punishment. Nevertheless, in 2005, the board of directors was uncertain whether previous statements by the APA or its Code of Ethics were sufficient to address the role of psychologists in supporting national security in the changed circumstances following the attacks of September 11, 2001. Hence the task force. (Most of the APA documents related to issues of interrogation and torture can be accessed through links at a webpage maintained by the association. That page is available at www.apa.org/news/press/statements/interrogations.aspx; accessed August 18, 2011.)

7. PENS report, 4. The style of APA ethics reports is that of a statement of fact, i.e., "psychologists do not," etc. This should be read as an imperative: psychologists must not . . .

8. PENS report, 1.

9. Mary Pipher, "Acting on Conscience," *Counterpunch*, November 2, 2007, www.counterpunch.org/2007/11/02/acting-on-conscience; Arrigo, "Psychological Torture"; Stephen Soldz, "Protecting the Torturers," *Counterpunch*, September 6, 2006, www.counterpunch.org/2006/09/06/protecting-the-torturers/.

10. A website associated with the movement to withhold dues from the APA can be found here: "Some History and Information about 'WithholdAPADues,'" Psychologists for an Ethical APA, accessed August 18, 2011, www.ethicalapa.com/Join_Withhold.html.

11. Olson, Soldz, and Davis, "Ethics of Interrogation and the American Psychological Association."

12. The text of the 2002 code can be found here: "Ethical Principles of Psychologists and Code of Conduct," APA, last modified October 8, 2002, available on the Pacific Union College website, www.puc.edu/__data/assets/pdf_file/0020/31529/APA-Ethics-Code.pdf. The 2002 code replaced the code from 1992 and was in turn replaced by a revision adopted in 2010. The APA website has links to sites that compare the 2002 version to the 1992 version: "Redline Comparison of APA Ethical Principles of Psychologists and Code of Conduct, December 1992 and December 2002," APA, last modified in 2002, www.apa.org/ethics/code/92-02codecompare.pdf.

13. 2002 APA Code of Ethics, 3.

14. PENS report, 2.

15. 2002 APA Code of Ethics, 3.

16. Olson, Soldz, and Davis, "Ethics of Interrogation," 8.

17. 2002 APA Code of Ethics, 2.

18. Ibid., 9.

19. "Email Messages from the Listserv of the American Psychological Association's Presidential Task Force on Psychological Ethics and National Security: April 22, 2005–June 26, 2006," accessed May 22, 2012, posted by ProPublica at http://s3.amazonaws.com/propublica/assets/docs/pens_listserv.pdf.

20. Ibid., 9.

21. Ibid., 16.

22. Ibid., 25.

23. PENS report, 5.

24. Ibid.

25. Wilks, "Stain on Medical Ethics," 430.

26. "Timeline of APA Policies and Actions Related to Detainee Welfare and Professional Ethics in the Context of Interrogation and National Security," APA, accessed May 22, 2012, www.apa.org/news/press/statements/interrogations.aspx.

27. "APA Council Endorses Ethical Guidelines for Psychologists Participating in National Security-Related Investigations and Interrogations," APA, August 29, 2005, www.apa.org/news/press/releases/2005/08/security.aspx.

28. "Reaffirmation of the American Psychological Association Position against Torture and Other Cruel, Inhuman, or Degrading Treatment or Punishment and Its Application to Individuals Defined in the United States Code as 'Enemy Combatants,'" APA, February 22, 2008, www.apa.org/about/policy/torture.aspx.

29. Minutes of APA Council of Representatives meeting, APA, February 20–22, 2009, accessed May 22, 2012, www.apa.org/about/governance/council/09feb-crminutes.aspx.

30. Wilks, "Stain on Medical Ethics"; Arthur Levine, "Collective Unconscionable: How Psychologists, the Most Liberal of Professionals, Abetted Bush's Torture Policy," *Washington Monthly*, January/February 2007, www.washington monthly.com/features/2007/0701.levine.html; Katherine Eban, "Rorschach and Awe," *Vanity Fair*, July 17, 2007, www.vanityfair.com/politics/features/2007/07/torture200707; Amy Goodman, "The Real Anti-torture President," *Seattle Post-Intelligencer*, April 10, 2008, www.seattlepi.com/local/opinion/article/The-real-anti-torture-president-1269918.php.

31. "Reclaiming Our Profession: Psychology Ten Years after 9/11," Coalition for an Ethical Psychology, July 2010, www.ethicalpsychology.org/resources/reclaiming-our-profession.php.

32. "Coalition Open Letter on APA Complicity in Torture Interrogations," Coalition for an Ethical Psychology, August 11, 2010, www.ethicalpsychology.org/re sources/goodheart-8-11-10.php.

33. Ibid.

Two

What's Wrong with Supporting National Security?

Psychology and the Pursuit of National Security

Rightly understood, professionalism has a civic dimension. The theory of democratic professionalism . . . holds that a number of key professions have civic roles to play in contemporary democracy and that such civic roles both strengthen the legitimacy of professional authority and render that authority more transparent and more vulnerable to public influence.

—Albert W. Dzur, *Democratic Professionalism*, 10

We saw in chapter 1 what a commitment to democratic deliberation looks like in the context of a debate among professionals about their role in serving the common good. At the core of the debate about whether psychologists should be involved with national security–related interrogations was a disagreement about whether the expertise gained through the study of human psychology could be used to design and implement coercive interrogations in the service of safeguarding the common good. For the majority of the members of the PENS task force the answer appeared to be that psychology could serve these ends, even if the means to those ends might sometimes be in tension with the code of ethics in the field. The leadership of the APA also appears to have held this view.

The fight that erupted within the APA demonstrates just how passionate democratic deliberation can be. Charges and countercharges were made, alliances were formed, and strategies for doing battle were devised. That violence did not ensue is perhaps testimony to the power of a code of professional ethics. Although battles were fought, the field of combat was the APA Code of Ethics. As we saw, both sides were constrained by that code, and both sought to interpret the code to support their position. As with all battles, there were winners and losers, and although both sides might dispute this assessment, in my view, the dissenters won.

Perhaps the most compelling piece of evidence supporting this assessment is the shift in rhetoric of one of the central figures in the debate, Gerald Koocher. From external appearances, Koocher is an unlikely warrior. With a boyish face, wire-rimmed glasses, and an ever-present bow tie, Koocher looks more the part of a kindly pediatrician than a tough political insider with an acid pen. Yet Koocher, a past president of the APA and an ex officio member of the PENS task force—he represented the APA Council of Representatives to the committee—was an outspoken advocate for the involvement of psychologists in interrogations, and initially he showed very little regard for constraints of international law. For example, in a notorious post to the PENS e-mail list, Koocher wrote: "I have zero interest in entangling APA with the nebulous, toothless, contradictory, and obfuscatory treaties that comprise 'international law.' Rather, I prefer to see APA take principled stands on policy issues where psychology has some scientific basis for doing so."[1] Nor did he seem inclined to condemn abusive practices alleged to have involved psychologists. Instead, he condemned the allegations. Writing in the "President's Column" in *Monitor on Psychology*, a publication of the APA, Koocher displayed his contempt. He described the opponents of the PENS report as "opportunistic commentators masquerading as scholars." He claimed that when the APA leadership asked for evidence of alleged abuses by mental health professionals, critics provided none. "No data have been forthcoming from these same critics," Koocher wrote, "and no APA members have been linked to unprofessional behaviors. The traditional journalistic dictum of reporting who, what, where and when seems notably absent."[2]

However, by 2009 Koocher appeared to recognize the need for a stronger (and broader) condemnation of interrogation techniques. Ethical standards in the mental health professions, he said, demand that psychologists not engage in either deception or coercion. "Deceptive and coercive interrogation techniques," he wrote, "violate these moral values."[3] From worrying only about whether psychologists may engage in coercive interrogations if they are following orders or not violating US law, Koocher had arrived at a position that "engaging in illegal, inhumane, cruel, degrading, or other torturous practices can never pass as ethically acceptable conduct under any rationale."[4]

Even if I am right that opponents of the PENS report prevailed in demonstrating that the report left too much room for psychologists to engage in abusive practices in national security–related interrogations, and even if the opponents are right that this is exactly what the APA leadership set out to do, the fact is that, in the end, the APA code was mobilized and revised to insure that psychologists could not engage in cruel, inhuman, or degrading interrogation practices and claim to be acting as professional psychologists. Ultimately, no one was prepared to dispute Robert Jay Lifton's observation that "if a professional society is unable to take a stand against torture, it is pretty much unable to take a stand against any immoral behavior."[5]

If Lifton's observation crystallizes one issue that faced the APA as it wrestled with the role of psychologists at Abu Ghraib and Guantánamo Bay, it is not particularly illuminating when we turn to the broader issues here. For it is one thing to claim that psychologists should not plan, implement, or even monitor cruel, inhuman, and degrading forms of interrogation; it is another thing to say that psychologists should not be involved with national security–related counterterrorism work at all. Yet critics of the PENS report have come awfully close to making a categorical moral judgment against any participation by psychologists in interrogations. We have not yet discussed this larger question of whether taking a stand against torture and cruel, inhuman, or degrading treatment also commits one to opposing any role for psychologists in national security–related work. It is to this question that I now turn.

Banning Psychologists from National Security–Related Work?

We can begin our consideration of this question by looking at the position of those who advocate for a national security role for psychologists. A good starting point for this examination is an article by Scott Shumate and Randy Borum, "Psychological Support to Defense Counterintelligence Operations," which provides both the institutional context for the emergence of "national security psychology" and a normative defense of this development.

The field of national security psychology is new and has emerged through the work of military and civilian psychologists who have served as consultants to the counterintelligence (CI) community. Historically, each branch of the military had CI responsibilities for its own branch, but in 2002 the Department of Defense (DOD) created the Counterintelligence Field Activity (CIFA) Agency with responsibilities for coordinating CI throughout all DOD operations. Within this agency there is a Directorate of Behavioral Sciences, which is staffed by a cadre of psychologists and others whose responsibility is to support traditional CI activities. The new agency's commitment to the behavioral sciences is thus substantial, and the need for psychologists, both military and civilian, to work with CIFA has steadily grown.

What precisely do the psychologists within the Directorate of Behavioral Sciences do? Shumate and Borum explicitly discuss four functions that national security psychologists may perform: (1) psychological risk assessment, (2) help in recruiting and training human assets, (3) help in managing the relationship between a case officer and his or her intelligence asset, and (4) consultation on the interrogation of an uncooperative source.

The first of the four, risk assessment, primarily involves screening and monitoring those involved with national security positions. Because employees who work in national security settings or agencies have access to vital intelligence information, it is important that they not be compromised or suffer work-related performance problems from psychological vulnerabilities that could be avoided or ameliorated. In a sense, the services that psychologists perform in this area are like ones they perform in other fields; for example, screening or designing screening tests for any job applicant or providing counseling for employees whose psychological problems are affecting job performance.

If the first function is quite similar to work psychologists perform in other organizations, the next three are fairly distinctive. Almost everyone in the intelligence community agrees that there is a need for greater human intelligence; that is, more agents who have intimate connections with groups that pose a national security threat. Recruiting such agents is thus a high priority, but successful recruitment is psychologically complex. For example, serving as a CI asset is likely to generate a sense of competing identities and conflicting loyalties. How individuals will handle the strain of such conflicts is important, but traditional psychometric tests are not designed to provide useful information in this area. National security psychologists are thus needed to help develop and refine tools for identifying potential recruits who will negotiate the role of intelligence asset successfully.

Once a CI asset is recruited, the relationship of this asset to his or her handler is likely to involve an elaborate dance that a psychologist might help to choreograph. The case officer will need to manage the relationship with careful attention to the credibility of the informant's information, as well as to ongoing threats to which the asset is vulnerable, including psychological threats. According to Shumate and Borum, psychologists can play a crucial role in helping a case officer manage an asset.

Finally, psychologists can play a role in interrogating uncooperative sources. Here Shumate and Borum make clear that they are not talking about the kind of abusive interrogations that were conducted at Guantánamo Bay and elsewhere. Instead, psychologists can use their insight into human behavior and cognitive function to assist with interrogations. And Shumate and Borum are categorical in their assessment that psychologists can assist with interrogations without violating codes of professional ethics. In a memorable formulation, they write, "It is absolutely possible for a trained psychologist to offer assistance with interrogation in an ethical manner."[6]

For example, psychologists can evaluate how a detainee is responding to a particular line of questioning or a particular interviewer. They can provide information about how memory functions and how various stressors may affect memory. In short, psychologists "can draw on the empirical literature bearing on persuasion and interpersonal influence to suggest potential strategies to counter and overcome a source's resistance," and they can offer an assessment of a source's credibility or attempts at deception.[7]

Because passions run deep on the subject of the treatment of detainees at Guantánamo Bay, it is important not to focus too narrowly on this last function of consulting on interrogations, for Shumate and Borum mean to defend a broad mandate for the involvement of psychologists in the war on terror, one that extends not only beyond interrogations but also beyond the other three functions identified in this article. For example, in another article, Shumate and Borum are joined by other counterterrorism professionals in noting the importance of research in behavioral science to counterterrorism efforts. And they call for that research to be "operationally relevant."[8] Although taken from outside the field of counterterrorism strictly speaking, the example they cite for operationally relevant research is instructive.

The example is research conducted by Robert Fein and Bryan Vossekuil that challenged traditional assumptions about those who seek to assassinate public officials.[9] Instead of asking what makes people become assassins—an important question but not one whose answer is necessarily helpful in preventing an imminent assassination threat—Fein and Vossekuil sought to discover whether there were discernible patterns of thinking and behavior that were correlated with actual instances of assassination or assassination attempts that might be used in the effort to prevent attacks. In the study, known as the Exceptional Case Study Project (ECSP), they reviewed the cases of eighty-three persons who had attacked or nearly attacked public officials in the United States over the previous fifty years. Their findings were surprising to many security officials and offered concrete recommendations for assessing and managing threats to public figures. For example, most attackers do not harbor a grievance toward the target, and in fact many consider multiple targets. Also, mental illness does not appear to be a critical factor, and none of those studied had issued a threat to the target prior to the attack.

As Borum et al. point out, the approach adopted in this study of assassinations can be used to study threats to national security, but the research must be driven by the needs of national security professionals and not by questions of general scientific and psychological interest. This point seems obvious enough, but it has a very significant implication. It means that those who conduct the study "must begin with an understanding of the key ultimate questions that end users (e.g., investigators, intelligence analysts, defense, and security decisionmakers, etc.) routinely are required to answer, the threshold decisions they are required to address, and the environment in which that process occurs."[10] The upshot is that those conducting behavioral science research must work closely with security professionals and in settings that may well be morally ambiguous.

Extending the model of the ECSP to address threats to national security allows us to see that the list of functions psychologists may serve in CI and counterterrorism is larger than we surveyed earlier.

Borum and his colleagues list five additional areas in which operationally relevant research could contribute to national security: information gathering, intelligence analysis, resource deployment, identification of intersystem relationships, and information integration. We do not need to go into detail about each of these areas to see that psychologists, and behavioral scientists generally, can contribute to the war on terror by helping to collect, organize, analyze, assess, and disseminate intelligence that may safeguard against attack.

If we now turn to the critics of the PENS report who advocate for a "bright-line prohibition" against psychologists' involvement in interrogation, we note that they face a number of hurdles in making their case. They need to show not only why involvement with interrogation is wrong, but why such involvement is different from the other sorts of involvement that we have just reviewed. Unless critics wish to rule out any role for psychologists in national security activities, they will need, for example, to explain why observing an interrogation in order to provide feedback to an interrogator about a source's behavior is different morally from analyzing the group behavior of a suspected terrorist cell for signs that an attack is imminent. What are the arguments here?

We see an example of the argument for a bright-line prohibition in the article that framed our original discussion of the PENS report in chapter 1. As we saw, Olson, Soldz, and Davis sought to show that abusive interrogations were not compatible with the APA Code of Ethics and that where the task force appeared to suggest otherwise, the committee had misinterpreted or misapplied the code. However, Olson, Soldz, and Davis went further than condemning clearly abusive interrogations; they suggested that a bright line is needed to demarcate unacceptable involvement by psychologists and that the only defensible line is between participation and nonparticipation. They write, "Because the risk of coercion and torture is inherent in these settings, the bright-line position of no psychologist participation in the interrogation process, at least for the time being, takes precedence over our best but highly unrealistic wishes that psychologists are there to minimize harm."[11]

The reasoning here is a classic example of a slippery-slope argument: Although there may be no intrinsic objection to psychologists' involvement with interrogations that are based on, say, rapport-building techniques, the current setting in which interrogations are conducted makes it likely that any form of interrogation will degenerate into abuse. In such circumstances, the argument goes, it is better not to be involved at all. Slippery-slope arguments are, of course, notoriously problematic, but in fairness to Olson, Soldz, and Davis, their argument is not simply that the slide into abusive behavior may occur; it is that such a slide is likely and that there is evidence to that effect to be found in the literature of social psychology.[12] Milgram's well-known obedience studies and Zimbardo's Stanford prison experiment are just two studies that show how easily good people may turn abusive when placed in an abuse-generating context.[13]

In a previously published piece, Olson and Soldz suggested that there are other arguments that support noninvolvement. They make this case in an essay in which they respond to an article that was originally produced by a task force appointed by the Society for the Psychological Study of Social Issues to examine research on interrogation and confessions. The authors of that article, Mark Costanzo, Ellen Gerrity, and M. Brinton Lykes, examined eight different ethics codes for psychologists, drawn from multiple continents, from which they identified five "cross-cutting" principles: (1) respect for the dignity and rights of persons, (2) caring for others and concern for their welfare, (3) competence, (4) integrity, and (5) professional, scientific, and social responsibility.[14]

Olson and Soldz claim that principles (1) and (2) are fundamentally incompatible with psychologists' participation in interrogations. "In even the best of circumstances, it is difficult to believe that psychologists involved in interrogations of alleged terrorists can follow these key ethical maxims."[15] And the settings in which detainees are being interrogated in the war on terror are not the best of circumstances. In the circumstances that prevailed at least through 2007, when their essay was published, it is "virtually inconceivable" that psychologists would respect the dignity of the detainee or safeguard his welfare.

In introducing their argument, Olson and Soldz indicate that they will draw on both ethical considerations and practical knowledge of the actions of the BSCTs at Guantánamo Bay to make their case. The problem with their argument is that it relies almost exclusively on the assumption that because the involvement of psychologists in interrogations at Guantánamo Bay violated both the principles that the APA

Code of Ethics sets out as well as the principles articulated by Costanzo, Gerrity, and Lykes, involvement with interrogation of any sort would also violate this principle. But what is the basis for that assumption?

That such an assumption is mistaken is suggested by the fact that the relevant international human rights conventions do not make this assumption. For example, the Geneva Convention Relative to the Treatment of Prisoners of War anticipates that prisoners will be interrogated, but seeks to set the limits of such interrogations. It thus specifies that "the questioning of prisoners of war shall be carried out in a language which they understand" (art. 17) and that "no physical or mental torture, nor any other form of coercion, may be inflicted on prisoners of war to secure from them information of any kind whatever" (art. 17).[16] The fact that (a) article 14 of the convention specifies that respect for prisoners and their honor must be shown in all circumstances and (b) questioning of prisoners is expected and accepted suggests that the framers of the convention repudiated the assumption that grounds the bright-line prohibition of Olson and Soldz.

At this point, Olson and Soldz face the second obstacle noted above; namely, that if they reject psychologists' participation in interrogations they are logically committed either to condemn other roles for psychologists in national security operations or to show that participation in interrogations is somehow different from these other roles. Unfortunately, the closest they seem to come to distinguishing interrogation of detainees from other activities of psychologists is in disputing the comparison between domestic forensic psychology and foreign intelligence work, a point they make in the essay written with Martha Davis.

They begin by noting that the PENS report seeks to understand the work of psychologists in national security settings by comparing it with the work of psychologists in other contexts. They note the report's contention that "it is consistent with the APA Ethics Code for psychologists to serve in consultative roles to interrogation . . . as psychologists have a long-standing tradition of doing in other law enforcement contexts."[17] Admittedly, there is a long tradition of forensic psychologists interviewing criminal suspects for assessment of mental status or general fitness to stand trial, as there is a tradition of psychologists conducting research on detecting deception and other aspects of criminal investigations.

Yet, according to Olson and Soldz, this comparison of the role of psychologists in law enforcement with their role in national security interrogations is flawed. They offer three reasons why the comparison is flawed. The first is that psychologists do not have supervisory responsibilities in domestic law enforcement settings. Further, psychologists do not sit in on interrogations. They may help train investigators by offering workshops on relevant topics, but they are not members of the interrogation teams.

Second, psychologists working within the criminal justice system operate in settings where the rule of law is firmly established. Prisoners have basic constitutional rights, and these rights are legally recognized and protected by the system itself. In contrast, psychologists involved with the interrogations of detainees in the war on terror work in settings where standard legal protections are not afforded to prisoners. They have no right to an attorney, no right against self-incrimination, no right even to know what the charges against them are. As Olson and Soldz put it in their article with Martha Davis, "such extreme violations of liberty are inevitably, in and of themselves, psychologically harmful and demeaning to the profession of psychology."[18]

Third, psychologists working in the criminal justice system have access to colleagues and resources they can consult in negotiating any ethical issues that might arise in their role as consultants. By contrast, psychologists working for the military or the CIA are constrained by secrecy, chain of command, and geographical distance, which makes consultation with independent psychologists nearly impossible.

As much as I sympathize with the position that Olson and Soldz are seeking to defend, I do not think that they have made their case. It is puzzling, for example, that they would claim in their first point that if psychologists participate in domestic interrogations they cease to be psychologists and become law enforcement officers instead, for one of the conclusions of the PENS report that they emphatically endorsed was that "all U.S. psychologists, regardless of their different applied, research-based, or practitioner roles, were to be held fully accountable to all sections of the APA ethics code."[19] In other words, psychologists do not cease to be accountable to the professional code of ethics simply because they function in nontraditional roles. Nor does their first line of argument address precisely how to distinguish morally the various roles psychologists may play, even in relation to interrogation. They say, for example, that one difference between the unacceptable participation in interrogations at Guantánamo Bay and the acceptable participation in domestic settings is that in the latter psychologists do not sit in on the interrogations or help shape the contours of the interrogations. Yet they acknowledge that, in domestic forensic work, psychologists "present the results of linguistic or behavioral analyses of prior interviews."[20] Presumably, however, these analyses are used in decisions about how to proceed with the investigation or prosecution, which may involve future interrogations. Does the moral judgment we make about the participation of psychologists thus come down to whether they are in the interrogation room? I doubt that Olson and Soldz would want to answer yes to this question, but it seems to be the logical conclusion of their argument.

The arguments in the second and third points also appear to be weak. In fact, they reproduce a problem that we already identified. They do not address the question of whether there is anything intrinsically problematic about psychologists being involved with interrogations, but instead focus on the problems that faced psychologists involved with interrogations at Guantánamo Bay and Abu Ghraib. The fact that psychologists working in settings where international human rights conventions are ignored is problematic does not mean that psychologists may not work in settings where the rule of law is in evidence.

Are there arguments that Olson and Soldz are missing? To answer that question, we might attempt to apply the principles identified by Costanzo, Gerrity, and Lykes to some cases of CI work. Shumate and Borum provide a useful case study for consideration. In the scenario they sketch, DOD investigators were monitoring the activities of a suspected terrorist cell when they discovered that one member of the cell had long-standing ties with an active-duty service member who appeared to be unaware of his friend's apparent terrorist involvement. The investigators sought to recruit the service member into the role of "access agent" to provide them with information about his friend and the friend's cell.

Recognizing that using the service member as an access agent would present a number of psychological issues, the investigators worked with an operational psychologist to develop a plan for evaluating the service member's suitability for the role, the best way to approach recruiting him, how to monitor his psychological status during the operation, and how to reintegrate him into his regular service responsibilities. Throughout the operation, the psychologist met with both the case officer and the access agent to evaluate the psychological dimensions of the ongoing operation.

Does the psychologist's involvement with this counterterrorism operation violate the five principles that Costanzo, Gerrity, and Lykes identified as the common norms governing the conduct of psychologists internationally? It is hard to see how it does. Both the case officer and the psychologist were concerned about the access agent's welfare, and they structured their approach to him in such a way that he would have a sense of what the operation would involve before he consented to the operation. As best as we can tell from Shumate and Borum's description of the case, the psychologist was competent to advise, monitor, and evaluate the operation, and the operation itself served a social good. There would undoubtedly be uncertainties in a case of this sort—was the friend really a member of a terrorist cell; might the psychological costs be higher than anticipated; and so forth—but assuming the psychologist was competent and acted with integrity, his or her actions do not appear to have violated the five principles. As in the case of interrogations, in this scenario a psychologist might succumb to the pressure of the situation and act irresponsibly—in this case recommending that the operation go forward even knowing that using a friend, even one who perhaps had already betrayed him, would be deeply emotionally traumatic for the access agent—but that such an outcome might result is not reason to believe that the psychologist's involvement is per se wrong.

A Rorschach Test

Although I disagree with Olson and Soldz that an absolute ban on the involvement of psychologists with interrogations and other national security–related activities is morally required, their concern is reasonable and should not be restricted to involvement with interrogation. In effect, I am advocating a middle-of-the-road position that accepts the involvement of psychologists in interrogations and other counterterrorism activities, but with serious concerns about the dangers that accompany this involvement. Regrettably, most of the literature on the professional responsibility of psychologists in national security clusters around the extreme positions, so mapping the middle ground is difficult. Acknowledging this reality, it may be useful to explore a mediating position in a case that tends to be a Rorschach test for identifying which of the extremes one finds attractive.

Unlike our previous case, this one is not hypothetical. We know the details of the case because it involved criminal prosecution for conspiracy to transmit information relating to national defense, attempted transmission of national defense information, and obtainment of national defense information, all of which are violations of federal law. The defendants, Theresa Marie Squillacote and Kurt Alan Stand, were convicted of these crimes and appealed their convictions all the way to the US Supreme Court, which declined to hear the case. Because of this legal history, we have a richly textured account of a national security–related operation that involved psychologists working with the FBI to catch and prosecute a spy. Indeed, even the dry recitation of the facts in the legal documents reads like a John le Carré novel.[21]

The Squillacote case raises difficult ethical and legal issues, and we need a fairly detailed account of the case before us if it is to be useful to our deliberations. Some of the facts of the case are disputed, but I will follow the account of the facts as rehearsed in the decision of the US Court of Appeals for the Fourth Circuit, which upheld the convictions of Squillacote and Stand. Even a mere chronology of the case is somewhat lengthy, but it is helpful to have a time line.[22]

- 1930s—Kurt Stand's parents flee Hitler's Germany.
- Early 1970s—Stand begins working for Lother Ziemer, a member of the Hauptverwaltung Aufklärung (HVA), the foreign intelligence arm of East Germany's intelligence agency.
- 1976—Stand recruits James Michael Clark to become an HVA source.
- 1979–81—Stand recruits his wife, Theresa Squillacote, to work for the HVA. Squillacote has an affair with Ziemer.
- 1985–89—The HVA trains Squillacote and Stand and pays $40,000 in travel expenses for them.
- 1991—Squillacote obtains a job as an attorney at the DOD and gets security clearance and access to classified documents.

- 1992—Ziemer is arrested and convicted but released. The FBI learns of the existence of three spies, two men and a woman, working out of Washington, DC.

- 1995—Squillacote obtains a PO box under the name "Lisa Martin" and sends Ronnie Kasrils, the deputy defense minister of South Africa, a letter hinting at a possible intelligence operation.

- 1996:
  - The FBI gets a Foreign Intelligence Surveillance Act (FISA) warrant for clandestine electronic surveillance of all calls to and from Squillacote's home and office.
  - The FBI Behavioral Analysis Program (BAP) profiles Squillacote and designs a "false flag" operation to catch her.
  - Posing as Kasrils, the FBI sends "Lisa Martin" a letter seeking a meeting between Squillacote and Kasrils's emissary.
  - An undercover FBI agent, posing as a South African intelligence officer, meets with Squillacote.

- 1997:
  - Squillacote turns over four classified DOD documents to the undercover FBI agent.
  - Squillacote and Stand are arrested.

For our purposes, of course, the focal point in the time line is the involvement of the FBI BAP, for it was at that point that psychologists were involved in this security operation. What precisely did the BAP do?

Essentially, the BAP reviewed all FBI files on Squillacote, including audio- and videotapes made under the FISA warrant. It also reviewed third-party psychological evaluations of Squillacote, and the point of the entire analysis was to construct a psychological profile of her that would inform FBI efforts to obtain evidence against her. A passage from the BAP reports provides a sense of its work. The BAP team assigned Squillacote the code name "Loftiest Shade" (LS), as we see in the following passage from the report.

LS walks with a limp due to her prosthetic right limb. She flaunts her handicap wearing clothing that highlights her limb, and she takes offense when someone makes a joke about handicapped people. She suffers from cramps

and depression and is taking the anti-depressants Zoloft and Diserel. . . . The
subject's family has been beset with depression; her mother was prone to
depression; her sister committed suicide; and her brother is taking anti-depressants. LS has wide mood swings. When things are going her way, on
her own agenda, she laughs, is very upbeat, and is full of energy. When she
feels as though she is losing control and is under stress (which is the majority of the time), she became [sic] hysterical, sobs, and screams.[23]

In a section titled "Personality Characteristics," we find the following: "This person reflects a cluster of personality characteristics often
loosely referred to as "emotional and dramatic." She needs constant attention and approval. She reacts to life events in a dramatic, over-emo-
tional fashion, calling attention to herself at every opportunity. . . . She
is totally self-centered and impulsive. She has no concern for applying
logic to thought or argument about long-term issues such as ethics,
loyalty or most other moral reasoning."[24]

On the basis of this analysis, the BAP recommended that the FBI
undertake an undercover operation in which an agent would pose as
a South African intelligence officer. The recommendation was precise
and detailed. The approach to Squillacote should be made within a year
of the loss of her East German contact, with whom she had been ro-
mantically involved, because this was the time when she would be most
vulnerable and thus most approachable. The agent should be a man
because "she appears to possess the mind of a newly pubescent child,
tending to seek an 'idealized' relationship with men who are not able,
for various reasons, to respond to her." The agent should be professional and somewhat aloof. He should bring her a personal gift, ideally
a biography, because that was Squillacote's favorite type of book. The
initial meeting should leave Squillacote "beguiled and craving more attention." The agent should not talk about money during the first meeting; he should appeal to "their shared desire to advance the 'New South
Africa' being built by the ANC dominated government."[25]

The BAP also provided recommendations for dealing with Squillacote after she was arrested. It suggested that two female FBI agents
should interview her and that their "approach should be matter-of-fact
businesslike (i.e., 'I need you to talk about this.') rather than appealing
to her emotions." It noted that once she was arrested she might attempt suicide, and it would thus "be prudent at the appropriate time to

advise individuals close to her (i.e., her husband, brother, and attorney) of the potential danger."[26] What should we make of the role of the BAP team, which included at least one psychologist, in this national security operation? As I suggested earlier, this case tends to be polarizing, and two commentaries on the case display the divisions pretty clearly. Charles Ewing and Michael Gelles, for example, argue that the psychologist's involvement is entirely consistent with APA ethical principles. Admittedly, some harm might have come to Theresa Squillacote, but that potential harm must be balanced against the harm to national security if she leaked classified material to foreign governments.[27] And the codes of both the American Psychiatric Association and the American Psychological Association recognize that a psychologist may have to balance competing goods or evils. By contrast, Philip Candilis reaches the exact opposite conclusion. He, too, acknowledges that cases like Squillacote's may require weighing of individual and social goods and that codes of professional ethics allow for such balancing. Nevertheless, Candilis strikes the balance very differently: "The doctrines of professional ethics, legal ethics, role morality, and social contract theory all oppose the actions of the FBI psychologist."[28]

Who is right here? Does the Squillacote case demonstrate the valuable (and ethical) contribution that psychologists can make to national security activities, or does it show precisely why psychologists must not participate in CI work? I hope it is clear by now that my answer to this question is going to be "neither." Although there are aspects of the Squillacote case that are deeply troubling, I do not believe that it supports those who would ban psychologists from national security–related work altogether.

The first thing to notice about this case is that it took place in a setting structured by the rule of law. To be sure, the operation was conducted in secret, but FBI surveillance is approved through proper legal channels, and, once she was arrested, Squillacote had the full array of legal rights provided for those under indictment for criminal misconduct, which is indeed why we know precisely what was done in this case. In this respect, the Squillacote case is a better vehicle for deliberating about the role of psychologists in the war on terror than is reflecting on whether psychologists should have been involved with interrogations at Guantánamo Bay. Olson and Soldz's worries about the abuse-producing context of national security interrogations should largely be absent here.

Once again, applying Costanzo, Gerrity, and Lykes's five principles may be useful. Recall the principles: (1) respect for the dignity and rights of persons, (2) caring for others and concern for their welfare, (3) competence, (4) integrity, and (5) professional, scientific, and social responsibility. When Olson and Soldz used these principles to assess the involvement of psychologists in the interrogation of detainees, they focused primarily on the first two principles, and there was a reason. As important as competence, integrity, and responsibility are, they largely address the question of how a professional's expertise is used and not the ends to which it is put or the means that bring about those ends. Yet it is often difficult to know whether a psychologist acted competently and with integrity in any given case.

For example, although we know a great deal about the Squillacote case, we may not know enough fully to assess whether the psychologist involved acted with integrity in helping to shape the BAP report, for we do not know exactly what role he or she played in the process. However, we do know what the BAP recommended, and we can ask whether its recommendations are consistent with a commitment to the first two principles. My answer to this question is mixed. On the one hand, the BAP team clearly treated Squillacote as a competent agent capable of making an autonomous, if treacherous, decision to betray her country. As far as we can tell, Squillacote's legal rights were not violated, and she initiated contact with a South African official even before the FBI launched its false-flag operation. On the other hand, I believe the BAP team may not have shown sufficient concern for Squillacote's welfare, given the plan it devised.

The irony here is that, in one sense, it may not have been possible fully to follow both the principle of respect for persons and that of caring for others and concern for their welfare in this case. By this I do not mean that treating Squillacote as a rational agent capable of making autonomous decisions would foreseeably result in harm to her when she was arrested and imprisoned. (A concern of this sort about imprisonment would involve a trivialization of the principle of care and concern for welfare.) Instead, I have in mind the palpable tension in the BAP report between the plan that treats Squillacote as a rational agent capable of making decisions for which she can be held morally and

legally liable and the portrait it paints of her as an extraordinarily dam-
aged and fragile human being. The fact that the report itself acknowledges that there was a possibility that Squillacote might attempt suicide
if the undercover operation was successful and she was arrested is perhaps the strongest piece of evidence here, but there are others as well.
The report makes clear, for example, that her family life was a mess.
We read that she ignored and neglected her two children, ages ten and
twelve, and that she frequently left them to care for themselves. Her
home is described as resembling a construction site, with closets so
jammed with stuff that they were unusable. We are told that she was
incapable of genuine friendship and was a loner who avoided social
contact when she could. We know that she was under the care of a psy-
chotherapist and was being treated for depression. Admittedly, I am not
competent to make a mental health assessment of Theresa Squillacote;
I have neither the training nor the access to the wealth of information
about her that was available to the BAP. Nevertheless, the unflattering
portrait of Squillacote painted in the BAP report certainly raises questions about her stability and whether there was not another way to discover if she was selling classified documents and, if so, to minimize the
damage done by those leaks and to prevent future ones, while at the
same time not pushing Squillacote to the brink of suicide.[29]

There are two other issues that merit consideration in discussing the
Squillacote case. Gerald Koocher framed the first in the essay "Ethics
and the Invisible Psychologist," from which I quoted earlier in the chapter. The general ethical issue to which Koocher draws our attention
is that psychologists are increasingly serving as consultants to clients
who seek psychological evaluation of third parties who are not the psychologists' clients and who are unaware that they are being evaluated.
Psychologists now routinely consult in litigation, consumer advertising
and marketing plans, employment and management decisions, political polling, and many other contexts where those being evaluated may
arguably be harmed by the work of psychologists about which they are
unaware. Koocher states the moral problem succinctly: "The invisible
psychologist's work may have direct dire consequences for third parties
who have no role in the confidential contract [between the psychologist
and the client]. In addition, the invisibility tends to shield such psychologists from clear lines of accountability for their own ethical behavior
because any evidence of their role may remain undetectable."[30] We

have seen this concern about accountability before. It is this concern that informs Olson and Soldz's argument that psychologists should not be involved in interrogations in settings that violate US or international law. Is this a genuine concern in the Squillacote case? Although the assessment of Squillacote was conducted in secret and without her knowledge or consent, there is, nevertheless, clear accountability here. The fact that there is such extensive documentation about the case allows for precisely the sort of review in which we are engaged. Certainly, too, the courts provided a detailed review of the activities of the FBI in this case.

Indeed, the second issue worth noting at this point emerges precisely because there was a process of review. In the appeal of her conviction, Squillacote's lawyers noted that among the conversations that were monitored under the FBI surveillance of Squillacote were privileged communications between Squillacote and her therapists. Moreover, the lawyers argued that these communications were used in preparing the BAP report and the undercover operation that ensnared Squillacote.[31] While the courts held that the conversations between Squillacote and her therapists were privileged, they did not agree that evidence obtained from actions based on BAP recommendations—which in turn may have been partly based on two privileged conversations—should be excluded.

Whatever one thinks of the legal ruling, there are questions that may be raised about the propriety of psychologists using privileged communications between Squillacote and her therapists as a basis for formulating a psychological profile of Squillacote and a plan to "take advantage of her emotional vulnerability" that "includes suggestions designed to exploit her narcissistic and histrionic characteristics."[32] We do not, of course, know precisely what the psychologist did when presented with the transcripts of the privileged conversations, and so we cannot conclude that he or she violated norms of professional conduct. For all we know, the psychologist may have objected and reported the problem to the agent supervising the operation. But we can make a general observation. The perception of impropriety may be as damaging as any actual impropriety, and it is hard not to be troubled knowing that the BAP team had access to confidential information and sought to exploit Squillacote's vulnerabilities, which may have been identified partly through access to that information.

Philip Candilis has stated the difficulty very powerfully: "The mere perception of a government psychologist's disavowing forensic protections and using deception against a suicidal individual is damaging. Are private thoughts and feelings, which a psychologist has special powers to exploit, fair game, or will the community view the intrusion as Orwellian? . . . The social contract with psychologists is not likely to tolerate the perception that government clinicians are secretly available to record and manipulate private thoughts."[33] The moral question is not the narrow one of whether any particular action of the FBI psychologist violated the APA Code of Ethics or principles distilled from various codes of professional ethics drawn from around the world. The question explores a broader horizon, for codes of ethics do not exist merely to regulate the behavior of members of a guild; they in fact signal a social contract that needs to be negotiated and maintained. This is a point Candilis makes in response to FBI special agent John Schafer's arguments that the FBI behavioral analysis team acted properly in the Squillacote case. The public statements of a profession's ethics as articulated in a code of ethics, Candilis writes, "are a public recognition of reciprocal obligations, a social contract that, although not absolute, frames the moral discussion."[34]

I will take up the issue of medical professionalism in a later chapter, but the comparison to the social responsibilities of physicians is helpful at this point as well.[35]

Those who have written on medical professionalism point out that physicians have a responsibility that extends beyond their relationship to individual patients, for societies can abandon the sick and vulnerable, just as individuals can. Medical professionalism thus protects social values as well as vulnerable persons. In committing as a profession to the sick and the vulnerable, even at the expense of individual interests, physicians provide a stabilizing social influence. Yet, as Wynia et al. point out in their treatment of medical professionalism, "the social role of professionalism as a stabilizing force is not unique to the medical profession. Complex societies in different times and places have had in common a need for meritocratic, dedicated sub-groups that function to keep private interests and government power in balance through attention to greater social goods." They continue: "Professions protect not only vulnerable persons but also vulnerable social values. Many values are vulnerable: individuals and societies may abandon the sick, ignore due process in judging guilt or innocence of a person accused of a crime, provide inadequate support for education, propagate information that suits those in power while stifling different perspectives, and so on."[36]

When Candilis writes that the "social contract with psychologists is not likely to tolerate the perception that government clinicians are secretly available to record and manipulate private thoughts," I believe he has something like this concern in mind. It is not just the fact that Squillacote was being manipulated and possibly entrapped with the help of psychologists that is morally troubling; it is that the social value of respect for persons and their autonomy appears to have been sacrificed in this case. As we will see in chapter 9, understanding the relationship between dignity and autonomy is important for addressing the appropriate limits of national security–related actions.

I asked earlier whether there was anything intrinsically problematic with the involvement of psychologists in interrogations, and the Squillacote case may now help us to answer this question. I do not believe that there is anything intrinsically wrong with psychologists consulting on interrogations or working with a BAP team to assess the best way to draw out a suspected spy. Where psychologists cross the line is in using their training in an effort to strip others of autonomy. At that point they move from applying their knowledge forcefully or even coercively to using it brutally. The effort to break the will, to turn a person's most acute psychological vulnerabilities against him to get him to do your bidding, is what unites the abusive interrogations at Guantánamo Bay and the Squillacote case. Both could have been handled differently, but psychologists in both cases violated a foundational social norm and thereby broke the social compact between psychology as a profession and a democratic commitment to autonomy and respect for persons.

Jeremy Waldron has cited Hannah Arendt in characterizing what is wrong with torture. It is not the fact that torture is coercive or abusive that makes it repugnant; it is that it reduces a human being to a "quivering mass of 'bestial, desperate terror.'"[37] I will return to this point at some length in chapter 9. For now, let me simply note that we tend to think of this effort to strip a person of his humanity as quintessentially accomplished through the infliction of physical pain, but it can be attempted without physical pain. Psychological manipulation or, for that matter, the administration of truth serum, may equally dehumanize another. If the profession of psychology is to serve a stabilizing function in society, it must clearly take a stand against such dehumanization.[38]

Notes

1. "Email Messages from the Listserv of the American Psychological Association's Presidential Task Force on Psychological Ethics and National Security: April 22, 2005–June 26, 2006," accessed May 22, 2012, posted by ProPublica at http://s3.amazonaws.com/propublica/assets/docs/pens_listserv.pdf, 159–60.

2. Koocher, "Speaking against Torture."

3. Koocher, "Ethics and the Invisible Psychologist," 102.

4. Ibid., 106.

5. Quoted in Peltz, "Learning from History," 715.

6. Shumate and Borum, "Psychological Support to Defense Counterintelligence Operations," 289.

7. Ibid.

8. Borum et al., "Role of Operational Research," 425.

9. Fein and Vossekuil, "Assassination in the United States."

10. Borum et al., "Role of Operational Research," 425.

11. Olson, Soldz, and Davis, "Ethics of Interrogation and the American Psychological Association."

12. In conversation, Brad Olson has suggested that his argument is not rooted in the idea of a slippery slope. Instead, the point is that in a situation where detention is unlawful or unethical, psychologists should not be involved, period. This is a fair reading of part of the argument, but the idea of a comprehensive bright-line prohibition is, I believe, ultimately rooted in worries about a slippery slope.

13. Milgram, *Obedience to Authority*; Zimbardo, *Lucifer Effect*.

14. Costanzo, Gerrity, and Lykes, "Psychologists and the Use of Torture," 8.

15. Olson and Soldz, "Positive Illusions."

16. Geneva Convention Relative to the Treatment of Prisoners of War (Third Geneva Convention), 75 UNTS 135, International Committee of the Red Cross, August 12, 1949, available on the UN High Commissioner for Refugees website, www.unhcr.org/refworld/docid/3ae6b36c8.html.

17. Olson, Soldz, and Davis, "Ethics of Interrogation and the American Psychological Association," 6.

18. Ibid.

19. Ibid., 2.

20. Ibid., 6.

21. David Grann, "The Stasi and the Swan," *New Republic*, April 19, 1999, 19–27.

22. United States v. Theresa Marie Squillacote, 221 F.3d 542 (4th Cir. 2000).

23. "National Security Division (NSD) Behavioral Analysis Program (BAP) Team Report Loftiest Shade," appendix D in Petition of Writ of Certiorari at 111a, *Squillacote*, 221 F.3d 542 (4th Cir. 2000) (No. 99-4088), available on the Federation of American Scientists website, www.fas.org/irp/ops/ci/squill/appendix.pdf.

24. Ibid., 112a.

25. Ibid., 113a, 8a, and 117a.

26. Ibid., 118a.

27. Ewing and Gelles, "Ethical Concerns in Forensic Consultation."

28. Candilis, "Reply to Schafer," 455.

29. Given that the goal of the sting operation was the arrest and prosecution of Squillacote, it is surprising that there is no explicit discussion of mens rea in the BAP report.

30. Koocher, "Ethics and the Invisible Psychologist," 98.

31. It is important to note that only the first two conversations between Squillacote and her therapists that were recorded were listened to and transcribed. Once the supervising FBI agent learned of the conversations she instructed agents not to listen to, index, or transcribe these conversations.

32. "National Security Division (NSD) Behavioral Analysis Program (BAP) Team Report Loftiest Shade," 112a and 8a.

33. Candilis, "Reply to Schafer," 455.

34. Ibid., 453.

35. In drawing on the idea of medical professionalism I do not mean to suggest that the norms of clinical psychology apply to all psychologists, whether they are seeing patients or not. Some of the criticism of the involvement of psychologists in national security work comes close to equating psychologists with doctors. I do not accept that equation.

36. Wynia et al., "Medical Professionalism in Society," 1612.

37. Waldron, "Torture and Positive Law," 1726.

38. The issue of administering a truth serum has not received enough attention. It might be counterintuitive, but I think using a truth serum may be understood as torture. On this point, see Gilbert Meilaender, "Stem Cells and Torture," *Weekly Standard*, June 2009.

Three

Interrogating Justice
The Torture Memos and the
Office of Legal Counsel

Torture is rarely solo work. It is a systematic practice, institutional-
ized by nations and states, supported hierarchically, and requiring
the participation of professionals of many stripes.
—Nancy Sherman, *The Untold War*, 147

In the first two chapters, we saw how professionals in the field of psychology became involved in interrogations of detainees in the war
on terror that arguably amounted to torture. Some psychologists facilitated abusive practices, but others sought to end any support for (or
participation in) abusive interrogations. In some cases, the very same
psychologists who facilitated abuse also belatedly sought to curtail it.
Yet, as Nancy Sherman rightly notes, torture and abuse are the end
points of an interlocking set of activities, which typically involve professionals of many stripes. Our discussion of the role of psychologists
thus needs to be supplemented by a consideration of the activities of
other professionals in the war on terror. And few can deny the profound role that attorneys have played in this war.

The Office of Legal Counsel

Given that our focus is on the use of coercive interrogations in the war
on terror, the natural starting point for our discussion is the so-called
torture memos and the work of the attorneys who produced them.[1]
Most references to "the torture memos" are restricted to three memoranda produced by the Office of Legal Counsel (OLC) at the DOJ—the
unclassified Bybee memorandum, the classified Bybee memorandum,

and the Yoo memorandum—and these three memoranda will be the focus of much our discussion below. Nevertheless, it is important to note that there are at least eight memoranda, produced under three different directors of the OLC, that address the issue of interrogation techniques, and we will need to examine some of the other memoranda as well. Three additional memoranda are particularly important. The memorandum issued by Daniel Levin, acting assistant attorney general, in December 2004 is significant because it explicitly repudiates the reasoning but not the conclusions of the unclassified Bybee memorandum. Similarly, two memoranda issued by Steven Bradbury, principal deputy assistant attorney general, in May 2005, known as the "Techniques" and "Combined Techniques" memoranda, merit attention.[2]

To gain a sense of the role the interrogation memoranda played in abusive interrogations, it is necessary to understand the function of the OLC. The OLC provides legal advice to the executive branch of the government, including the president, and OLC opinions are binding on the executive branch. The OLC website provides a very clear description of the office's responsibilities:

> The Office of Legal Counsel provides authoritative legal advice to the President and all the Executive Branch agencies. The Office drafts legal opinions of the Attorney General and also provides its own written opinions and oral advice in response to requests from the Counsel to the President, the various agencies of the Executive Branch, and offices within the Department. . . . The Office also is responsible for providing legal advice to the Executive Branch on all constitutional questions and reviewing pending legislation for constitutionality. All executive orders and proclamations proposed to be issued by the President are reviewed by the Office of Legal Counsel for form and legality, as are various other matters that require the President's formal approval.[3]

Because the OLC is effectively the unit within the federal government to which executive-branch agencies turn when novel legal questions arise, it is not surprising that it fell to the OLC to determine the legality of various interrogation techniques that federal counterterrorism units considered using in the aftermath of the attacks of September

11, 2001. The immediate occasion of the interrogation memos was a request from John Bellinger III, the legal adviser to the National Security Council, to the OLC seeking clarification about what techniques the CIA could legally use in interrogating suspected terrorists captured in Afghanistan and elsewhere. Specifically, the CIA sought clarification about twelve techniques that it considered using on captured al-Qaeda member Abu Zubaydah.[4]

Work on the questions raised by the CIA is found in OLC log sheets as early as April 2002, and John Rizzo, the acting general counsel for the CIA at the time, is listed as the client. As OLC lawyers began to work on the questions raised by the National Security Council, the CIA, and the White House counsel, drafts of two different memoranda—one classified, the other unclassified—emerged. By all accounts, although the memoranda went out over the signature of Jay Bybee, the head of the OLC at the time, John Yoo, deputy assistant attorney general with the OLC, was the principal author of both memoranda. Both were issued in August 2002.

In addition to the two memoranda, on August 1, 2002, John Yoo sent a six-page letter to Alberto Gonzales, the White House legal counsel, which summarized the findings of the OLC memoranda. Yoo's statement of the questions addressed by the OLC is thus a nice roadmap for navigating the two memoranda. Yoo writes:

> You have requested the views of our Office concerning the legality, under international law, of interrogation methods to be used during the current war on terrorism. More specifically, you have asked whether interrogation methods used on captured al Qaeda operatives, which do not violate the prohibition on torture found in 18 U.S.C. § 2340-2340A, would either: a) violate our obligations under the Torture Convention, or b) create the basis for a prosecution under the Rome Statute establishing the International Criminal Court (ICC). We believe that interrogation methods that comply with § 2340 would not violate our international obligations under the Torture Convention, because of a specific understanding attached by the United States to its instrument of ratification. We also conclude that actions taken as part of the interrogation of al Qaeda operatives cannot fall within the jurisdiction of the ICC, although it would be impossible to control the actions of a rogue prosecutor or judge.[5]

Effectively, the memoranda took up the question of what standards of conduct should be applied in deciding appropriate action under the antitorture provisions of federal law. This in turn raised questions about the history of US support for the UN CAT, because the sections of the US Code under consideration are those that serve to implement American responsibilities under the CAT agreement.

The unclassified Bybee memorandum addressed the complex issues raised by an analysis of the CAT agreement and US law. The memorandum is divided into six parts. Parts 1 through 4 discuss the text and history of section 2340 of title 18 of the US Code, the text, ratification, and negotiating history of CAT, the Torture Victims Protection Act, and international legal cases that have addressed the question of what interrogation techniques rise to the level of torture. Parts 5 and 6 of the memorandum discuss whether the president's commander-in-chief powers may override section 2340 and whether a necessity or self-defense argument may justify the use of interrogation methods that violate section 2340.[6]

The unclassified Bybee memorandum concluded that none of the interrogation techniques proposed by the CIA could be classified as torture under section 2340 and that even if they were torture, either the president, exercising his powers as commander in chief, could still authorize their use, or a necessity defense would defeat any effort at prosecution under federal law. Less well known is the response in the legal community to the arguments in both Bybee memoranda when those memoranda became public in June 2004.

To be sure, Yoo, Bybee, and other lawyers who supported the aggressively permissive interpretation of US and international law were vilified in some quarters. But as in the case of psychologists who facilitated abusive interrogations, the more interesting professional responses were collective or institutional or both. For example, in August 2004, 130 attorneys sent an open letter to President George W. Bush condemning the lawyers who prepared the Bybee memoranda for failing "to meet their professional obligations."[7] The list of signers included seven past presidents of the American Bar Association (ABA), twelve former federal judges, and a former director of the FBI.

Among the signers was the chair of the ABA Task Force on the Treatment of Enemy Combatants. It is worth noting that the ABA resolution condemning torture appeared almost simultaneously with the open letter to President Bush. The resolution, adopted August 9, 2004, is striking for its full-throated condemnation of torture, but also for its condemnation of those who sought to authorize torture.[8] The first item of the resolution makes this clear. It reads, "RESOLVED, That the American Bar Association condemns any use of torture or other cruel, inhuman or degrading treatment or punishment upon persons within the custody or under the physical control of the United States government (including its contractors) *and any endorsement or authorization of such measures by government lawyers, officials and agents*" (italics mine). If there was any question whether the ABA statement had as one of its targets the Bybee memorandum and its authors, that doubt is dispelled when the statement calls for amending sections 2340(1) and 2340A of title 18 of the *United States Code* so that they prohibit torture "regardless of the underlying motive or purpose," and for initiating "appropriate proceedings against persons who may have committed, assisted, *authorized*, condoned, had command responsibility for, or otherwise participated in such violations [of law]."[9]

At this point, we could turn to an examination of the work of the Task Force on the Treatment of Enemy Combatants and the role the ABA played in assessing the conduct of the lawyers involved in the torture memos, just as we did in the case of psychologists and the APA. But professional accountability takes place both at a macro level—for example, with the application of a general code of professional ethics—and at a micro level, with the application of specific codes that are expected to govern particular work environments. In the case before us, examining the standards to which lawyers of the OLC are held is particularly illuminating. This examination is facilitated by the fact that the DOJ conducted an investigation of the work of Yoo and Bybee in preparing the interrogation memoranda, and it is to that investigation that we turn.

The Investigation of the Office of Professional Responsibility

Although I will focus below on the review conducted within the DOJ on whether the work of Yoo and Bybee constituted professional misconduct, we should not lose sight of the fact that it was the concern of other professionals—expressed both individually and institutionally—about the work of Yoo and Bybee that led to the DOJ investigation.

Indeed, the report of the investigation specifically cites the criticisms of Harold Koh, then dean of Yale Law School, Scott Horton, past chairperson of the International Human Rights Committee of the New York Bar Association, and the open letter discussed above as providing the context for the investigation.[10] The concerns, widely expressed, about the quality of the work in the interrogation memoranda, combined with an official request for an investigation by Congressman Frank Wolf, led the OPR to initiate a formal investigation in October 2004.[11]

The OPR is the unit within the DOJ responsible for investigating allegations of misconduct by DOJ attorneys and for recommending changes in policies and procedures if an investigation reveals that changes are needed. Although it does not have subpoena power over those outside the DOJ, it can compel testimony of those within the DOJ, and it has the authority to collect department documents. At the conclusion of an OPR investigation, the office issues a finding of whether an attorney has engaged in professional misconduct or merely shown poor judgment, or neither. The policy of the DOJ is to notify relevant bar authorities when a lawyer has been found guilty of professional misconduct at the end of an OPR investigation. And it is important to note that the end of an OPR investigation comes when its findings are reviewed by a senior-level DOJ official and either accepted or rejected. As we will see, Associate Deputy Attorney General David Margolis did not accept the findings of the OPR investigation of Yoo and Bybee, and the DOJ did not refer the findings of the investigation to the relevant state bar authorities for disciplinary action.[12]

The OPR's report of its findings acknowledges with exquisite understatement that "this was not a routine investigation."[13] One hundred thirty of the country's most distinguished attorneys condemned the work of Yoo and Bybee as unprofessional; the ABA recommended amending a federal statute so that it could not be misread as it had been by Yoo and Bybee; and the United States was vilified as a torture regime for actions authorized by the Yoo and Bybee memoranda. This was the environment in which the OPR conducted its investigation.

The investigation was, to say the least, not swift. Begun in October 2004, it did not conclude with the issuance of the final report until July 2009. As the report makes clear, there were many obstacles to a quick and complete investigation. There were delays in obtaining security clearances for OPR personnel; many witnesses from the CIA and

White House refused to meet with the OPR; important e-mails of John Yoo and Patrick Philbin, deputy assistant attorney general at the OLC, were lost; and additional revelations about the CIA interrogation program emerged during the course of the investigation. As we will see, there were other problems as well.

The findings of the OPR investigation can be stated succinctly by quoting the report. John Yoo "committed intentional professional misconduct when he violated his duty to exercise independent legal judgment and render thorough, objective, and candid legal advice." Jay Bybee "committed professional misconduct when he acted in reckless disregard of his duty to exercise independent legal judgment and render thorough, objective, and candid legal advice."[14] No other DOJ officials were found to have committed professional misconduct.

In reaching its conclusions, the OPR drew upon a variety of sources, including a document titled "Principles to Guide the Office of Legal Counsel"; the Model Rules of Professional Responsibility; title 28, part 77, of the Code of Federal Regulations; Ethical Standards for Attorneys for the Government; and the OPR's own "Analytical Framework." For example, the OPR's "Analytical Framework" sets out the elements necessary to a conclusion of professional misconduct as well as defining what an "intentional" violation includes and what constitutes "reckless disregard" of an obligation. The elements of professional misconduct are as follows: "A Department attorney engages in professional misconduct when he or she intentionally violates or acts in reckless disregard of an obligation or standard imposed by law, applicable rule of professional conduct, or Department regulation or policy. The elements essential to a conclusion that an attorney committed professional misconduct, then, are that the attorney (1) violated or disregarded an applicable obligation or standard (2) with the requisite scienter. A violation or disregard of an obligation or standard does not necessarily constitute professional misconduct if, under the circumstances, it is *de minimis*."[15] If this is the standard, what are the arguments that Yoo and Bybee violated it? The OPR's answer to that question is found in part 3 of its report, in which it analyzes various OLC memoranda regarding interrogation techniques. For our purposes, we can focus on its analysis of the unclassified Bybee memorandum.

The OPR begins its analysis by noting that both the unclassified and classified Bybee memoranda and the Yoo memorandum were withdrawn by the OLC as inadequate before the OPR completed its investigation. It thus relied to some degree on the analysis of OLC lawyers other than Yoo and Bybee who repudiated the legal argumentation found in the unclassified Bybee memorandum, but it did not confine its analysis solely to the problem sections identified by others. In particular, the OPR focused on six areas discussed in the memorandum: (1) specific intent, (2) severe pain, (3) the ratification history of the CAT, (4) US judicial interpretations, (5) international legal decisions, and (6) the commander-in-chief powers and possible defenses to a charge of torture. Effectively, the OPR concluded that, when viewed together, the discussion of these six topics in the memorandum "did not represent thorough, objective, and candid legal advice."[16]

The reasons were various. The section on specific intent, for example, left the impression that an interrogator who inflicted severe pain would not violate the torture statute even if his intention were to cause pain, so long as the goal of causing pain was to obtain information. The reason it was important to define specific intent is that under federal antitorture statutes a defendant violates the law only if he specifically intends to cause the severe pain that is constitutive of torture. By treating specific intent as it did, therefore, the unclassified Bybee memorandum in effect concluded that there could be no such thing as interrogational torture. In supporting this conclusion the memorandum misleadingly and erroneously conflated intent and motive, and it treated specific intent as if there were an unambiguous and precise standard acknowledged in the law. Yet, according to the OPR, the Supreme Court has repeatedly commented on the lack of precision in the distinction between "general intent" and "specific intent," a fact that the memorandum either ignores or glosses over.

For similar reasons, the OPR found the unclassified Bybee memorandum's analysis of "severe pain" badly inadequate. Once again, the conceptual, legal analysis is crucial, because for an act to be torture it must cause severe pain and suffering. Unfortunately, the memorandum's treatment of severe pain is so contrived that it is hard to read it as objective. The memorandum begins this treatment by noting that the Supreme Court accepts a plain-meaning-of-the-words starting point for construing statutory language, and this is the starting point that the memorandum uses as well. It notes various dictionary definitions of "severe" and concludes that severe pain is pain that is "difficult for the subject to endure." Then, notoriously, the memorandum turns to a section of the US Code that defines medical emergencies to help clarify the meaning of severe pain. The reasoning found in the memorandum is worth quoting at length.

Significantly, the phrase "severe pain" appears in statutes defining an emergency medical condition for the purpose of providing health benefits. These statutes define an emergency medical condition as one "manifesting itself by acute symptoms of sufficient severity (including severe pain) such that a prudent lay person, who possesses an average knowledge of health and medicine, could reasonably expect the absence of immediate medical attention to result in—placing the health of the individual . . . (i) in serious jeopardy, (ii) serious impairment to bodily functions, or (iii) serious dysfunction of any bodily organ or part." Although these statutes address a substantially different subject from Section 2340, they are nonetheless helpful for understanding what constitutes severe physical pain. They treat severe pain as an indicator of ailments that are likely to result in permanent and serious physical damage in the absence of immediate medical treatment. Such damage must rise to the level of death, organ failure, or the permanent impairment of a significant body function. These statutes suggest that "severe pain," as used in Section 2340, must rise to a similarly high level—the level that would ordinarily be associated with a sufficiently serious physical condition or injury such as death, organ failure, or serious impairment of body functions—in order to constitute torture.[17]

P. F. Strawson once concluded about a passage in Kant's *Critique of Pure Reason* that it contained "a non sequitur of numbing grossness."[18] The OPR report does not dismiss the unclassified Bybee memorandum's reasoning in such memorable terms, but the critique is the same. As the report points out, the medical benefits statutes at issue do not define "severe pain," but rather medical emergency, and they do so in terms of "serious jeopardy" to health, "serious impairment to bodily functions," and "serious dysfunction of any bodily organ or part." Moreover, according to the OPR report, the language used to gloss the medical benefits statutes is deeply (and perhaps intentionally) misleading. "The words chosen to paraphrase the statute," the OPR writes, "tended to heighten the severity of the listed consequences . . . 'serious jeopardy' became 'death,' 'serious dysfunction of any bodily organ' became 'organ failure,' and 'serious impairment of bodily functions' became 'permanent damage.'" The OPR thus concludes that the memorandum's authors rephrased the language of the statutes "to add further support to their 'aggressive interpretation' of the torture statute," when in reality the medical benefits statutes provide almost no support for the conclusion that, to be severe, pain must rise to the level associated with death, organ failure, or serious impairment of bodily function.[19]

We do not need to review each of the other sections individually to summarize the OPR report accurately by saying that the basic conclusion is that Yoo and Bybee deployed shallow, biased, and sloppy legal argumentation to justify a preordained position without acknowledging alternative interpretations of the law or the tenuousness of their own conclusions. This summary objection has sometimes been characterized by saying that Yoo and Bybee engaged in ends-driven legal reasoning, by which critics mean that Yoo and Bybee knew that the Bush administration wanted complete latitude in interrogating detainees in the war on terror and therefore cobbled together implausible legal arguments to authorize what the administration wanted.

Although the substance of this critique has some merit, dismissing Yoo and Bybee's approach as ends driven may not be the most perspicuous way of framing the point, for even the OPR report acknowledges that OLC guiding principles indicate that the office should take executive-branch goals into account and "assist their accomplishment within the law."[20] The problem is thus not that Yoo and Bybee sought to serve the ends of the Bush administration in making the strongest case possible for a position the administration wanted; it is that the means by which they undertook this task did not serve other ends or goals set by professional standards for lawyers at the DOJ and by the Model Rules of Professional Responsibility. Although the guidelines for OLC lawyers were promulgated after, and at least in part in response to, Yoo and Bybee's work at the OLC, they capture what former OLC lawyers understood to be their professional responsibility. The guidelines are quite clear about the necessity of not simply giving a green light to executive-branch desires. "When providing legal advice to guide contemplated executive branch action," the guidelines read, "OLC should provide an accurate and honest appraisal of applicable law, even if that advice will constrain the administration's pursuit of desired goals."[21]

And the OPR report makes it clear that providing an accurate and honest appraisal of applicable law is not just an aspirational goal set out by the OLC after the fact; for example, the District of Columbia Bar Association's "Rules of Professional Conduct" require that "a lawyer shall exercise independent professional judgment and render candid advice."[22]

Unfortunately, this is precisely what Yoo and Bybee failed to do in the memoranda they wrote on the legality of particular interrogation techniques. Indeed, this is the central conclusion of the OPR report. The professional misconduct that Yoo and Bybee committed was not approving the use of the EITs requested by the CIA; it was failing to support their conclusions with the thoroughness, objectivity, and candor that professional standards require.[23] This is an important point to which I will return shortly.

The Justice Department Rejects the OPR's Findings

The failure of Yoo and Bybee to support their conclusions with solid legal reasoning is no small matter, but it is in some ways a procedural problem and not a substantive one. This may in fact explain why Associate Deputy Attorney General Margolis did not accept the findings of the OPR and why the DOJ did not refer Yoo or Bybee for disciplinary action. The reason I say this is that, in setting out his reasons for not accepting the OPR's findings, Margolis does not in fact endorse the legal work of Yoo and Bybee; instead, he raises process issues about the OPR investigation itself. It is almost as if Margolis reasons as follows: The OPR concluded that professional misconduct was committed because Yoo and Bybee had an end in view from the start and they used every means—that is, every legal argument—possible, however specious, to reach that end. But the OPR seems to have done the same thing. It believed Yoo and Bybee should be found guilty of professional misconduct and it compromised the integrity of the process by seeking to find them guilty, whatever it took.

Examining the main contours of his case for not accepting the OPR recommendations reveals that many of Margolis's objections are process issues. For example, Margolis notes that the OPR contacted then–attorney general Michael Mukasey on December 23, 2008, to inform him of its plan to release the report on January 12, 2009. It asked that a sensitivity review be conducted before the release date and that a meeting be scheduled with the attorney general so that the OPR could review its findings with him before the OPR report was released. Margolis then quotes Mukasey's and Deputy Attorney General Mark Filip's response to the OPR, in which they noted that the period between December 23 and January 12 would not be enough time to do a thorough review of the 191-page, single-spaced report, even if it did not fall during the Christmas and New Year's holiday season. Moreover, Margolis points out, the custom is for a draft of the OPR's findings to be given to the subject of the investigation so that he or she can respond. This would not have occurred in this case, had the Office of the Attorney General not intervened. Even had Yoo and Bybee been given a draft when the attorney general received one, the scheduled release date of January 12, 2009, "would have precluded any meaningful opportunity for such review" by Yoo and Bybee.[24]

Even more damning in terms of process, says Margolis, is that the final version of the OPR report is dramatically different from the December 2008 draft that the OPR was prepared to release in January 2009. This is significant because the basis for an OPR finding of misconduct needs to be rooted in the analytical framework governing OPR investigations, and there is no discussion of the analytical framework in the December 2008 draft. Margolis's reaction might fairly be characterized as astonishment. He writes: "In a departure from standard practice and without explanation, OPR in its initial two drafts analyzed the conduct of the attorneys without application of OPR's own standard analytical framework. . . . I have held my current position with the Department for nearly seventeen years. During that time, I have reviewed almost every OPR report of investigation. OPR developed its framework over a decade ago and to the best of my recollection has applied it virtually without exception since that time."[25]

In addition to the fact that in the early drafts the OPR did not tether its findings to the analytical framework that is supposed to govern such investigations, it made substantial changes in its arguments after receiving Yoo's and Bybee's responses to the December 2008 draft. Margolis documents these changes in reasoning and is clearly and appropriately sympathetic to Yoo's complaint that the OPR had done precisely what it accused Yoo and Bybee of doing. In his response to the draft of the OPR report, Yoo anticipated this outcome. Margolis quotes Yoo's response: "OPR goes to great lengths to criticize what it asserts was ends-driven legal reasoning in the Bybee Memoranda, but dressing up OPR's Draft Report with newly concocted postmortem 'findings' will but prove that OPR has itself engaged in exactly this alleged sin."[26] On this point, Margolis found Yoo to be prescient; this is exactly what OPR did in its final report, and in Margolis's view this shows that the standard that was used to reach the OPR's findings was "neither known nor unambiguous," as the OPR's general guidelines require. It is worth quoting Margolis's conclusion at length:

The fact that OPR's standard for analysis changed from a second draft, which [was] issued four and half years after it began its investigations, to the final report in and of itself likely establishes that the standard that it ultimately applied was neither known nor unambiguous. There are, however, similarities between OPR's description of the standards that it applied in the drafts and in the final report even though the drafts specifically reached findings of identified bar rules and the final report reached a finding of violation of an obligation to be thorough, candid, and objective. Nonetheless, the evolution of the analytical standard combined with the fact it was gleaned in part from a "best practices" memorandum issued after these events, the fact that OPR's analysis failed to address other potentially applicable rules and opinions from the District of Columbia, and the fact that evidence in the records calls into question the appropriateness of applying broad standards of conduct reflected in after-the-fact "best practices" to attorneys answering novel and difficult legal questions for a limited audience at a time of national crisis lead me to conclude that the standard at which OPR arrived in its final report, to wit the highest standard of thoroughness, candor and objectivity, is not unambiguously established by law, policy, rule, or the record and fails to distinguish between the Department's expectations of its attorneys and the less stringent minimal requirements established by Rules of Professional Conduct.[27]

We saw in the first two chapters that process issues can have important substantive consequences, and we see that again with Margolis's findings. He does not agree with the legal analysis found in the Yoo and Bybee memoranda, but if in fact there was professional misconduct in this case, the OPR failed to prove it because the process by which the OPR conducted its investigation and reached its conclusions was deeply flawed. Not only did the OPR not use the appropriate analytical framework in reaching its original conclusions, and not only did the office fail in providing Yoo and Bybee sufficient time to respond before the OPR's planned release of its findings, there were other problems as well. When Yoo and Bybee did respond, the OPR failed to demonstrate in its final report that their arguments were inadequate to defeat the findings; it instead found new reasons for condemning Yoo and Bybee's work.

What conclusions, then, should we draw at the end of this prolonged investigation into professional responsibility? One conclusion might be that the whole process was a waste of time, talent, and money. Margolis himself seems to have anticipated the frustration that his decision was likely to generate, and he clearly wanted to avoid the conclusion that the OPR investigation was a waste of time. Toward the end of the nearly seventy-page memorandum explaining his conclusion, Margolis writes, "OPR's findings and my decision are less important than the public's ability to make its own judgments about these documents and to learn lessons for the future."[28]

I agree with Margolis about this, but I would add that the professionals at the DOJ who conducted the investigation, however flawed it was, provided a public service with this investigation if only by framing the issues for public review and by pushing for high standards of professional conduct within the OLC, even if they themselves did not meet the highest standards for which one might hope. We will have to wait to see whether the OPR learned any lessons from its investigation of Yoo and Bybee, but it is clear that the OLC sought to implement higher standards for legal argumentation after this review of its attorneys' work.

Margolis reasonably questioned the OPR's use of OLC documents produced after Yoo and Bybee left the DOJ, but that does not detract from the fact the OLC sought greater clarity about the responsibilities of its attorneys after the Bybee memoranda came to light. Within six months of the release of the memoranda to the public, nineteen former OLC attorneys had drafted and signed the "Principles to Guide the Office of Legal Counsel."[29] The document does not attempt to assess the work of any particular OLC lawyers; it rather sets out ten principles that may serve as standards for attorneys working for the OLC.

There were also other efforts within the OLC to clarify expectations of office lawyers. For example, on May 16, 2005, Steven Bradbury, principal deputy assistant attorney general, issued a memorandum for attorneys of the OLC with the subject heading "Best Practices for OLC Opinions."[30] The memorandum included sections on evaluating opinion requests; soliciting the views of interested agencies; researching, outlining, and drafting opinions; conducting secondary review of draft opinions; finalizing opinions; and publishing opinions.

Although neither this memorandum nor the statement about guiding principles for the OLC included any mention of the Yoo and Bybee memoranda, the OPR clearly thought the standards set out in these documents were violated by Yoo and Bybee. Whether the work of Yoo and Bybee would have been different had these standards been explicitly articulated before their work on the interrogation memoranda is a question to which we cannot know the answer. Nevertheless, as David Cole points out in an important article, although the reasoning of Yoo and Bybee was repudiated by the OLC after their memoranda came to light, the substantive conclusions that they sought to justify with their flawed arguments were not abandoned. It is well and good to talk about their memoranda as a "slovenly mistake," as "riddled with error," and as a "one-sided effort to eliminate any hurdles posed by the torture law" (as other OLC lawyers did),[31] but, at the end of the day, the conclusions Yoo and Bybee reached were upheld in subsequent OLC opinions written after the clarification of guidelines and principles for OLC attorneys was promulgated.

Cole's point is that Yoo and Bybee's OLC critics have focused attention on the scantily clad legal arguments of Yoo and Bybee to distract attention from the fact that the rule of law has disappeared through the trapdoor of subsequent OLC memoranda. Why, Cole asks, are we not focused on the fact that the subsequent memoranda issued by the OLC all upheld the legality of the CIA engaging in torture and cruel, inhuman, and degrading interrogation techniques? Why, he asks, "did the OPR and Margolis [both] fail to consider the legality of the brutality itself?"[32]

Cole notes the irony in the fact that, however critical of Yoo and Bybee the OLC lawyers who came after them were, these lawyers always emphasized the necessity of taking into account that Yoo and Bybee worked in crisis circumstances in which another terrorist attack was thought to be imminent. Yet, even if this is a mitigating circumstance in evaluating the work of Yoo and Bybee, it cannot explain the conclusions reached in the memoranda of Levin and Bradbury. And there is an additional irony in the fact that the same attorney who authored the "Best Practices" memorandum for attorneys at OLC in May 2005 also authored, six days earlier, a memorandum upholding the use of all of the interrogation techniques authorized by the Yoo and Bybee memoranda.

Consider, for example, table 3.1, which compares the classified August 2002 Bybee memorandum with the May 10, 2005, Bradbury "Techniques" memorandum.

A close comparison of the two memoranda shows that the Bradbury "Techniques" memorandum is much more carefully argued. Just as in the Levin memorandum that preceded it, and with which it is said to be "fully consistent," the Bradbury "Techniques" memorandum abandons the analysis of "severe pain" found in the unclassified Bybee memorandum and any discussion of the commander-in-chief powers or any arguments based on possible defenses of necessity or self-defense. Nevertheless, with regard to the question of whether the CIA may use the EITs, it is entirely consonant with the classified Bybee memorandum. "We conclude," the memorandum reads, "that the separate authorized use of each of the specific techniques at issue, subject to the limitations and safeguards described herein, would not violate sections 2340-2340A."[33]

A reader of this memorandum might be inclined to highlight the language in the above conclusion that only the separate use of individual interrogation techniques is approved, for this point is in fact highlighted in a footnote in the memorandum itself. The footnote reads, "The present memorandum addresses only the separate use of each individual technique, not the combined use of techniques as part of an integrated regimen of interrogation."[34] But as the footnote goes on to point out, the CIA acknowledges that the "authorized techniques are designed to be used with particular detainees in an interrelated or combined manner as part of an overall interrogation program." For that reason, the memorandum indicates that a separate memorandum will address the combined use of EITs.[35]

Given the comment in the footnote of the "Techniques" memorandum, one might expect that the OLC was going to conclude that the combined use of the EITs is prohibited. That is not the case. Whether used individually or in combination, the EITs that I have listed in table 3.1 are held not to violate sections 2340–2340A, and in fact the May 2005 "Techniques" and "Combined Techniques" memoranda

Table 3.1 Comparison of OLC Memoranda

Interrogation Technique	Classified Bybee Memorandum	Bradbury Memorandum
	(Allowed?)	(Allowed?)
Walling	Yes	Yes
Facial hold	Yes	Yes
Facial slap	Yes	Yes
Cramped confinement	Yes	Yes
Wall standing	Yes	Yes
Stress positions	Yes	Yes
Sleep deprivation	Yes	Yes
Insects placed in confinement box	Yes	Yes
Waterboarding	Yes	Yes
Dietary manipulation	—	Yes
Nudity	—	Yes
Attention grasp	—	Yes
Abdominal slap	—	Yes
Water dousing	—	Yes

authorize five techniques not addressed in the classified Bybee memorandum. Yet, although Yoo and Bybee have been vilified, Bradbury, for the most part, has not been. David Cole's observations about the Bradbury memoranda strike me as correct. The conclusion reached in these memoranda "is truly a remarkable conclusion—namely, that the CIA could deprive a suspect of sleep for days on end, repeatedly slap him in the stomach and face, force him into painful stress positions for hours at a time, and waterboard him, without inflicting cruel, inhuman, degrading treatment."[36]

Remarkable or not, the opinion that these combined interrogation techniques did not constitute torture or cruel, inhuman, or degrading treatment of detainees remained the position of the OLC until April 15, 2009, when the office withdrew both the "Techniques" and the "Combined Techniques" memoranda.

Noninstitutional Responses

Thus far we have focused primarily on the institutional responses to the interrogation memoranda issued by John Yoo and Jay Bybee. But David Cole's analysis of these memoranda is illustrative of the response of individual professionals to the work of attorneys to facilitate the war on terror. It is worth looking at some other individual responses. Although it took place within an institutional context, perhaps the most striking individual response to the interrogation memoranda came from Alberto Mora, the general counsel of the navy, during the time that the memoranda were being operationalized.

Mora's response to the memorandum that Yoo wrote for William J. Haynes II, the general counsel at the DOD, on March 14, 2003, is chronicled in a memorandum that Mora wrote to the inspector general of the navy, Vice Admiral Albert Church, dated July 7, 2004.[37] It is an unusual document in part because it is clearly an effort to get on the record the steps that the Office of the General Counsel of the navy took in response to concerns about enhanced interrogations. It is also unusually personal in that it documents what actions Mora himself took. As Mora writes, the memorandum "is largely an account of my personal actions or knowledge."[38]

After explaining why the issue of detainee interrogation came to his attention, even though the Office of the General Counsel of the navy would not typically be involved in such matters, Mora documents the concerns that were raised with him by the director of the Naval Criminal Investigative Services (NCIS) that some detainees at Guantánamo Bay were being physically and emotionally abused. In late December 2002, Mora met with the director of NCIS, David Brant, and Michael Gelles, the chief NCIS psychologist. Gelles described conditions at Guantánamo Bay that violated US military interrogation guidelines and expressed his concerns that the treatment of detainees was likely to escalate to torture unless something was done.

Mora was disturbed by the reports of Brant and Gelles and immediately sought a clarification of official policy on interrogation. This led him to contact Steven Morello, his counterpart at the Department of the Army. Morello provided Mora with a number of documents, including a legal brief by Lieutenant Colonel Diane Beaver that concluded that the enhanced techniques complied with the law, and a memorandum from Secretary of Defense Donald Rumsfeld authorizing some EITs. Because he found the Beaver brief "a wholly inadequate analysis of the law" and because the memorandum authorizing enhanced techniques was based on this analysis, Mora sought a meeting with Haynes, the general counsel of the DOD, to urge him to withdraw the Rumsfeld memorandum. By mid-January 2003, Mora felt that no progress had been made in reviewing or moving to rescind the interrogation policy, and he drafted a memorandum laying out his serious objections to the policy. Only when Mora told Haynes that he would sign off on this memorandum, thus making it part of the documentary evidence about the interrogation policy, did Haynes convince Secretary Rumsfeld to suspend the use of the previously approved techniques.

In his "Statement for the Record," as he captioned his memorandum, Mora documents how Haynes and Rumsfeld then convened a working group to review the DOD interrogation policy and how the working group followed the advice set out in the Yoo memorandum to Haynes, which contained the same analysis of the law contained in the Bybee memoranda that we reviewed earlier in this chapter. Because Mora anticipated the need for an alternative approach to interrogation policy, he arranged for three memoranda to be drafted that set one out. Yet Haynes and Rumsfeld appeared set on the Yoo analysis. Mora writes:

> It became evident to me and my OGC [Office of the General Counsel] colleagues that the Working Group report being assembled would contain profound mistakes in its legal analysis, in large measure because of its reliance on the flawed OLC Memo. In addition, the speed of the Working Group process and the division of responsibility among the various services made it difficult to prepare detailed comments or objections to those sections not assigned to OGC. My intent at this stage was to review the final draft report when it was circulated for clearance but, based on the unacceptable legal analysis contained in the early draft versions that were likely to be retained in the final version, I anticipated that I would non-concur with detailed comments.[39]

Unfortunately, the final working group report was never circulated, at least not to those who had criticized the reasoning of early drafts. Thus Mora, who was a member of the working group, never saw the version on which Secretary Rumsfeld signed off.

I have characterized Mora's actions as noninstitutional partly because this is how Mora himself frames his "Statement for the Record" memorandum and partly because his opposition to the interrogation policy justified in the Yoo and Bybee memoranda is not rooted in institutional norms at the DOJ or the Department of the Navy. Instead, it is his personal and professional commitment to what he describes as American values and the rule of law that led him to oppose the Yoo and Bybee memoranda. In Mora's view, the conclusions reached in these memoranda violated the core commitments of his professional life. What precisely, then, were his objections?

As we have seen, there were clearly process concerns documented in the "Statement for the Record" memorandum. Neither the original formulation of the policy nor the restatement of the policy undertaken by the working group involved serious input from those who questioned the policy. Military lawyers were cut out of the process of deliberation and little consultation was sought. As we saw when we considered the development of APA policy on interrogation, process matters, and Mora certainly would not deny that. Nevertheless, Mora's central objections were not procedural.

There are parts of Mora's analysis of the Yoo memorandum that echo concerns set out in the OPR report and elsewhere. For example, he raises concerns that the memorandum's treatment of the *Ireland v. United Kingdom* case was not adequate. It is true, Mora points out, that the court said that the interrogation techniques in question in this case—ones that are virtually the same as those authorized in the Yoo and Bybee memoranda—did not rise to the level of torture. Nevertheless, the court found that these techniques constituted cruel, inhuman, and degrading treatment, a fact that the Yoo and Bybee memoranda did not seriously engage. Nor did the memoranda take seriously the likelihood that the courts would reject the claim of Guantánamo's special jurisdictional status. As Mora puts it, "The coercive interrogations in Guantánamo were not committed by rogue elements of the military acting without authority, a situation that may support a finding of lack of jurisdiction." On the contrary, at Guantánamo "the authority and direction to engage in the practice issued from and was under review by the highest DOD authorities, including the Secretary of Defense." What, asks Mora, "precluded a federal district court from finding jurisdiction along the entire length of the chain of command"?[40]

More importantly, however, the Yoo memorandum provides almost no sense of the legal and political significance of authorizing the techniques in question. Even if one might find a narrow legal justification for these EITs, one must consider the broader implications. Because the mistreatment of detainees was "contrary to American values," when the abuse was made public, there would be "severe policy repercussions." Mora is emphatic about the likely reaction to the abusive practices: "The public and the military would both repudiate them; public support for the War on Terror would diminish; [and] there would be ensuing international condemnation." The consequences, Mora concludes, "were incalculable but certain to be severe."[41]

The basic problem, Mora argues, is that even if one wanted to authorize coercive interrogations, to do so would profoundly alter the relationship between the law and the character of the military. The law embodies fundamental values and helps to shape the character of military men and women. Military training inculcates virtues and respect for the rule of law and American values. To authorize the military to conduct coercive interrogations is to undermine military training. Part of that training, not to mention American foreign policy, has been support for human rights. Can we, Mora asks, continue to support human rights while engaged in practices that we routinely condemn?

Notice that Mora has significantly broadened the range of considerations to which we ought to attend in asking about the legality of enhanced interrogations. In doing so, he draws attention to the fact that professional responsibility involves more than staying within a prescribed set of guidelines in the conduct of one's labors. He is, in effect, asking how a legal professional could defend an interpretation of the law that appears profoundly at odds with the values the law is meant to serve. This is obviously an important question, and we turn to it in the next chapter.

Notes

1. Some critics of interrogation techniques used by the United States at Guantánamo Bay treat the designation "torture memos" as descriptive of what the memoranda authorized. That is, they refer to them as torture memos because they authorized torture. But it is possible to refer to the memoranda as the torture memos without implying a moral judgment, for the memoranda explored the issue of what constitutes torture. I will typically refer to these memoranda as the interrogation memoranda as a reminder that one fundamental question that the memoranda sought to answer is what interrogation techniques could be considered torture under the controlling legal documents.

In particular, I will focus on two memoranda issued by Jay Bybee and a memorandum and letter issued by John Yoo. Yoo was the principal author of all four documents, and although these documents were written for different recipients and slightly different purposes, they set out a consistent view that enhanced interrogation is legal under both domestic and international law. The two Bybee memoranda and the Yoo letter were dated August 1, 2002. The Yoo memorandum is dated March 14, 2003. One of the Bybee memoranda is addressed to Alberto Gonzales, counsel to the president. This memorandum is conventionally referred to as the unclassified Bybee memorandum. The other Bybee memorandum is addressed to John Rizzo, acting general counsel of the CIA. This memorandum is usually referred to as the classified Bybee memorandum.

2. Most of the declassified memoranda on the interrogation of detainees can be found at an electronic Freedom of Information Act "reading room" established by the DOJ at "OLC FOIA Reading Room," last modified April 2012, www.justice.gov/olc/olc-foia1.htm. The Levin memorandum is available here: Daniel Levin, acting assistant attorney general, to the deputy attorney general, memorandum, OLC, December 30, 2004, www.justice.gov/olc/18usc23402340a2.htm. Bradbury's memoranda can be found here: Steven G. Bradbury to John A. Rizzo, "Techniques" memorandum, OLC, May 10, 2005, www.justice.gov/olc/docs/memo-bradbury2005-3.pdf; Steven G. Bradbury to John A. Rizzo, "Combined Techniques" memorandum, OLC, May 10, 2005, www.justice.gov/olc/docs/memo-brad bury2005-2.pdf.

3. "About the Office," OLC, last modified March 2012, www.justice.gov/olc/.

4. The history of OLC involvement with the interrogation memoranda is narrated differently in different sources. Here I draw upon the account in the DOJ's review of the work of the OLC found in the OPR report "Investigation into the Office of Legal Counsel's Memoranda Concerning Issues Relating to the Central Intelligence Agency's Use of 'Enhanced Interrogation Techniques' on Suspected Terrorists," July 29, 2009, available on the US House of Representatives Committee on the Judiciary website, http://judiciary.house.gov/hearings/pdf/OPRFinalRe port090729.pdf (hereafter, OPR report).

5. John Yoo to Alberto R. Gonzales, OLC, August 1, 2002, www.justice.gov/olc/docs/memo-gonzales-aug1.pdf.

6. Jay S. Bybee to Alberto R. Gonzales, memorandum, OLC, August 1, 2002, www.justice.gov/olc/docs/memo-gonzales-aug2002.pdf.

7. The letter is summarized in Jim Lobe, "130 Jurists Condemn White House Torture Memos," Antiwar.com, August 7, 2004, www.antiwar.com/lobe/?articleid=3261.

8. "Report to the House of Delegates" (resolution condemning torture), ABA, August 9, 2004, www.abanow.org/2004/08/aba-house-of-delegates-torture-resolution-2004/.

9. Ibid., 1–2.

10. There is considerable irony in the fact that Harold Koh went on to become legal adviser to the State Department and a staunch defender of the Obama

administration's targeted killing policy. The fact that a secret OLC memorandum provides the legal authorization for targeted killing appears not to have deterred Koh from defending the policy. See "Interview with Harold Koh, Obama's Defender of Drone Strikes," *Daily Beast*, April 8, 2012, www.thedailybeast.com/articles/2012/04/08/interview-with-harold-koh-obama-s-defender-of-drone-strikes.html.

11. OPR report, 2–4.

12. David Margolis, associate deputy attorney general, to the attorney general, memorandum, January 5, 2010, available on the US House of Representatives Committee on the Judiciary website, http://judiciary.house.gov/hearings/pdf/DAGMargolisMemo100105.pdf.

13. OPR report, 13.

14. Ibid., 11.

15. "Analytical Framework," OPR, accessed May 22, 2012, www.justice.gov/opr/framework.pdf, 1–2.

16. OPR report, 160.

17. Bybee to Gonzales, pt. 1, sec. B, 5–6.

18. Strawson, *Bounds of Sense*, 28.

19. OPR report, 178.

20. Ibid., 16, quoting from "Principles to Guide the Office of Legal Counsel," OLC, December 21, 2004, www.acslaw.org/files/2004%20programs_OLC%20principles_white%20paper.pdf, 5.

21. "Principles to Guide the Office of Legal Counsel," 1.

22. "Rules of Professional Conduct," DC Bar Association, accessed May 22, 2012, www.dcbar.org/for_lawyers/ethics/legal_ethics/rules_of_professional_conduct/amended_rules/.

23. It is important to note in this regard that the OLC memoranda that replaced the Yoo and Bybee memoranda did not repudiate the conclusion that the CIA could use all of the EITs it requested. They did, however, repudiate the questionable legal reasoning deployed by Yoo and Bybee. The OPR discussed the Levin and Bradbury memoranda, but did not conclude that Levin or Bradbury committed professional misconduct. I will return to this point later in this chapter.

24. Margolis to the attorney general, 5.

25. Ibid., 6.

26. Ibid., 8.

27. Ibid., 25–26.

28. Ibid., 67–68.

29. In fairness to the OPR, it should be noted that this document itself claims that the principles it sets forth "are based in large part on the longstanding practices of the Attorney General and the Office of Legal Counsel, across time and administrations." To the degree that the principles were in fact widely accepted within the OLC before the promulgation of this document, it was not unreasonable of

the OPR to assess Yoo and Bybee in relation to these principles. See "Principles to Guide the Office of Legal Counsel," 1.

30. Steven G. Bradbury to "Attorneys of the Office," memorandum, Office of the Principal Deputy Assistant Attorney General, May 16, 2005, available at the Federation of American Scientists website, www.fas.org/irp/agency/doj/olc/best -practices.pdf.

31. Quoted in Cole, "Sacrificial Yoo," 455.

32. Ibid., 458.

33. Bradbury to Rizzo, "Techniques" memorandum, 3.

34. Ibid., 5.

35. It is important to note that the "Techniques" and "Combined Techniques" memoranda were issued on the same day with nearly identical subject lines: "Application of 18 U.S.C. Sections 2340–2340A to Certain Techniques That May Be Used in the Interrogation of a High Value al Qaeda Detainee" and "Application of 18 U.S.C. Sections 2340–2340A to the Combined Use of Certain Techniques in the Interrogation of High Value al Qaeda Detainees."

36. Cole, "Sacrificial Yoo," 459.

37. Alberto Mora to inspector general, memorandum, Department of the Navy, July 7, 2004, available at the Center for Constitutional Rights website, www.ccrjus tice.org/files/Mora%20memo.pdf. Jane Mayer's account of Mora's role in opposing coercive interrogation should be required reading in courses on professional responsibility; see her essay "The Memo," *New Yorker*, February 27, 2006, www .newyorker.com/archive/2006/02/27/060227fa_fact. The Yoo memorandum to which Mora responds is consistent with both Bybee memoranda and the letter Yoo wrote to Alberto Gonzales on enhanced interrogation. John Yoo to William Haynes, memorandum, OLC, March 14, 2003, www.justice.gov/olc/docs/memo -combatantsoutsideunitedstates.pdf.

38. Mora to inspector general, 1.

39. Mora to inspector general, 18. In a footnote in this passage (n. 12), Mora notes, "The DON [Department of the Navy] legal leadership was united in its view that the OLC Memo was rife with mistaken legal analysis. . . . For that matter, the senior leadership among DON civilian and military attorneys shared a common view of virtually all the legal and policy issues throughout the debate on detainee interrogation."

40. Ibid., 12.

41. Ibid., 10.

Four

Ticking Bombs and Dirty Hands
Coercive Interrogation and the
Rule of Law

Coerced confessions offend the community's sense of fair play and decency. So here [in this case], to sanction the brutal conduct which naturally enough was condemned by the court whose judgment is before us, would be to afford brutality the cloak of law.
> —Rochin v. California, 342 U.S. 165, 172 (1952)

Among legal academics, a near consensus has emerged: coercive interrogations must be kept "illegal," but nonetheless permitted in certain circumstances.
> —Eric A. Posner and Adrian Vermeule, "Should
> Coercive Interrogation Be Legal?" 673

One of the striking claims Alberto Mora makes in his "Statement for the Record" memorandum is that, while he is uncertain about the morality of torture in a "ticking bomb" case, he can imagine a scenario in which he might be prepared to torture a suspected terrorist. In such a case, he says, he would apply the torture himself, but "with full knowledge of potentially severe personal consequences."[1] Even in that case, however, he argues that the laws and values of the nation should not be changed to render torture lawful.

Discussions of the ticking bomb scenario have been pervasive in debates about coercive interrogations, and for that reason, we will need to take up the arguments around this scenario.[2] Before we turn to the ticking bomb, however, it is important to note that the arguments about whether torture should be legal if it might prevent a horrific terrorist attack are not merely framed as matters of law. As Mora makes clear, the values for which the law stands and to which legal professionals must be committed are implicated in the debate. Professional responsibility thus requires engaging the larger questions of values that are at stake in the debate about coercive interrogation. Just as we must assess the argument that Yoo and Bybee failed to provide thorough, objective, and candid advice, we must assess the claim that legal professionals cannot embrace a practice that is contrary to the rule of law.

Eric Posner and Adrian Vermeule, quoted in an epigraph above, are probably right that most legal academics have defended the view that torture must remain illegal, but not all have. Perhaps the best-known arguments for legalizing torture have come from Alan Dershowitz, and his arguments merit serious consideration.[3] What is particularly interesting about Dershowitz's position for our purposes is that he defends his view by appealing to democratic values. He would disagree with Mora that legalizing torture compromises core democratic values; on the contrary, according to Dershowitz, authorizing torture in rare cases is the best way of preserving those values.

The Ticking Bomb Scenario

Dershowitz's proposal is born from what he believes to be a tough-minded and realistic assessment: if the United States and other democratic countries can prevent terrorist attacks on innocent civilians by torturing known terrorists, they will. If that assessment is correct, Dershowitz argues, then we need to ask ourselves whether it would be better to torture in secret or openly within a system that demands and provides accountability. According to Dershowitz, a scenario in which a known and uncooperative terrorist has information about a ticking bomb that is set to explode imminently—and that is likely to kill many innocent civilians—pits at least three democratic values against one another in a way that leads to tragic choice. The first value is the safety and security of a country's citizens; the second value is a commitment to human rights; the third value is democratic openness and accountability.[4]

In the face of this tragic choice, Dershowitz's position is unwavering: we must preserve the first and third values. While violations of human rights should be minimized, they are not prohibited. Indeed, the state must explicitly and openly permit the use of torture to safeguard the lives of its citizens. Nor does he flinch at recommending types of torture. Here is the specific scenario Dershowitz sketches, along with his advice for what should be done.

Suppose that the FBI had actually searched the computer of Zacarias Moussaoui in the weeks before September 11, 2001, and found that there was a plan to destroy a number of occupied buildings in the coming weeks.[5] Further, let us also suppose that Moussaoui was interrogated, offered immunity from prosecution, and even injected with truth serum; still, no additional information about the planned terrorist attacks was forthcoming.[6] Dershowitz believes that in such circumstances most Americans would repudiate an absolutist commitment to human rights in favor of protecting innocent civilians. In such a case, if the FBI proposed inserting a sterilized needle under Moussaoui's fingernails to produce unbearable but nonlethal pain—or, similarly, if they proposed drilling through an unanesthetized tooth to get Moussaoui to talk—Dershowitz believes that it would be hard to argue against doing so. In his own words, "Pain is a lesser and more remediable harm than death; and the lives of a thousand innocent people should be valued more than the bodily integrity of one guilty person."[7]

Given this reasoning, the only remaining question is whether the torture should be done secretly, in violation of existing laws, or whether the laws should be changed to permit legal torture after a torture warrant had been granted by the proper authorities. Again, Dershowitz's stance is clear: no democracy should allow its leaders to undertake actions that are illegal. If we believe torture is necessary, we should change our laws to accommodate the practice. To be sure, this is a difficult—even tragic—choice: "If we do not torture, we compromise the security and safety of our citizens. If we tolerate torture but keep it off the books and below the radar screen, we compromise principles of democratic accountability. If we create a legal structure for limiting and controlling torture, we compromise our principled opposition to torture in all circumstances and create a potentially dangerous and expandable situation."[8] This last choice is unwelcome, but Dershowitz nonetheless believes that it is the one we should make.

By contrast, consider Michael Walzer's account of the relation of torture and law, a view that is close to the one that Alberto Mora apparently holds.[9] Walzer joins Dershowitz in his concern about political leaders who must make hard decisions to do evil so that good may come.

Indeed, one of Walzer's examples is essentially equivalent to Dershow-itz's ticking bomb scenario. Imagine, says Walzer, a recently elected political leader whose country is embroiled in a prolonged colonial war that he opposes; moreover, the leader campaigned on a platform of decolonization and is genuinely committed to seeking peace. Unfortu-nately, one of the first decisions that he confronts is whether to autho-rize the torture of a rebel leader who apparently knows the location of a number of bombs set to explode within the next twenty-four hours.

The political leader in Walzer's case believes "that torture is wrong, indeed abominable, not just sometimes, but always."[10] Nevertheless, he orders the man tortured in the hope that he can save the lives of those who might otherwise die if the bombs go off. Having set up his ex-ample, Walzer invites his readers to consider a question that may help us decide between the contrasting positions of Dershowitz and Mora: How should the leader who has ordered the torture view his action? How should he regard himself morally and legally?

The Problem of Dirty Hands

One possible answer to the question of how a torturer should regard himself morally and legally is that he should deny that any wrong has been done. Such a leader might, for example, think of his decision as difficult—indeed, extremely difficult—but nevertheless view it as the right decision. Such a leader might feel burdened by having had to make the hard choice, but he would not feel guilty about having done something wrong. Walzer argues that this is the utilitarian response to the ticking bomb scenario: the leader may need to overcome his moral inhibitions about ordering torture in such a case, but he should not feel guilty since—on this view—he has done nothing wrong; because torturing the terrorist may save many innocent lives, it is the right thing to do. In John P. Reeder Jr.'s terminology, this is a "righteous torturer" who overrides the prohibition against torture because he believes that "torture is morally justified overall."[11]

The obvious problem with this answer is that it effectively eliminates what philosophers refer to as the problem of dirty hands; namely, the dilemma created when correct political action may require violating fundamental moral norms. If the leader believes he has simply weighed the alternatives and calculated that the consequences of torturing are better than those of not torturing, then he has not committed a crime. Rather, he has merely done what he ought to have done—as distasteful as that is. According to Walzer, the problem with this way of understanding the situation is that it is strikingly at odds with how we tend to think about the moral life. It is certainly at odds with the conception of law that Mora appears to hold. If we genuinely believe that ordering torture is the right thing to do in a particular case, we are just as likely to offer reasons to excuse the action as we are to justify it: "When rules are overridden we do not talk or act as if they had been set aside, canceled, or annulled. They still stand and have this much effect at least: that we know we have done something wrong even if what we have done was also the best thing to do on the whole in the circumstance."[12] For Walzer, then, it is clear that the leader who orders torture must understand that what he has done is a crime and accept the moral burden of having committed a crime. This presumably is what Mora meant when he spoke of "potentially severe personal consequences."

By contrast, Dershowitz's proposal would effectively eliminate any consequences for the torturer or those who order torture, so long as the torture is judicially approved. This does not, of course, mean that the person who conducts torture under an appropriate warrant will not feel bad about either torturing or authorizing the torture. The same holds for the judge who issues the warrant. Both may be troubled by what they have done. Nevertheless, as Walzer points out, it does not seem substantial enough simply to say that someone who tortures should feel bad. It is interesting that, in making this point, Walzer cites the position of Saint Augustine, who believed that, although killing in a just war was not wrong, a soldier might still be saddened by having to kill in such a war since killing remains a terrible thing to have to do. Dershowitz's torturer might very well feel sad even if torture is not a crime; however, on this view, he should not feel guilty.

The question at this point is whether we should follow Dershowitz in thinking that torture should be rare but legal or Walzer (and Mora) in believing that torture is always a crime, even if it may occasionally be required of a good leader. I side with Walzer in this debate, and it is important to understand why regret on the part of the leader who authorizes torture is not enough. Walzer's explanation is compelling:

Surely we have a right to expect more than melancholy from him now. When he [the duly elected political leader] ordered the prisoner tortured, he committed a moral crime and he accepted a moral burden. Now he is a guilty man. His willingness to acknowledge and bear (and perhaps to repent and do penance for) his guilt is evidence, and it is the only evidence he can offer us, both that he is not too good for politics and that he is good enough. Here is the moral politician: it is by his dirty hands that we know him. If he were a moral man and nothing else, his hands would not be dirty; if he were a politician and nothing else, he would pretend that they were clean.[13]

In reaching the conclusion that the political leader who orders a prisoner tortured should acknowledge and bear his guilt for committing a crime, Walzer draws upon Albert Camus's play *The Just Assassins*. In deciding whether to side with Walzer or Dershowitz, Camus is instructive.[14]

Camus's play is a dramatization of the assassination of Grand Duke Sergei Alexandrovich of Russia in 1905. Although Camus says that he tried to achieve dramatic tension in the work by creating characters of equal strength who disagree about the role of assassination in the pursuit of a more just social order, he also makes it clear that he ultimately sides with the assassins—that is, those in the play who are attempting to overthrow the despotic government of tsarist Russia. "My admiration for my heroes, Kaliayev and Dora," Camus writes, "is complete" (x). Nevertheless, it is also clear that Camus admires Kaliayev and Dora precisely because they are willing to accept responsibility for their actions—even to the point of preferring to be executed rather than pardoned.

Walzer acknowledges that Camus's position is extreme, but he insists that the logic of this view is sensible. If political leaders choose to do evil to protect the innocent, they must simultaneously be prepared to accept what Mora referred to as the "potentially severe personal consequences" of the evil they do. In this way, torturing terrorists to defuse a ticking bomb is like an act of civil disobedience. In both cases, Walzer writes, political actors "violate a set of rules, go beyond a moral or legal limit, in order to do what they believe they should do. At the same time, they acknowledge their responsibility for the violation by accepting punishment or doing penance."[15]

This is the very position of Ivan Kaliayev in *The Just Assassins*. Although Kaliayev is prepared to—and does—assassinate the grand duke, he does not undertake this action lightly: he recognizes that, in throwing the bomb that kills Sergei, he becomes a criminal. "When we kill," Kaliayev says, "we're killing so as to build up a world in which there will be no more killing. We consent to being criminals so that at last the innocent, and only they, will inherit the earth" (245). Indeed, when Sergei's widow, the grand duchess, visits Kaliayev in prison and offers to have him pardoned, he refuses. Their exchange is instructive:

> THE GRAND DUCHESS. Won't you join with me in prayer and repent? Then we should be less lonely.
> KALIAYEV. Let me prepare myself to die. If I did not die—it's then I'd be a murderer. (288)

In the end, Kaliayev rejects the pardon because he believes that accepting death as punishment for his crime is the only thing that prevents him from being simply a murderer. Yes, he has killed a man. However, he has done so in the pursuit of a just cause, and he is willing to sacrifice his life in recognition of the fact that doing so is the only way to atone for his crime. It is precisely Kaliayev's acceptance of responsibility for his crime that Walzer describes as Camus's sensible but exaggerated view that a torturer or assassin must accept death if his actions are going to be expiated. According to Walzer, the reason this view is sensible is that it sets the stakes of violating the rules against torture or assassination very high and thus ensures that we properly value these prohibitions.

Although Walzer focuses primarily on Kaliayev's willingness to accept death as support for his position that the rules against torture should not be relaxed, there are many other aspects of the play that also support this position. It is significant, for example, that both Dora and Kaliayev insist on imposing limits on what they are prepared to do in pursuit of the overthrow of the government. Thus, when Kaliayev first goes out to bomb the grand duke's carriage, he fails in his mission because Sergei's niece and nephew are in the carriage with Sergei and Kaliayev cannot bring himself to kill these innocent children. A heated debate then ensues among the revolutionaries who have plotted the assassination about whether or not Kaliayev should have hesitated as he did:

> DORA. Open your eyes, Stepan, and try to realize that the group would lose all its driving force, were it to tolerate, even for a moment, the idea of children being blown to pieces by our bombs.
>
> STEPAN. Sorry, but I don't suffer from a tender heart; that sort of nonsense cuts no ice with me. . . . Not until the day comes when we stop sentimentalizing about children will the revolution triumph, and we be masters of the world.
>
> DORA. When that day comes, the revolution will be loathed by the whole human race. (256)

A little further on:

> DORA. Yanek's ready to kill the Grand Duke because his death may help to bring nearer the time when Russian children will no longer die of hunger. That in itself is none too easy for him. But the death of the Grand Duke's niece and nephew won't prevent any child from dying of hunger. Even in destruction there's a right way and a wrong way—and there are limits.
>
> STEPAN, *vehemently.* There are no limits! . . .
>
> KALIAYEV. Stepan, I am ashamed of myself—yet I cannot let you continue. I am ready to shed blood, so as to overthrow the present despotism. But, behind your words, I see the threat of another despotism which, if ever it comes into power, will make of me a murderer—and what I want to be is a doer of justice, not a man of blood. (258–59)

As this exchange indicates, Camus's heroes, Dora and Kaliayev, are not prepared to accept the proposition that anything goes. Indeed, with the exception of Stepan, Camus has all of the revolutionaries struggle mightily with the prospect of killing the grand duke. Although they try in various ways to distance themselves emotionally from what they are about to do, they never manage to achieve the detached commitment to the killing that characterizes Stepan. In fact, one of the characters, Voinov, realizes that he cannot go through with the assassination. It is one thing to plan to kill a man, he tells the group's leader, Annenkov;

however, "it's a very different matter going down into the street when night is falling on the city, taking your stand among the crowds of people hurrying home to their evening meal, their children, the wife who's watching on the doorstep—and having to stand there, grim and silent, with the weight of the bomb tugging at your arm—and knowing that in three minutes, in two minutes, in a few seconds, you will dash out toward a carriage, bomb in hand" (265–66). Significantly, Annenkov tells his compatriots that the decision that Voinov will not throw the bomb was not Voinov's but his own; further, Annenkov defends Voinov in the face of Stepan's accusation that Voinov has lost his nerve.

Although Walzer focuses on the characters of Dora and Kaliayev to support his position that the prohibition against torture should not be loosened, it is actually the character of Stepan who may provide the most significant insight on this matter. As we have seen, Stepan is fanatically committed to assassinating the grand duke. He would not have hesitated in throwing the bomb, even if it meant killing the grand duke's wife or his niece and nephew. In fact, Stepan is the only character in the play that seems to lack a kind of basic humanity. He says at one point, "I do not love life; I love something higher—and that is justice" (244). Yet his single-minded commitment to killing the grand duke seems to be born not from a love of justice, but rather from hatred—a hatred that has clearly overtaken his life.

It is thus worth noting that Stepan's hatred seems to have grown from his experience of being tortured while in a tsarist prison. When Kaliayev insists that the only justification for the assassination is that it is being done for the good of the Russian people, Stepan responds fiercely: "Don't prate of justification! I got all the justification I need three years ago, one night in the convict prison" (ibid.). Not only does Camus display the repugnant self-righteousness of someone for whom everything is permitted in the pursuit of an apparently just cause, but additionally, he suggests that it was legally sanctioned torture that created such a fierce and misshapen personality.

This hint about the relationship between law and character is suggestive. Law can shape or deform character. Ideally, respect for the rule of law promotes character formation that serves democratic values, but not always. The idea that the rule of law is incompatible with certain democratic dispositions, emotions, and character traits is a theme that appears in various critiques of torture. Consider, for example, Jeremy

Waldron's arguments against legalizing interrogational torture.[16] Waldron develops his position partly in response to Dershowitz, and one reason Waldron's analysis of Dershowitz's proposal is so compelling is that he places the plan in the context of other legal responses to the war on terror rather than treating it as an isolated legal initiative. For Waldron, it is important to see Dershowitz's response to the prospect of torturing detainees as similar to those made by John Yoo and Jay Bybee. Although Dershowitz's plan would sanction far fewer instances of legitimate torture than did Yoo's or Bybee's, the important point remains that it provides legal sanction to any at all. According to Waldron, the real problem is that torture is repugnant to the spirit of American law. Furthermore, there is an important link or nexus between the prohibition of torture and the rule of law, which, if severed, threatens the very rule of law itself. In different but related ways, all three theorists—Yoo, Bybee, and Dershowitz—rend the fabric of American law by severing this crucial connection.[17]

In arguing for this conclusion, Waldron highlights the various ways all three legal theorists basically ignore the normative background that informs prohibitions of torture. That background is best understood as a "felt and well-established sense that certain abuses are beyond the pale, whether one is dealing with criminal suspects, political dissidents, or military detainees, and [that] they remain beyond the pale even in emergency situations or situations of armed conflict."[18] On Waldron's view, something like this fundamental conviction informs every legal instrument, both domestic and international, that seeks to outlaw torture.

That said, lawyers who have defended the use of torture or its equivalent have treated antitorture law on the legal model of *malum prohibitum* rather than *malum in se*. In other words, laws against torture have been construed as limiting actions that would be permitted in the absence of specific antitorture laws. By contrast, if the normative background to antitorture statutes and conventions were taken seriously, we would then recognize that torture is *malum in se*—that is, wrong regardless of whether positive law prohibits it or not.

The significance of not taking seriously the normative commitments that stand in the background of human rights law—and thus of construing torture as merely *malum prohibitum*—is that particular actions undertaken to gain "actionable intelligence" from detainees are presumed to be acceptable unless they can be shown to be ruled out by a relevant statute or convention. After all, this is why Yoo and Bybee insisted that the Geneva conventions do not apply to al Qaeda and Taliban detainees; similarly, this explains why the interrogation memoranda sought to define torture so narrowly. By contrast, Dershowitz is not nearly as willing as Yoo or Bybee to ignore the background beliefs that inform legal prohibitions of torture. Nevertheless, his insistence that democratic governments will torture in the face of terrorist threats leads him to the same place. Waldron frames the issue as follows: Since they want "to turn the existing vague standard into an operationalized rule," all three theorists seek a kind of precision in defining torture by clarifying who can be tortured and specifying how severe the torture can be.[19]

Waldron makes a second argument against legitimating torture; namely, that torture is inherently at odds with our legal system. In developing this argument, Waldron articulates and defends the concept of legal archetypes. According to Waldron, a legal archetype is a rule or positive law that transcends an individual law or statute in that it captures the spirit of an area of law. As Waldron puts it, an archetype "expresses or epitomizes the spirit of a whole structural area of doctrine and does so vividly, effectively, and publicly, establishing the significance of that area for the entire legal enterprise"; for example, habeas corpus statutes serve as legal archetypes because they express our laws' profound respect for an individual's freedom from physical confinement.[20]

In the case of rules against torture, the archetype is "expressive of an important underlying policy of the law, which we might try to capture in the following way: Law is not brutal in its operation. Law is not savage. Law does not rule through abject fear and terror, or by breaking the will of those whom it confronts." To be sure, law is coercive. However, the prohibition against torture is emblematic of a commitment not to coerce by dehumanizing those against whom the force of law must be brought. As Waldron states, there is "an enduring connection between the spirit of law and respect for human dignity" that is severed when torture is legalized. While force and coercion are intrinsic to the nature of law, a prohibition against torture symbolizes the recognition that law should not compel compliance by reducing human beings to "a quivering mass of 'bestial, desperate terror.'"[21]

Waldron's argument at this point is strikingly similar to those made by David Luban in a series of essays in which he argues that torture is incompatible with values embedded in our legal system. Luban begins his argument by noting that, at least on first inspection, torture appears especially abhorrent to those who believe in limited government and the importance of human dignity and individual rights—that is, to liberals broadly construed.[22] This is notable in itself because liberals are not equally horrified by the death, maiming, and suffering caused by war. Why, then, does torture appear to strike at the core of American values, when the death and destruction of war does not?

The answer, says Luban, "lies in the relationship between torturer and victim." He continues: "The self-conscious aim of torture is to turn its victim into someone who is isolated, overwhelmed, terrorized, and humiliated. Torture aims to strip away from its victim all the qualities of human dignity that liberalism prizes."[23] Torture is thus a kind of tyranny, and tyranny is incompatible with a political system that makes human dignity central. That is why none of the political ends that torture has traditionally served can be defended given a commitment to a liberal polity. The infliction of torture in order to terrorize, extract confessions, punish, or relish in victory involves a repudiation of a liberal commitment to human dignity. The only possible exception to the condemnation within liberalism of the political use of torture, says Luban, is its use to prevent future harm. This is why Dershowitz's ticking bomb scenario gains traction. Unlike other forms of torture, interrogational torture alone appears to bear no essential connection with tyranny.[24]

Luban's analysis here helps us to see that, in one important respect, Dershowitz's argument is very close to Walzer's. Dershowitz's argument has found supporters because it breaks the nexus between torture and tyranny. Intelligence gathering to prevent a catastrophe is not a tyrannical use of power, even if torture is involved, so long as a court has approved the torture. Walzer, of course, arrives at the same place via a different route. The leader who orders a suspected terrorist tortured is not acting tyrannically, because he is not above the law. He breaks the law and is willing to accept the consequences of so doing.

While Dershowitz and Walzer may thus agree that interrogational torture is not (necessarily) tyrannical, they differ in that Walzer acknowledges the dark reality of torture in a way that Dershowitz does not. The problem with the ticking bomb scenario is that it fosters a profound self-deception about the nature of torture. By presenting torture in "a highly stylized and artificial way,"[25] ticking bomb scenarios obscure the link between torture and the violation of human dignity and lead us to think that torture can be restricted to isolated and exceptional cases. Henry Shue has provided an argument for why the case for exceptional cases of torture is deeply flawed.[26] According to Shue, torture confronts us with an either/or choice. We can either defend torture by arguing that interrogational torture will provide us with the kind of counterintelligence we need to prevent catastrophic attacks, in which case we need a practice of torture that is effective, or we can defend an absolute ban on torture. "The moderate position on torture," Shue writes, "is an impractical abstraction—it is torture in dreamland." This either/or is compelled by another one. "Either 'torturers' are just thugs who have no clue what they are doing, in which case we need not allow for exceptional cases in which they rapidly and effectively extract invaluable catastrophe-preventing information, or some can have genuine expertise."[27] The problem, of course, is that in order to have expertise, in order to be proficient in extracting information through torture, one would have to torture regularly. In the case of torture, as with other activities, practice makes perfect. In short, the logic of interrogational torture precludes the exceptional case.

Luban makes a similar point when he writes that torture cannot be an improvisational act. "The real world," he says, "is a world of policies, guidelines and directives. It is a world of *practices,* not of ad hoc emergency measures."[28] Putting the point this way helps us to see why legalizing torture tears at the moral fabric of society. We cannot justify even the exceptional case of torture without also justifying a torture culture. If we accept torture, we will need torture experts, new instruments of torture, torture research, and a pedagogy of torture. It is just not possible to quarantine torture in the way that advocates for the exceptional use of torture require.

We see this vividly in the adoption of EITs at Guantánamo Bay and elsewhere. Because the techniques used by the CIA and military interrogators were not considered legal before the OLC issued the interrogation memoranda, there was effectively no knowledge base for deploying these techniques successfully. The government thus turned to the closest experience it had with torture; namely, the training that US military personnel receive in survival skills that should be used if they are captured and interrogated. Known as survival, evasion, resistance, escape (SERE) training, this structured course was designed in part based on the experience of former prisoners of war who had been captured, interrogated, and tortured.

Although for a time there was some dispute about whether SERE training was reverse engineered to provide a template for US interrogation of detainees, there is no longer any doubt about this fact. As the 2005 "'Techniques'" memorandum from the OLC makes clear, the techniques about which the CIA wanted clarification "have all been imported from military Survival, Evasion, Resistance, Escape ('SERE') training, where they have been used for years on U.S. military Personnel."[29] To see the significance of this fact for our purposes, we need to note several important aspects of the use of SERE training. First, SERE courses include training in how to resist harsh and abusive interrogations. Coercive interrogations are thus simulated, and training to resist interrogation has included the use of waterboarding to see how soldiers responded to this interrogation technique. Second, research has been conducted on SERE soldiers who consented to being monitored as they went through the training course. There is thus a body of published scientific knowledge on which those designing enhanced interrogation methods in the war on terror could draw.[30] Third, professionals in the fields of both psychology and law did in fact draw on this research in justifying and undertaking a regime of abusive interrogation in Guantánamo Bay and elsewhere.

I will return to the third point shortly, but note that the use of the experience with SERE training is exactly what would be predicted by Luban's (and Shue's) argument that torture is not a one-off activity. If we do not know what we are doing when we use coercive interrogations then we are simply engaged in thuglike activity. But the only way we can know what is effective and what is not is to engage in and to practice abusive interrogation. It should thus come as no surprise that once coercive interrogations were authorized, a whole apparatus of research and instruction on using EITs followed.

This is precisely what Physicians for Human Rights (PHR) documents in its June 2010 white paper titled *Experiments in Torture: Evidence of Human Subject Research and Experimentation in the "Enhanced" Interrogation Program.* Specifically, PHR cites documentary evidence that demonstrates at least three instances of experimentation. The white paper summarizes the experiments as follows:

1. Medical personnel were required to monitor all waterboarding practices and collect detailed medical information that was used to design, develop, and deploy subsequent waterboarding procedures;

2. Information on the effects of simultaneous versus sequential application of the abusive interrogation techniques on detainees was collected and used to establish the policy for using tactics in combination. These data were gathered through an assessment of the presumed "susceptibility" of the subjects to severe pain;

3. Information collected by health professionals on the effects of sleep deprivation on detainees was used to establish EIP [Enhanced Interrogation Program] sleep deprivation policy.[31]

It is notable that the evidence for experimentation in relation to waterboarding consists in part of how the procedures for waterboarding were changed from its original use, which followed the techniques used in SERE training, to subsequent applications of the technique that drew upon what was learned from medical monitoring of the process. For example, water was typically used in SERE training, where trainees were waterboarded only once. When the waterboard technique was used repeatedly, the medical monitoring revealed that detainees were susceptible to contracting pneumonia or suffering from extremely low sodium levels, or both. Saline solution was thus substituted for water. In addition, PHR documents that the systematic medical monitoring of this EIT resulted in multiple improvements, so to speak, over the use of waterboarding in SERE training. These include the use of a specially designed gurney to move a detainee to an upright position quickly and of a blood oximeter to measure a detainee's vital signs and the administration of a liquid diet that lowers the risk of choking if a detainee vomits during the interrogation.

Similarly, the collection of observational data involving the comparison of individual use of techniques with their combined use and the effects of various lengths of sleep deprivation on detainees was used in calibrating the application of EITs for maximum effect without violating OLC guidelines. This last point is especially important.

As we saw in chapter 3, the original interrogation memoranda defined torture in relation to severe pain, and they cited the SERE studies to suggest that the use of EITs did not rise to the level of severe pain.

As SERE techniques were adapted and applied in ongoing interrogations, CIA medical monitoring and OLC legal decisions became ever
more intertwined. Thus, although by 2005 the original interrogation
memoranda had all been withdrawn, the Bradbury memoranda that
replaced them explicitly cited the evolving use of EITs to justify their
continued legality.

Indeed, a good part of the case that PHR makes in claiming that
the CIA has conducted unethical and illegal human-subjects research
comes from the "Techniques" and "Combined Techniques" memoranda issued by Bradbury in May 2005. For example, both the use of
a combination of EITs and the use of sleep deprivation with detainees
are upheld on the basis of the medical monitoring of interrogations
that the CIA had undertaken through its Office of Medical Services
(OMS). It is worth quoting the "Combined Techniques" memorandum at length. Discussing the possibility that EITs used in combination
might result in greater susceptibility to severe pain than when used individually, Bradbury writes:

> We recognize the theoretical possibility that the use of one or more tech-
> niques would make a detainee more susceptible to severe pain or that the
> techniques, in combination, would operate differently from the way they
> would individually and thus cause severe pain. But as we understand the
> experience involving the combination of various techniques, the OMS
> medical and psychological personnel have not observed any such increase
> in susceptibility. Other than the waterboard, the specific techniques under
> consideration in this memorandum—including sleep deprivation—have
> been applied to more than 25 detainees. See [redacted] *Fax* at 1-3. No ap-
> parent increase in susceptibility to severe pain has been observed either
> when techniques are used sequentially or when they are used simultane-
> ously—for example, when an insult slap is simultaneously combined with
> water dousing or a kneeling stress position, or when wall standing is simul-
> taneously combined with an abdominal slap and water dousing. Nor does
> experience show that, even apart from changes in susceptibility to pain,
> combinations of these techniques cause the techniques to operate differ-
> ently so as to cause severe pain. OMS doctors and psychologists, moreover,
> confirm that they expect that the techniques, when combined as described
> in the *Background Paper* and in the *April 22* [redacted] *Fax*, would not operate

in a different manner from the way they do individually, so as to cause severe pain.[32]

If we recall the passage from Nancy Sherman with which we began chapter 3, we see here precisely the point Sherman seeks to make in saying that torture is not solo work. The "Techniques" and "Combined Techniques" memoranda show the interlocking roles of professionals in facilitating interrogation practices that are arguably abusive. Lawyers, doctors, and psychologists interacted in ways that provided mutual support for the practice of abusive interrogations. As Luban and Shue point out, it makes little theoretical sense to conceptualize torture as an exceptional event, and the experience with interrogations at Guantánamo Bay and elsewhere provides an empirical case study of how difficult it is to avoid systematizing abusive interrogations.

How Many Dirty Hands?

Criticism of US interrogation practices in the war on terror has tended to crystallize around the role of Yoo and Bybee, but the assessment of their work in terms of the norms of professional responsibility is not enough. As we have seen, the interrogation memoranda were not produced in a vacuum, and Yoo and Bybee were not alone in drafting them. Lawyers at the National Security Council, the DOD, the White House counsel's office, and others were involved in vetting the work of Yoo and Bybee. And their work took place against a backdrop in which prominent legal academics like Alan Dershowitz were arguing for the necessity of torture to preserve democratic values. Add to this the fact that, although the reasoning of Yoo and Bybee was repudiated by their successors at the OLC, the substantive conclusions they reached about the legality of EITs were not repudiated, and the need to stress the incompatibility of torture with the rule of law becomes clear. Waldron, Luban, and Shue present different arguments for why torture is a threat to the rule of law and why, therefore, lawyers must not facilitate the use of torture or cruel, inhuman, and degrading treatment, even if the interest of national security appears to be at stake.

What these critics of torture in effect suggest is that the proper functioning of the rule of law is undermined when the core values embedded in the law—avoidance of brutality, tyranny, arbitrary detention, and so forth—are threatened by a practice that, by its nature, works brutally and tyrannically, and that is unlikely to be contained within neat legal categories. Indeed, examining the effort to legalize but constrain torture and cruel, inhuman, and degrading treatment of detainees may offer the best argument for the position of Waldron and others. Jonathan Rothchild has put the point nicely. "The practice of torture and its intended purposes of expediency, clarity, and utility," he writes, "lose all connections to the social and moral fabric of a society; torture segregates law and morality in pernicious and hyperbolic ways."[33] We can see this by attending to the consequences of legalizing torture. For example, if torture is legal then there ought to be nothing wrong with the government patenting torture devices. Yet to patent torture devices is surely to sever the legitimate connection between morality, law, and the common good.

The deep tension that exists when we imagine a government that embraces human rights and the rule of law while simultaneously patenting torture devices is heightened when we read the actual interrogation memoranda, and not just those produced by Yoo and Bybee. These memoranda attempt to calibrate the delivery of pain and suffering so that legal thresholds preventing torture and cruel, inhuman, and degrading treatment will not be reached. Consider, for example, this passage from the "Combined Techniques" memorandum:

> In one specific context, monitoring the effects on detainees appears particularly important. The *Background Paper* and the *April 22* [redacted] *Fax* illustrate that sleep deprivation is a central part of the "prototypical interrogation." We noted in *Techniques* that extended sleep deprivation may cause a small decline in body temperature and increased food consumption. *See Techniques* at 33-34. Water dousing and dietary manipulation and perhaps even nudity may thus raise dangers of enhanced susceptibility to hypothermia or other medical conditions for a detainee undergoing sleep deprivation. As in *Techniques*, we assume that medical personnel will be aware of these possible interactions and will monitor detainees closely for any signs that such interaction are developing. *See id.* at 33-35. This monitoring, along with quick intervention if any signs of problematic symptoms develop, can be expected to prevent a detainee from experiencing severe pain.[34]

Perhaps even more extraordinary is the discussion of EITs found in the "Techniques" memorandum. Consider, for example, the following summary of the technique of water dousing taken from that memorandum:

> *Water dousing.* Cold water is poured on the detainee either from a container or from a hose without a nozzle: This technique is intended to weaken the detainee's resistance and persuade him to cooperate with interrogators. The water poured on the detainee must be potable, and the interrogators must ensure that water does not enter the detainee's nose, mouth, or eyes. A medical officer must observe and monitor the detainee throughout application of this technique, including for signs of hypothermia. Ambient temperatures must remain above 64° F. If the detainee is lying on the floor, his head is to remain vertical, and a poncho, mat, or other material must be placed between him and the floor to minimize the loss of body heat. At the conclusion of the water dousing session, the detainee must be moved to a heated room if necessary to permit his body temperature to return to normal in a safe manner. To ensure an adequate margin of safety, the maximum period of time that a detainee may be permitted to remain wet has been set at two-thirds the time at which, based on extensive medical literature and experience, hypothermia could be expected to develop in healthy individuals who are submerged in water of the same temperature.[35]

The memorandum then goes on to give examples. For a water temperature of 41°F, a maximum exposure of twenty minutes is allowed; for 50°F, fifty minutes; for 59°F, sixty minutes.

Apart from the unsavory quality of government attorneys worrying about calibrating food intake and body temperature so that they dovetail with legal standards of severe pain, there is the ugly specter here of those whose profession it is to uphold the rule of law demonstrating greater concern for interrogators not crossing a line that might leave them vulnerable to criminal prosecution than for those whom the state seeks to humiliate and physically abuse for national security reasons. The attempt to draw the line between torture and nontorture so precisely is itself disturbing. That the state must control calorie intake and basal body temperature more precisely than would be done in any intensive care unit in order to stay just this side of the line on torture surely is an indicator that something is deeply wrong. For government lawyers to be writing briefs stating that a detainee can be doused with water that is 41°F but not water that is 40°F is troubling. What interest is served by such definitional legal precision? Waldron suggests that no legitimate interest is served. Claiming that the interrogator has a legitimate interest in having a precise legal definition of torture is like a husband saying he has an interest in pushing his wife around and therefore needs to know precisely how much he can push her before it counts as domestic violence.[36]

As I noted above, attending to how precisely the treatment of detainees must be monitored in order to avoid crossing the legal boundary of criminal behavior also drives home the close nexus between law and medicine in the interrogation regime that emerged at Guantánamo Bay and elsewhere. If, as I believe, Waldron and other legal scholars are right that professional responsibility for attorneys includes a commitment not to facilitate torture or cruel, inhuman, and degrading treatment under the cover of law, we must also ask about the role of medicine in monitoring detainees. Is not the close monitoring of detainees that the "Techniques" and "Combined Techniques" memoranda describe also a violation of professional responsibility? Is the medical monitoring required by the CIA's OMS guidelines and documented in OLC memoranda an unethical violation of the protections afforded human research subjects under national and international norms, as PHR alleges? It is to these and similar questions that we next turn.

Notes

1. Alberto Mora to inspector general, memorandum, Department of the Navy, July 4, 2004, available at the Center for Constitutional Rights website, www.ccrjustice.org/files/Mora%20memo.pdf, 11.

2. Parts of this chapter have appeared in my previous essay "Torture Warrants and Democratic States."

3. Dershowitz develops his arguments in a series of essays: "Should the Ticking Bomb Terrorist Be Tortured?"; "Reply: Torture without Visibility and Accountability Is Worse Than with It"; "Torture Warrant"; and "Tortured Reasoning."

4. Dershowitz, "Should the Ticking Bomb Terrorist," 151–52.

5. Moussaoui was arrested in August 2001 after officials at a flight-instruction school in Minnesota notified the FBI about their suspicions regarding Moussaoui.

He was charged with immigration violations, but the laptop and computer discs found among his belongings were not searched at the time.

6. Note that Dershowitz sees the use of truth serum as relatively innocuous. I think he is mistaken about this. Chapter 9 suggests why the use of truth serum may be worse than the infliction of pain.

7. Dershowitz, "Should the Ticking Bomb Terrorist," 144.

8. Ibid., 153.

9. Walzer, "Political Action."

10. Ibid., 167.

11. Reeder, "What Kind of Person Could Be a Torturer?" 81.

12. Walzer, "Political Action," 171.

13. Ibid., 167–68.

14. Page references for quotations from this work are given in the text below.

15. Walzer, "Political Action," 178.

16. Waldron, "Torture and Positive Law," 1727.

17. Although I understand Waldron's argument that the work of Yoo, Bybee, and Dershowitz should be read together, I take Dershowitz's arguments much more seriously. I do not agree with Dershowitz, but he provides a careful argument for accepting torture in rare cases consistent with the rule of law. Indeed, his arguments are framed in terms of foundational democratic values. In this way, Dershowitz's position contrasts starkly with that developed in the interrogation memoranda.

18. Waldron, "Torture and Positive Law," 1694.

19. Ibid., 1698.

20. Ibid., 1723–24.

21. Ibid., 1726, 1727.

22. Luban, "Liberalism, Torture, and the Ticking Bomb," 1426.

23. Ibid., 1430.

24. Ibid., 1439.

25. Ibid.

26. Shue, "Torture in Dreamland."

27. Ibid., 237.

28. Luban, "Liberalism, Torture, and the Ticking Bomb," 1445.

29. Steven G. Bradbury to John A. Rizzo, "'Techniques'" memorandum, OLC, May 10, 2005, www.justice.gov/olc/docs/memo-bradbury2005-3.pdf, 8.

30. See, e.g., Morgan et al., "Symptoms of Dissociation in Humans Experiencing Acute, Uncontrollable Stress."

31. Physicians for Human Rights, *Experiments in Torture*, 7.

32. Steven G. Bradbury to John A. Rizzo, "'Combined Techniques'" memorandum, OLC, May 10, 2005, www.justice.gov/olc/docs/memo-bradbury2005-2.pdf, 61.

33. Rothchild, "Moral Consensus," 146.

34. Bradbury to Rizzo, "Combined Techniques" memorandum, 62.

35. Bradbury to Rizzo, "Techniques" memorandum, 11–12.

36. Waldron, "Torture and Positive Law," 1701.

Part II

Five

Treating Terrorists
The Conflicting Pull of
Role Responsibility

The United States is a country of law, and international human
rights laws regarding prisoners cannot be ignored or routinely
violated without the active cooperation, or at least acquiescence, of
lawyers and physicians, including military lawyers and physicians.

　　　　　　—George Annas, "Human Rights Outlaws," 428

It is in the nature of torture that the two ubiquitously present [pro-
fessions] should be medicine and law, health and justice, for they are
the institutional elaborations of body and state.

　　　　　　—Elaine Scarry, *The Body in Pain*, 42

We saw in the last chapter how tightly legal analysis of coercive interrogations was tied to medical monitoring and assessment of the health
needs of detainees. Interrogation techniques that are arguably abusive
were justified, in part, by the fact that doctors would carefully monitor
the medical status of detainees who were undergoing such treatment.
Medical findings were also used to calibrate coercive interrogations so
that long-term, permanent physical damage or death would not result
from interrogation techniques.[1] Indeed, reading the OMS guidelines together with the Bradbury "Techniques" and "Combined Techniques"
memoranda provides a concrete sense of Elaine Scarry's assertion,
quoted in an epigraph above, that medicine and law are destined to
be the two ubiquitous professions when a society moves toward the
legalization of torture or cruel, inhuman, and degrading interrogation
techniques. Lawyers cite the involvement of doctors as evidence that
the threshold levels of pain and suffering (in terms of which torture
and cruel, inhuman, and degrading treatment are defined) will not be

reached, and physicians can be involved in coercive or abusive interrogations because lawyers have defined the EITs as not constituting torture.

The mutually reinforcing claims of law and medicine are important here because the profession of medicine, more than that of either psychology or law, has condemned the participation of physicians in torture. Steven Miles has traced the evolution of statements of medical societies and human rights organizations on the role of physicians in the treatment of prisoners in the post–World War II period, and demonstrates both an increasing recognition of the role physicians have played in facilitating torture or cruel, inhuman, and degrading treatment of detainees and the need to put a stop to physician participation in torture.[2] For example, below is a list of various statements and proclamations aimed at addressing the role of physicians.

- Declaration of Geneva (1948)
- World Medical Association, Regulation in Time of Armed Conflict (1956)
- Declaration of Tokyo (1975)
- UN Principles of Medical Ethics (1982)
- World Psychiatric Association, Declaration of Madrid (1996)

This list could be dramatically expanded, but with virtually every new statement there is movement toward harsher condemnation of the involvement of medical personnel in coercive interrogations. The UN Principles of Medical Ethics, whose full title is "Principles of Medical Ethics Relevant to the Role of Health Personnel, Particularly Physicians, in the Protection of Prisoners and Detainees against Torture and Other Cruel, Inhuman or Degrading Treatment or Punishment," are especially clear. Indeed, the document is striking in its brevity and clarity. The entire statement reads as follows:

> Principle 1: Health personnel, particularly physicians, charged with the medical care of prisoners and detainees have a duty to provide them with protection of their physical and mental health and treatment of disease of the same quality and standard as is afforded to those who are not imprisoned or detained.
>
> Principle 2: It is a gross contravention of medical ethics, as well as an offence under applicable international instruments, for health personnel, particularly physicians, to engage, actively or passively, in acts which constitute

participation in, complicity in, incitement to or attempts to commit torture or other cruel, inhuman or degrading treatment or punishment.

Principle 3: It is a contravention of medical ethics for health personnel, particularly physicians, to be involved in any professional relationship with prisoners or detainees the purpose of which is not solely to evaluate, protect or improve their physical and mental health.

Principle 4: It is a contravention of medical ethics for health personnel, particularly physicians: (a) To apply their knowledge and skills in order to assist in the interrogation of prisoners and detainees in a manner that may adversely affect the physical or mental health or condition of such prisoners or detainees and which is not in accordance with the relevant international instruments; (b) To certify, or to participate in the certification of, the fitness of prisoners or detainees for any form of treatment or punishment that may adversely affect their physical or mental health and which is not in accordance with the relevant international instruments, or to participate in any way in the infliction of any such treatment or punishment which is not in accordance with the relevant international instruments.

Principle 5: It is a contravention of medical ethics for health personnel, particularly physicians, to participate in any procedure for restraining a prisoner or detainee unless such a procedure is determined in accordance with purely medical criteria as being necessary for the protection of the physical or mental health or the safety of the prisoner or detainee himself, of his fellow prisoners or detainees, or of his guardians, and presents no hazard to his physical or mental health.

Principle 6: There may be no derogation from the foregoing principles on any ground whatsoever, including public emergency.[3]

Suppose we assume that something like this commitment to avoid any participation in interrogation is a consensus view among medical professionals. What should we make of the apparent gap between such a view and the OMS guidelines for medical personnel associated with the CIA or the army regulations for medical personnel? We have already looked briefly at the OMS guidelines. Looking at the situation of military medical personnel also helps us to answer this question.

Military Doctors and the Treatment of Detainees

As was true of psychologists, army medical personnel were accused of misconduct in their participation in the interrogation of detainees in the war on terror, and the accusations triggered investigations and accompanying reports. One such report was conducted by the Office of the Surgeon General of the Army and provides an assessment of detainee medical operations for Operation Enduring Freedom, Guantánamo Bay, and Operation Iraqi Freedom.[4] Because the assessment focuses on medical policies and procedures as well as alleged detainee abuse, it provides a useful introduction to the situation of military medical personnel in the war on terror.

The team conducting the assessment interviewed medical personnel in twenty-two states and five countries. They sought input from personnel who had served in the past, were then deployed, or were preparing for a future deployment. Several findings are particularly striking. For example, the assessment found that serious inconsistencies were present across theaters regarding pre- and postinterrogation screenings. Frequently, such screenings were not documented in detainee medical records, and some medical personnel were uncertain about whether interrogations could be stopped for medical reasons.[5] There were also wide variations among units in the use of physical restraints, with little clarity about the need to distinguish security-based restraint from medically based restraint.[6]

In evaluating military medical operations, the assessment team refers to relevant army policies, and the picture that emerges is one of fairly clear policies that are not always clearly followed. According to the assessment team, the applicable standard for medical care of detainees is found in army regulation 40-400, dated 2001. Section 3-38 reads, "Members of the enemy armed forces and other persons captured or detained by U.S. Armed Forces are entitled to medical treatment of the same kind and quality as that provided U.S. Forces in the same area."[7] Unfortunately, the assessment team found, "not one single interviewee, nor any team member prior to this assessment, knew of the existence of paragraph 3-38."[8]

Specific regulations for the treatment of detainees were also quite clear and largely unknown. Army regulation 190-8, which governs the treatment of "enemy prisoners of war, retained personnel, civilian internees, and other detainees," states:

> All prisoners will receive humane treatment without regard to race, nationality, religion, political opinion, sex, or other criteria. The following acts are

prohibited: murder, torture, corporal punishment, mutilation, the taking of hostages, sensory deprivation, collective punishments, execution without trial by proper authority, and all cruel and degrading treatment. All persons will be respected as human beings. They will be protected against all acts of violence to include rape, forced prostitution, assault and theft, insults, public curiosity, bodily injury, and reprisals of any kind. They will not be subjected to medical or scientific experiments. This list is not exclusive. EPW/RP [enemy prisoners of war/retained personnel] are to be protected from all threats or acts of violence.[9]

At this point we face a conundrum. The report by the Office of the Surgeon General, while acknowledging some cases of abuse, generally paints a positive picture of the role of medical personnel in all three theaters. Indeed, at several points the report makes categorical claims that are hard to square with other compelling evidence. For example, the report states that "there is no indication that BSCT personnel participated in abusive interrogation practices." Similarly, the report claims that "there is no indication that any medical personnel participated in abusive interrogation practices."[10] Discussing the team's findings about Guantánamo Bay, the report states that no interviewees, nor other medical personnel that the interviewees knew of, were ever present at or participated in an interrogation.

The problem with the claim that no medical personnel were present during interrogations is that there is significant evidence to the contrary. To take just one example, the interrogation log for Detainee 063 makes it clear that BSCT members helped plan interrogation strategies and that medical personnel provided frequent medical checks of detainees during interrogations.[11] Is the surgeon general's report just a cover-up? It would be easy to reach this conclusion, but I think it would be a mistake to do so. The better interpretation is to acknowledge the assessment team's desire to present the work of the medical corps in the best possible light. The report thus highlights the positive work of the medical corps, while acknowledging that the training for medical personnel did not prepare them for the reality they faced once the DOJ and the secretary of defense approved EITs.

This interpretation does not explain the apparent contradiction between the report's claims that medical personnel were not present and did not participate in interrogations and what we know to be the facts of the case. The (unsatisfactory) explanation for why the report makes these claims is found in a footnote to section 18-27. The footnote is worth quoting in full: "For purposes of this recommendation the term 'participating in interrogations' refers to the *active* participation by medical personnel during an interrogation. For example, asking questions would be active participation. Medical personnel who assist in developing the plan of interrogation are not deemed to be 'participating in an interrogation.' Likewise, actual presence in the interrogation room may not constitute 'participating in an interrogation.' For example, personal observation by medical personnel to ensure the health and welfare of the detainee is not deemed to be 'participation in the interrogation.'"[12] This footnote refers to the specific recommendation of section 18-27 that the DOD prohibit medical personnel from participating in interrogations, but the definition of "participating in interrogations" appears to apply to the whole document. Something like this definitional gerrymandering seems also to be embedded in the claim that medical personnel were not present during interrogations. Medical personnel certainly came to interrogation rooms to examine the detainees' vital signs and other indicators of physical well-being, but being present in this way apparently does not count as being "present."

Again, this kind of definitional maneuvering can be interpreted as a form of prevarication, but the better explanation is that the assessment team sought to uphold the highest ideals of military medicine and to reconcile these ideals with the actual behavior of medical personnel in the war on terror, which did not always match up. This effort at reconciliation does not work, but the interesting fact to take away from the attempt to reconcile theory and practice, ideals and reality, is that little effort was made to change the ideals. Indeed, the report repeatedly calls for reinforcing the restrictions on medical personnel found in existing regulations and doing a better job of training medical personnel so that they will know and act on the regulations.

To say that little effort was made to change the ideals is not to say that no effort was made. Recall, for example, the principles set out in the UN guidelines on medical ethics. Principles 2 and 4(b) can be summarized as follows:

> Principle 2: It is a violation of medical ethics for health personnel, particularly physicians, to participate in torture or other cruel, inhuman, or degrading treatment or punishment.

Principle 4: It is a violation of medical ethics for health personnel, particularly physicians, to certify prisoners as fit for torture or cruel, inhuman, or degrading treatment.

It is probably worth noting at this point that it is not just the Principles of Medical Ethics adopted by the UN that prohibits physicians from certifying prisoners as fit for interrogations; the Code of Ethics of the American Medical Association (AMA) does so as well. The AMA code reads, "Physicians must oppose and must not participate in torture for any reason. Participation in torture includes, but is not limited to, providing or withholding any services, substances, or knowledge to facilitate the practice of torture. Physicians must not be present when torture is used or threatened. Physicians may treat prisoners or detainees if doing so is in their best interest, but physicians should not treat individuals to verify their health so that torture can begin or continue."[13] If we compare footnote 4 from the surgeon general's report with either UN principle 2 or the passage above from the AMA Code of Ethics, we see an apparent effort to narrow the application of the moral norm that physicians not be involved with interrogations. And in the case of the UN guidelines this effort appears to have been anticipated, for the guidelines make clear that passive participation is still participation. Arguably, then, this move to narrow the application of the principle could be construed as an effort to change the ideal, especially given that planning an interrogation is defined as not participating in the interrogation.

Yet it must also be noted that there is tension between the expansive prohibition against physician participation in interrogations found in both the UN principles and the AMA code and the expectation that physicians will treat detainees in need. If medical personnel are checking the vital signs of detainees regularly to ensure their well-being, how will their actions not involve the certification of the fitness of detainees for interrogation? If a physician detects a precipitous spike or drop in a detainee's blood pressure and insists that an interrogation session be stopped, how is this not decertifying a detainee for interrogation, just as to report a normal blood pressure would be to certify one?

Conflicting Medical Duties

The problem with the code is that physicians cannot insure the safety of detainees without effectively verifying whether or not a particular detainee is fit to be interrogated. And physicians arguably have a responsibility to care for detainees. The philosopher Fritz Allhoff has noted the paradox in claiming that professional responsibility would preclude physician involvement in coercive interrogation. The paradox is that, if one takes seriously the traditional tenets of medical ethics, not only are physicians not prohibited from participating in interrogations, they must participate. "The principle of beneficence," Allhoff writes, "*requires* at least minimal physician participation in hostile interrogations, namely, in those cases where physician intervention would be in the medical interest of the interrogatee."[14] The paradox is thus that physicians both must and must not participate in interrogations.

Allhoff is not, however, interested in grounding the moral constraints on physicians in a code of professional ethics; he wishes instead to challenge this very idea. And he develops two arguments here. The first we have just seen. Although most medical codes strictly prohibit the involvement of physicians with torture or cruel, inhuman, and degrading treatment of prisoners, such a conclusion appears inconsistent with other value commitments enshrined in these codes. In effect, Allhoff argues that there is an irreconcilable contradiction between the medical profession's commitment to beneficence and its prohibition on physician participation in abusive interrogations. This argument is important and deserves a response, but Allhoff's second argument is even more important for our project.

His second argument is that doctors acting as interrogators should be understood to be medically trained interrogators who have no medical duties to those being interrogated. His arguments merit attention because they are in fact directed at the social-trustee model of professionalism that is at the heart of this study.

Effectively, Allhoff takes aim at the social-trustee model of professionalism because he suggests that the command of medical knowledge does not bring with it any moral responsibilities. He cites David Tornberg, former deputy assistant secretary of defense for health affairs, who claims that a medical degree is not a "sacramental vow," but is, in Allhoff's words, simply a "certification of technical merit."[15]

Allhoff is not making a standard appeal to the idea of dual loyalty. He is not claiming that a physician's obligation to national security might override his or her obligation to do no harm. He is claiming that a physician has no obligation *as* physician, because medical knowledge does not generate obligations.

Allhoff offers an analogy by asking how knowledge works in other professions. Do chemical engineers have a duty not to construct chemical weapons by virtue of the fact that they have the technical knowledge that would allow them to build such weapons? Allhoff believes that the answer to this question is no. There is, he says, "nothing *intrinsic* about their technical knowledge that would morally prohibit them from doing something."[16] If that is true of chemical engineers, it is also true of physicians.

Allhoff acknowledges that one response to his argument by analogy might be to suggest that it is not knowledge that generates obligations but the role that one plays in using one's knowledge. Medical knowledge does not generate an obligation to avoid participating in interrogations, but the role of physician is incompatible with participating in abusive interrogations. The problem with this move is that, if a physician participates in an interrogation, he is serving not in the role of physician but in the role of medically trained interrogator. In other words, the role responsibilities of a physician get traction only if a medically trained person agrees to that role. But doctors are not required to serve the role of physician to everyone.

Although I do not agree with Allhoff's position here, it highlights an interesting issue for those who wish to argue that physicians may be involved with interrogations. The difficulty raised by Allhoff's view that a physician participating in an abusive interrogation is only performing the role of medically trained interrogator is that the legal justification for approving EITs was premised on the assumption that medical personnel would be present and would function in a medical role. In the case of waterboarding, a physician must be present.

Recall that the Bradbury "Techniques" memorandum required a physician to be present, in case there is a medical emergency. The memorandum is quite specific. "It is conceivable (though, we understand from OMS, highly unlikely) that a detainee could suffer spasms of the larynx that would prevent him from breathing even when the application of water is stopped and the detainee returned to an upright position. In the event of such spasms, a qualified physician would immediately intervene to address the problem, and, if necessary, the intervening physician would perform a tracheotomy."[17]

Given the reasoning embedded in the OLC memoranda, the OMS guidelines, and the surgeon general's report, Allhoff's argument is not available to justify the participation of medical personnel in abusive interrogations, at least not the participation of physicians. The framework for EITs requires that doctors function in the role of physicians when they participate in interrogations; they do not function merely as medically trained interrogators.

This point is even clearer when we consider other activities engaged in by physicians at Guantánamo Bay. Consider, for example, the role played by physicians in responding to hunger strikers. The hunger strikes at Guantánamo Bay are well documented, as is the work of physicians at the facility in force-feeding detainees. Indeed, as recently as January 2009, nearly a fifth of detainees at Guantánamo Bay were on hunger strikes. And the position of the DOD on responding to hunger strikes is clear. A DOD instruction issued in June 2006 explicitly authorizes tube-feeding of detainees without their consent. Section 4.7.1 of the instruction reads: "In the case of a hunger strike, attempted suicide, or other attempted serious self-harm, medical treatment or intervention may be directed without the consent of the detainee to prevent death or serious harm. Such action must be based on a medical determination that immediate treatment or intervention is necessary to prevent death or serious harm, and, in addition, must be approved by the commanding officer of the detention facility or other designated senior officer responsible for detainee operations."[18]

Although the DOD authorizes military doctors to force-feed hunger strikers and clearly expects them to do so, force-feeding violates numerous codes of medical ethics, including the Declarations of Tokyo and Malta. If force-feeding rises to the level of torture, as a report of the UN Commission on Human Rights concluded about force-feeding at Guantánamo Bay, then it also violates numerous other codes, including those discussed earlier in this chapter.[19] Does Allhoff's argument provide a justification for physician involvement?

Once again, I think Allhoff's argument is deeply problematic. As the DOD instruction makes clear, in force-feeding detainees, physicians are acting as physicians, not in some other role, and they are delivering medical treatment. Although there is evidence to suggest that it is not always a "medical determination" that triggers force-feeding, nevertheless that is the policy of the DOD, and it is hard to see how medically trained individuals here are acting in any role other than that of physician.[20]

Although I do not think that Allhoff's argument is successful, it might appear to threaten a social-trustee model of professionalism. Even if Allhoff is right that one can separate the roles of medically trained interrogators by distinguishing when they function as interrogators and when they function as physicians and then restricting their medical obligations to the (limited) role they play as physicians, the social-trustee model of professionalism remains intact. When they occupy the role of physician, doctors have professional medical responsibilities *as* physicians. To be sure, if one can separate roles as easily as Allhoff thinks, then a social-trustee model of professionalism has weaker normative force than otherwise. Yet even a weak normative force is better than none. Can this normative force be explained?

Accounting for Role Responsibilities

The best treatment of the normative dimensions of role responsibilities I know is found in Arthur Applbaum's book *Ethics for Adversaries: The Morality of Roles in Public and Professional Life.*[21] Applbaum's account of role responsibilities is worth setting out in some detail. Applbaum is concerned with adversarial institutions in our society. Law, business, government, and medicine are all, at one time or another, adversarial in the sense that acting as a professional within the field is understood to require engaging in practices that would not be considered acceptable outside of a particular role. A lawyer's zealous defense of a client may include manipulation and deception; a politician may engage in a slanderous negative advertising campaign; a business manager's commitment to the bottom line is praised even when profits are raised at the expense of workers; and a doctor working for a managed health care system may be required not to mention transplants as treatment options for certain conditions. Given that acting in adversarial fashion will often result in harm to others, how can such actions be justified?

The answer typically given to this question is that, when one acts in an adversarial fashion, she or he is fulfilling the requirements of a role. Occupying certain roles—or, for our purposes in this study, being a member of certain professions—brings with it both requirements and constraints that do not apply to those who are not in those roles or professions. While an expertise-professionalism paradigm that separates expert knowledge from social responsibility might pose a challenge to this claim, the conviction that a doctor, for example, has particular responsibilities that come with being a doctor is widely accepted. Applbaum certainly agrees that roles have normative significance, but he urges caution in how we account for this significance. He begins with an arresting case.

The example he discusses at length is that of the executioner of Paris, Charles-Henri Sanson, who was appointed by Louis XVI. Louis XIV had appointed Sanson's great-grandfather to the post, and the position of executioner was something of a family business. All six of Sanson's brothers, as well as his son, were executioners. By all accounts, Sanson was conscientious in discharging his role responsibilities, which included torturing, mutilating, hanging, and beheading. And he functioned in this role through changing political regimes. He executed both Louis XVI and Robespierre. As Applbaum observes, any coherent account of Sanson's life and work must explain two facts: "first, every revolutionary faction that gained momentary ascendancy viewed Sanson as a practitioner of a necessary profession; second, Sanson viewed himself precisely this way" (19).

To provide a sense of Sanson's approach to his work, Applbaum imagines a conversation between one of Sanson's contemporaries, Louis Sébastien Mercier, and Sanson, in which Sanson defends himself against the charge that he is a serial murderer.

You have recently wondered about me, "what an instrument—what a man!" But that question misunderstands me in two ways. On the job, I am neither an instrument nor a man. Let me explain.

I am not a mere instrument, if by that you mean one who takes no responsibility for what his superiors demand of him. . . . I am not an instrument devoid of mind or conscience, but a *professional*. Professions are committed to the realization of important values. My profession is the guardian of a political value that is of utmost moral importance. . . . To this good I have dedicated my life, and my practice as executioner has aimed at it through all the changing regimes to which you accuse me of whoring. My devotion is not to any one regime or political ideology, but to the good of social order and the stability and security it brings. . . . To realize the good of social order, my profession is committed to a simple principle: the state must maintain its monopoly over violence. (36)

Applbaum imagines Sanson continuing his defense as follows:

What I mean by saying that on the job I am not a man is that I do not act as a man simply. In exercising my professional duties I must set aside personal considerations . . .

I do not mean simply that the executioner *may* not take personal consideration into account, but that the executioner *cannot*, and still be the executioner. . . . The act of execution that the executioner performs on the scaffold does not exist apart from his professional role—it is constituted by it. You would not describe what a surgeon does as stabbing, what a lawyer does as robbing, or what a prosecutor does as kidnapping, would you? (39)

In order to understand Sanson's claims here, we need to ask how role responsibilities connect to moral evaluation. Applbaum suggests that there are two ways to think about this connection. The first, "direct moralization," equates role prescriptions with moral prescriptions for those who occupy the relevant role. The problem with this approach is evident from Sanson's role responsibilities. If direct moralization is the correct account, then the fact that Sanson has a role responsibility to lop off someone's head means he has a moral responsibility to do so, which is not plausible. Moreover, even in roles that have moral force, not every role prescription has moral content.

The second account of the connection between role responsibilities and moral evaluation Applbaum calls "mediated moralization." On this account, the obligations that come with a role are not themselves moral prescriptions, and the standards for assessing excellence internal to particular roles are not moral standards. Instead, "if one occupies a role that has moral force, one has one big reason to follow the role's nonmoral prescriptions." Applbaum continues, "If one's role has moral force of a certain sort, part of being a morally good person is to be good at one's role" (52).

Of course, this account of the connection between role responsibilities and moral evaluation does not presuppose that a particular role has moral force. Nor does this account provide a means of determining what roles have moral force. Indeed, although mediated moralization has some advantages over direct moralization, it is not satisfactory on its own. Both accounts provide pieces of the puzzle; both capture part of the truth. The truth in direct moralization is that "though actual role prescriptions are not themselves moral prescriptions, reasonable role prescriptions may be. To the extent that what the role is tracks what the role morally should be, the role is, in this sense, directly moralized" (54). The truth in mediated moralization is that "there can be moral reasons that obligate a role occupant to comply with the actual substantive prescriptions of roles, even when the content of what the role is does not track the content of what the role should be" (55).

Applbaum concludes from this analysis that one way of understanding the constraints imposed by role responsibilities is clearly mistaken. Roles should not be understood on analogy with natural law. It is a mistake, for example, to think that a doctor occupies a natural role such that, because humans are the kind of creatures that fall ill and suffer, those who have the skills to prevent or alleviate suffering have a natural moral obligation to do so. Instead, what Applbaum proposes is a position he calls "practice positivism." Practice positivism is the view that practices comprised by a role or profession are not natural but conventional; they are stitched together by the social meanings of those who engage in the practices and those who rely on the practices. As Applbaum puts it in several places: "The rules of a practice simply are what they are, not what they ought to be or what we want them to be" (51).

Does this mean that Sanson is correct when he says that because he executes not as a man but as an executioner, his role swallows up his responsibility for killing another human being? Does acting in an institutional role change the description or the possible moral evaluation of one's action such that one can render a judgment only from within the practice or by condemning the practice as a whole? The answer to these questions is no, because acts always have more than one description and because a role never totally eclipses the person occupying the role. Sanson both executes and kills (often in a gruesome fashion), and it is never just Sanson the executioner that performs these acts, but Sanson the person.

Nevertheless, practice positivism complicates the relation between roles and moral evaluation in that practices can change in ways that undercut the normative purchase of particular roles. The example that Applbaum explores in this regard is, in fact, medicine. Applbaum asks us to reflect on the fact that various activities that physicians undertake appear to violate role responsibilities internal to the profession of medicine. If doctors' first commitment is to the health of individual patients, then a variety of professional activities appear to conflict with this commitment. For example, clinician-researchers treat patients as subjects, which potentially conflicts with treating them as patients. Managed-care physicians are frequently gatekeepers more concerned with the bottom line than with individual patient care. Does a physician's role responsibility preclude him or her from being a researcher or gatekeeper? To answer this question, Applbaum says, consider the case of *Spaulding v. Zimmerman.*[22] The facts of the case are as follows. John Zimmerman had a serious car accident, which resulted in extensive injuries to David Spaulding, a passenger in the car. Spaulding sought damages from Zimmerman, and Zimmerman's insurance company had Spaulding examined by a company doctor. The doctor discovered a life-threatening aneurysm that Spaulding's own doctors had missed. The insurance-company physician did not reveal the condition to Spaulding or his doctors and instead informed the insurance company and Zimmerman's lawyer. Not surprisingly, the lawyer recommended that the insurance company settle with Spaulding before the aneurysm was discovered or burst.

We might think that this physician had an intrinsic role responsibility that would require him to inform Spaulding of the aneurysm. The problem with this thought is that it conflicts with the view of practice positivism that a practice is what it is and not what it ought to be or what we want it to be. The upshot is that even if current role responsibilities of physicians are understood to preclude failing to disclose a life-threatening aneurysm, the insurance-company doctor might respond by saying: "Fine. If you don't think my work for the insurance company meets the standards of doctoring, call what I do schmoctoring." Applbaum claims that there is nothing preventing a doctor from making this "doctor/schmoctor" response. As long as he does not violate the law or any pre-professional moral obligations, he is free to employ his training and knowledge as he sees fit. Call it schmoctoring, if you don't want to call it doctoring.

At this point, it might seem that Applbaum has embraced an expertise model of professionalism, for, as he concedes, in effect, professionals can deploy their expertise as they see fit. Is this not the view that expertise is untethered to any conception of the common good? Yes and no. There is no intrinsic connection between expert knowledge and the common good, but a practice establishes a conventional connection. The insurance-company physician can act as a schmoctor, but not as a doctor, at least not as long as those who doctor define their practice as requiring one to notify a person one has examined of a life-threatening condition. Thus, in one sense, Applbaum's rejection of the notion of a natural role for a physician heightens the importance of professional associations and codes of ethics. For if a practice is what it is and not what it ought to be, then if enough doctors feel unconstrained by a previous generation's understanding of doctoring and instead understand themselves as schmoctors, then schmoctors will become doctors.

At this juncture, it is worth noting that, although I have distinguished between a social-trustee model of professionalism and an expertise model, the more precise formulation of the contrast would be social trusteeship vs. *neutral* expertise.[23] The qualifier "neutral" is important at this stage of the argument, because the assumption behind an expertise model of professionalism is that knowledge itself is neutral and so can be mobilized in any way a professional chooses. Someone who has been medically trained can use his knowledge to heal or to interrogate. The fact that he has expert medical knowledge does not itself constrain the expert's action.

In one sense, of course, an account of professionalism that relies on practice positivism cannot deny this claim. I have already indicated, for example, that there is nothing about the nature of medical knowledge that itself constrains how physicians act. Practice positivism is, in this way, antiessentialist. Yet to talk of neutral professional expertise, as if neutrality equals lack of constraint, is profoundly misleading. To see why, recall the discussion in the introduction about how to define professions. We saw that Eliot Freidson provides one important, but fairly typical, account. He identifies five elements of professions:

1. specialized work in the officially recognized economy that is believed to be grounded in a body of theoretically based, discretionary knowledge and skill and that is accordingly given special status in the labor force;

2. exclusive jurisdiction in a particular division of labor created and controlled by occupational negotiation;

3. a sheltered position in both external and internal labor markets that is based on qualifying credentials created by the occupation;

4. a formal training program lying outside the labor market that produces the qualifying credentials, which is controlled by the occupation and associated with higher education; and

5. an ideology that asserts greater commitment to doing good work than to economic gain and to the quality rather than the economic efficiency of work.[24]

Points 1–4 suggest why it is misleading to talk about neutral expertise, even if one accepts a nonessentialist account of the normative character of the professions. Freidson could be clearer here, for he assumes a lot when he says that discretionary knowledge and skill are "accordingly given special status in the labor force." This "accordingly" needs to be unpacked, for it gestures toward the relationship between professions and the social recognition of professional practices. Indeed, what is implicit in elements 1–4 is the reality of state licensing of professions. Yes, professions have a special (protected) status in the labor market on the basis of knowledge that is typically associated with higher education, and professions are self-policing, in part because one needs the specialized knowledge of the professional in order to evaluate professional competence. Note, however, that the vehicle for market protection is a credentialing and licensing system that is coordinated through the state. And the state does not create such a system to protect every group that has specialized knowledge.

The fact that many occupations are loosely called professions tends to obscure the role of the state in valuing certain kinds of expertise and not others. If, for example, you enter "film critics association" in an internet search engine, you will get results for the Los Angeles Film Critics Association, the Southeastern Film Critics Association, and other such groups. Further, the websites for these groups will indicate that their associations are organizations of "professional" film critics. But to speak of a professional film critic in this way is only to say that a particular individual earns his or her living through film criticism. It is not to speak of a profession as we have used the term in this study.

In one sense, of course, to refer to individuals who earn their living through film criticism as professional critics is to acknowledge the fact that such individuals often have extensive knowledge of film history, of literature, of the technical demands of cinematography, and of much else besides. In fact, the best film critics probably have command of a body of knowledge far exceeding that of a typical psychologist. But we would not speak of the film critic as a member of a profession in a way that we would of a psychologist. The reason is that the psychologist, but not the film critic, is licensed by the state on the basis of a credentialing system put in place and monitored by fellow professionals.

The difference between a profession that is state recognized and state licensed and a profession understood as merely a particular kind of occupation, even one that demands highly specialized knowledge, is that only the latter can be understood as value neutral. The professions of psychology, medicine, and law are not value neutral because society has recognized them as involving matters so important to the common good that they require both protection and oversight. For this reason, there is a check on the position of practice positivism articulated by Applbaum. Yes, a profession is what it is and not necessarily what it ought to be. And, yes, professions can change if practitioners as a group begin to practice differently. Nevertheless, because the expertise mobilized by professionals is valued by society and therefore recognized and restricted by the state, the state could withdraw its recognition in ways that could reduce a profession to an occupation. To put this point in Applbaum's terms, doctors could become schmoctors, but in doing so they might forfeit their status as professionals that society values, rewards, and regulates.

Once we acknowledge the tight connection between expertise that is socially valued and the regulation of professions embedded in codes of professional ethics that are partly enforced by the state, we see how talk of neutral expertise is misleading. We also see that a profession could come to define itself out of existence by effectively repudiating the social contract to use its expertise for the common good. Thus, practice positivism can, just as an essentialist view of the professions can, account for why there are certain actions that physicians or psychologists may not perform. The obligation to maintain the social contract also falls to those who are charged with regulating professions. For those who would change a profession in ways that threaten to undermine the social role the profession plays may not represent the profession as a whole. This is why it is important for those who monitor professional standards to do their jobs. Oversight boards need to discipline departures from the established norms of professional practice. It is to this point that we next turn.

Notes

1. "Office of Medical Services Guidelines on Medical and Psychological Support to Detainee Rendition, Interrogation and Detention," OMS, May 17, 2004, available on the American Civil Liberties Union website, www.aclu.org/torturefoia/released/103009/cia-olc/2.pdf.

2. Miles, *Oath Betrayed*.

3. "Principles of Medical Ethics Relevant to the Role of Health Personnel, Particularly Physicians, in the Protection of Prisoners and Detainees against Torture and Other Cruel, Inhuman or Degrading Treatment or Punishment," Office of the United Nations High Commissioner for Human Rights, December 18, 1982, www2.ohchr.org/english/law/medicalethics.htm.

4. Office of the Surgeon General, *Assessment of Detainee Medical Operations*.

5. Ibid., 1-4.

6. Ibid., 1-7.

7. "Army Regulation 40-400: Patient Administration," Department of the Army, March 12, 2001, available on the Washington Research Library Consortium Aladin Research Commons website, http://dspace.wrlc.org/doc/get/2041/63339/00100display.pdf, sec. 3-38, p. 25.

8. Office of the Surgeon General, *Assessment of Detainee Medical Operations*, 7-3.

9. "Army Regulation 190-8: Enemy Prisoners of War, Retained Personnel, Civilian Internees and Other Detainees," Department of the Army, October 1, 1997, http://armypubs.army.mil/epubs/pdf/r190_8.pdf, sec. 1-5 (b) and (c), p. 2.

10. Office of the Surgeon General, *Assessment of Detainee Medical Operations*, 18-12, 18-16.

11. "Interrogation Log: Detainee 063," Secret Orcon, November 23, 2002, available on the *Time* website, www.time.com/time/2006/log/log.pdf.

12. Office of the Surgeon General, *Assessment of Detainee Medical Operations*, 18-22, n. 4.

13. "Opinion 2.067—Torture," AMA Code of Ethics, December 1999, www.ama-assn.org/ama/pub/physician-resources/medical-ethics/code-medical-ethics/opinion2067.page.

14. Allhoff, "Physician Involvement in Hostile Interrogation," 395.

15. Ibid.

16. Ibid., 398.

17. Steven G. Bradbury to John A. Rizzo, "'Techniques" memorandum, May 10, 2005, www.justice.gov/olc/docs/memo-bradbury2005-3.pdf, 15.

18. "Medical Program Support for Detainee Operations," instruction no. 2310.08E, DOD, June 6, 2006, www.dtic.mil/whs/directives/corres/pdf/231008p .pdf, sec. 4.7.1.

19. Economic and Social Council (Commission on Human Rights), "Situation of Detainees at Guantánamo Bay," February 15, 2006. Reprinted in *International Legal Materials* 45 (2006): 716–41.

20. Annas, "Hunger Strikes at Guantanamo."

21. Page references for quotations from this work are given in the text below.

22. 263 Minn. 346, 116 N.W. 2d 704 (1962).

23. The discussion that follows is indebted to Dave Ozar, who pressed me to explore the question of value neutrality.

24. Freidson, *Professionalism*, 127.

Six

Discipline and Punish
The Importance of
Professional Accountability

> The foundation on which the analysis of a profession must be based
> is its relationship to the ultimate source of power and authority in
> modern society—the state.
>
> —Eliot Freidson, *Professional Dominance*, 83

If the argument in the previous chapter is correct, the efforts of those who resisted the participation of psychologists, lawyers, and doctors in abusive interrogations were an attempt, in Eliot Freidson's words, to save the soul of their professions. In speaking of the "soul" of a profession, I am not invoking any metaphysical or essentialist claim about the nature of particular professions. On the contrary, as I said in chapter 5, I take very seriously Applbaum's view that professions are what they are and not what they ought to be or what we want them to be. If Applbaum is right about this, then the effort to prevent professionals from participating in abusive interrogations is an attempt to shape professions so that what they are coincides with what we believe they ought to be, while recognizing that they could be different. This is why the fight about the APA Code of Ethics that we examined in chapter 1 was so significant: it was about what psychology is and will be. This is also why the fierce resistance to the work of Yoo and Bybee, even by those who agreed with the conclusions reached in the interrogation memoranda, is important. Allowing the legal arguments of Yoo and Bybee to go unchallenged threatened to define the standards of the profession downward and thus erode public confidence in lawyers and ultimately in the rule of law.

If the actions of professionals in debates about whether to authorize or participate in abusive interrogations was a defining moment for several professions, it is important to acknowledge that the work of professionals in defining their profession did not end when the interrogations ended, if indeed they have. The struggle for the "soul" of various professions continues in ways that have not been sufficiently appreciated. It is to some of those struggles that I turn in this chapter.

The Role of Professional Licensure

In order fully to understand the significance of the postinterrogation activism of critics of abusive interrogations, we need to return to the point on which we ended the previous chapter; namely, the role of licensing and disciplining professional practice. If an essentialist view of professions is rejected, then some mechanism for identifying and, more importantly, overseeing professional practice is necessary. Apart from stabilizing professional identity, regulating professional life is central to insuring that the professions actually promote the common good, a commitment that is central to a social-trustee model of the professions.

As with accounts of professionalism generally, there are primarily two views of professional licensure. The first, a public interest model, corresponds to the social-trustee approach to the professions. The second, a "capture" model, dovetails with expertise professionalism. And just as expertise professionalism is the preferred view among sociologists, so do economists champion the capture model.

Mario Pagliero states the contrast between the two models succinctly in his attempt to understand the effects of licensing requirements for various occupations. He notes that there has been a proliferation of such requirements and that "more than 800 occupations are licensed in at least one U.S. state."[1] Why, he asks, has there been an explosion of licensing requirements, and what effect has this sort of state regulation had?

To answer these questions, Pagliero considers both the typical rationale for, and the typical result of, "professional" licensing.[2] If one focuses on the typical rationale for licensing, the public interest model emerges; if one focuses on the results of licensing, the capture model appears more compelling. The idea behind the public interest model is that the services provided by some professions are such that only professionals in that field are capable of determining who is a competent practitioner of the profession. In the technical jargon of economic theory, there is an information asymmetry that can lead to market failure. Consider the application of this model to medicine. Because doctors, but not patients, are able to distinguish those who are highly qualified to practice medicine from those who are quacks, without a system of licensing overseen by physicians, patients will suffer at the hands of quacks, and quacks and qualified physicians will compete in the marketplace, which in turn will lower the price of medical services. When compensation declines, more qualified doctors will either leave or not enter the market.

The public interest model of licensing thus takes its name from the conviction that screening prospective professionals for at least minimal competence and disciplining established professionals for falling below minimal standards of competence provides a mechanism for protecting both individuals and society from potentially harmful incompetence. And, indeed, as many theorists have pointed out, almost all attempts to defend licensing requirements for occupations have been justified by appealing to the notion of public interest. Consider, for example, the objectives of licensing lawyers, as set out by the ABA and the National Conference of Bar Examiners: "The public interest requires that the public be secure in its expectation that those who are admitted to the bar are worthy of the trust and confidence clients may reasonably place in their lawyers."[3]

By contrast, the capture model looks more to the economic effects of licensing and concludes that the standard justification in terms of the public interest is not supported by empirical evidence. If licensing is not defensible in terms of the public interest, there must be some other interest it serves. There is, say capture theorists: it serves the interest of professionals in a field by increasing salaries through the restriction of the supply of qualified professionals. As Pagliero puts the point, the approach of capture theory is "that professional examinations are intended to limit the number of professionals, increase prices, and weaken competition, thereby introducing the typical inefficiencies caused by market power."[4]

If capture theory appears to adopt a cynical view of professional licensure, there is reason for the cynicism. Any number of studies, going back to the 1960s, provide reasons for doubting the public interest argument and accepting the capture model. Pagliero's own study of professional licensing for attorneys suggests that the main effect of licensing requirements is roughly a $10,000 increase in starting salaries for lawyers, which "implies a total transfer from consumers to lawyers of 19% of lawyers' wages and a total welfare loss of over $3 billion."[5] This line of argument can be traced back at least as far as Alex Maurizi's 1974 article "Occupational Licensing and the Public Interest." Maurizi contends that, despite the rhetoric that licensing safeguards the public interest, the reality is that licensing promotes the interests of those who are licensed and not of the public. He summarizes his findings by noting that "a 10 percent increase in excess demand generates a decrease in the pass rate [in licensing exams] varying primarily from 1 percent to 10." Similarly, "a 10 percent increase in average practitioner incomes produces up to a 10 percent decrease in the pass rate." The evidence thus appears to confirm the notion that "the power of licensing boards is often used to prolong the period of higher incomes resulting from increases in excess demand for the services of the occupation in question and that the instrument then used to accomplish this purpose is alteration of the pass rate on the licensing examination."[6]

Walter Gellhorn reaches a similar conclusion in his study titled "The Abuse of Occupational Licensing." He writes: "That restricting access is the real purpose, and not merely a side effect, of many if not most successful campaigns to institute licensing schemes can scarcely be doubted. Licensing, imposed ostensibly to protect the public, almost always impedes only those who desire to enter the occupation or 'profession'; those already in practice remain entrenched without a demonstration of fitness or probity."[7]

This last point Gellhorn makes is particularly relevant to our current study. I do not doubt that imposing a system of licensing is, and in many cases may well be intended to be, a way to capture a market for the benefit of those who are so licensed. There is a lot of empirical evidence to support the view that licensing has deleterious labor-market effects. This is especially true in the imposition of credentialing and licensing requirements that control entry to an occupation. Notice, however, that entry requirements are only one aspect of professional licensing. Licensing and disciplinary mechanisms go together. Unfortunately, Gellhorn is probably also right when he says that those already licensed who are in fact unfit to practice a profession are rarely disciplined or expelled from the profession.

In my view, the lack of oversight of professional practice and the failure to sanction alleged misconduct is a much more serious threat to the public good than the monopolistic practices of overregulating access to a particular occupation. Certainly if licensing boards raise standards on certifying exams in response to an increase in the supply of applicants, then some who are in fact qualified to practice medicine or law will not be given the opportunity to do so and the diminished supply of competent professionals may keep the cost of professional services unnecessarily high. But this harm is small compared to the harm an incompetent or unethical professional may cause.

Capture theorists may be right that professional standards frequently serve the interests of those licensed and not the public, but as I have insisted a number of times in this study, to acknowledge a reality is not to accept it. Professionals may view themselves as experts for hire, and they may even cynically manipulate a licensing system to insure a higher standard of living than they otherwise would have. But our discussion of the responses of various professional groups to the war on terror suggests that many professionals see their work in very different terms.

This is why the work of professionals to hold their colleagues accountable for alleged violations of professional standards is important. Our brief examination of professional licensure thus provides a context for the postinterrogation activism of professionals seeking to hold their colleagues accountable, for accountability is central to insuring that professions do serve the public interest.

The Importance of Professional Accountability

Consider the efforts by some psychologists to hold accountable their fellow psychologists who participated in abusive interrogations at Guantánamo Bay. Just as there are mechanisms for screening applicants who seek membership in a profession, so, too, are there oversight mechanisms as part of state licensing laws. For example, in the state of New York, the Board of Regents and New York State's Education Department oversee regulation of the professions through the Office of the Professions. The Office of the Professions in turn administers state regulation of professions through twenty-nine State Boards for the Professions.

We can see how these state boards function by examining the New York Board of Psychology's review of the complaint brought to it in the aftermath of abusive interrogations at Guantánamo Bay. The complaint was brought by the Center for Justice and Accountability on behalf of Steven Reisner, a board-licensed psychologist in New York, against John Leso, another licensed psychologist in the state. In his letter to the board, Reisner states his complaint succinctly:

> Under the authority of his New York license, Dr. Leso has used his expertise for the purpose of harming rather than protecting the health of detainees at Guantánamo Bay, Cuba. Dr. Leso used his training in psychology to exploit the weaknesses of detainees not only in the context of specific interrogations, but also in a systematic fashion; recommending that U.S. personnel use a series of increasingly abusive interrogation techniques designed to degrade, dehumanize, and disrupt the cognitive function of detainees held in U.S. custody, and to increase their mental pain and suffering, for the purpose of modifying their behavior, punishing, or intimidating them. As such, I believe he should be investigated and disciplined accordingly.[8]

To understand the complaint that Reisner lodges, it is important to know that John Leso led the first BSCT at Guantánamo Bay from June 2002 until January 2003. In this role, he coauthored an interrogation policy memorandum that drew upon SERE training in outlining an interrogation strategy that was physically and psychologically abusive. He personally participated in the interrogation of Mohammed al Qahtani, a fact that is documented in the interrogation log for Detainee 063.[9] The complaint alleges that, in serving in the role of BSCT psychologist, Leso violated various New York State laws.

Even if Leso violated the sections of the law enumerated in the complaint, it might reasonably be asked whether the New York State Board of Psychology has jurisdiction to review Leso's action as a military officer stationed in Cuba. In fact, the New York Office of Professional Discipline denied jurisdiction, but not because Leso acted as a military officer outside the state of New York. Instead, jurisdiction was denied because the alleged misconduct does not constitute the practice of psychology as defined by the state. The reasoning of the director of the Office of Professional Discipline, Louis Catone, is particularly interesting in light of our discussion of role responsibility in chapter 5. He writes: "While the military (or a civilian employer) is free to require that one hold a particular professional license as a condition of obtaining a position, that, without more, does not mean that some or all of the activities performed for that employer constitute the practice of a profession. The fact that Dr. Leso may have possessed special knowledge gained through his education, training, and/or experience as a psychologist that made him useful to the military in developing interrogation techniques does not mean that Dr. Leso's conduct in that regard constituted the practice of psychology."[10]

There is a peculiar logic at work in the decision of the Office of Professional Discipline. Although the army established BSCTs precisely for the purpose of utilizing the expertise of psychologists in interrogations, and although the army requires military psychologists to be licensed in at least one of the fifty states (and the army's own clinical quality assurance guidelines indicate that a license is valid only where the "issuing authority accepts, investigates, and acts upon quality assurance information, such as practitioner professional performance, conduct, and ethics of practice, regardless of the practitioner's military status or residency"[11]), the Office of Professional Discipline said it did not have jurisdiction because Leso was not acting as a psychologist.

Despite the fact that this office declined to investigate Leso, the possibility that it might have done so highlights the interconnections between professional codes, state and federal law, and military regulations that we have seen repeatedly in this study. The complaint against Leso is possible because the military recognizes the authority of states to license professionals and states recognize the importance of professional codes in setting state licensing requirements. The allegations of misconduct brought against Leso are framed in terms of New York State law, but they are, at bottom, allegations that Leso violated the APA Code of Ethics. Indeed, state standards typically embed professional standards, which is precisely what we see in New York. For example, the rules of the Board of Regents governing unprofessional misconduct in New York define misconduct, in part, by reference to standards in the professions themselves. "Unprofessional conduct in the practice of any profession licensed, certified or registered pursuant to title VIII of the Education Law," we read, "shall include willful or grossly negligent failure to comply with substantial provisions of Federal, State or local laws, rules *or regulations governing the practice of the profession.*"[12]

The fact that state licensing requirements for psychologists reflect professional standards of conduct set out by the APA should come as no surprise. Since the 1950s, the APA has provided states with a Model Licensing Act (MLA) designed to be a template for state law governing licensing and regulation of psychologists. The APA adopted the first MLA in 1955, when only nine states licensed psychologists. Between 1955 and the first revision of the MLA in 1967, twenty-three additional states adopted licensing requirements. By 1977, the goal of promulgating the MLA had been accomplished; all fifty states and the District of Columbia had enacted licensing requirements.[13]

Keeping this in mind, we see that the effort to get New York's Office of the Professions to investigate allegations of professional misconduct against John Leso and to discipline him if he was found guilty of the allegations made against him was an attempt to uphold standards of conduct within the profession of psychology. There is, I think, a tendency to interpret this effort at discipline as unnecessarily vindictive or inappropriately punitive. Those who adopt this position are inclined to argue that while it is admirable to fight for specific policy positions within the APA or to fight to revise the Code of Ethics to prohibit (or permit) specific actions of psychologists in the war on terror, it is misguided to seek sanctions against Leso and others. Leso was doing the best he could in an ambiguous situation, and he should not be punished for attempting to follow orders and safeguard national security by facilitating abusive interrogations.

We have seen the problem with this view above. If licensure is to serve the public interest, as the APA, ABA, and almost every other professional association say that it should, then professionals must be held accountable for violations of codes of conduct. Thus, as important as the fight within psychology was to define the standards of conduct set out in the APA Code of Ethics as they apply to the role of psychologists in coercive interrogations, the effort to sanction psychologists who are perceived to have violated the code is perhaps even more important. It is thus not surprising that some of the same advocates for restricting APA endorsement of participation in the war on terror have been actively pursuing complaints against the psychologists involved at Guantánamo Bay and elsewhere.

In addition to the complaint filed against John Leso in New York, complaints have been filed against Larry James in Ohio and James Mitchell in Texas.[14] None of these complaints has been greeted with much enthusiasm by the state agencies responsible for professional oversight, and the regulatory provisions in state law are sufficiently loose that significant disciplinary action is unlikely in these or other cases that may be brought in the near future. Nevertheless, these efforts to hold psychologists accountable are important to professional identity, even if the failure by states to take disciplinary action threatens that identity and undermines claims about professions serving the public interest.

The recognition of the importance of oversight of the conduct of professionals by the state has led not only to complaints to state boards of professional review, but to efforts to change state law to make disciplinary action easier. The most striking example comes from California, where, in a joint resolution with the state assembly, the state senate passed Joint Resolution 19, which resolved that California's licensed health professionals could be prosecuted for participation in abusive or enhanced interrogations, torture, or other forms of cruel, inhuman, or degrading treatment of those in US custody. The declaration further resolved "that in view of the ethical obligations of health professionals, the record of abusive interrogation practices, and the Legislature's interest in protecting California-licensed health professionals, the Legislature hereby requests the United States Department of Defense and the Central Intelligence Agency to remove all California-licensed health professionals from participating in any way in prisoner and detainee interrogations that are coercive or 'enhanced' or that involve torture or cruel, inhuman, or degrading treatment or punishment, as defined by the Geneva Conventions, CAT, relevant jurisprudence regarding CAT, and related human rights documents and treaties."[15]

Although not as far-reaching as the California law, an effort has also been made by legislators in New York explicitly to prohibit the involvement of health care professionals in abusive interrogations. A5891, introduced into the general assembly in March 2011, seeks to amend the education law in New York to eliminate professional participation in interrogation. Section 4(D) reads: "No Health Care Professional shall participate in the interrogation of a prisoner, including being present in the interrogation room, asking or suggesting questions, advising on the use of specific interrogation techniques, monitoring the interrogation, or medically or psychologically evaluating a person for the purpose of identifying potential interrogation methods or strategies."[16]

If we return to the complaint against John Leso, we can see that A5891 would remove any ambiguity about whether Leso's action involved professional misconduct. For example, the complaint notes that Leso prepared a memorandum proposing strategies of interrogation that were subsequently adopted at Guantánamo Bay. A5891 does permit psychologists to develop effective interrogation techniques and to train others in their use, as long as the techniques do not involve torture or improper treatment and as long as the training is "not provided in support of specific ongoing or anticipated interrogations."[17] But Leso was involved with ongoing interrogations, and the techniques set out in the memo are problematic.

The memorandum identified three categories of interrogation techniques, two of which would clearly be prohibited. Category II techniques included "stress positions; the use of isolation for up to 30 days (with the possibility of additional 30 day periods, if authorized by the Chief Interrogator); depriving a detainee of food for up to 12 hours (or as long as the interrogator goes without food during an interrogation); the use of back-to-back 20 hour interrogations once per week; removal of all comfort items including religious items; forced grooming; handcuffing a detainee; and placing a hood on a detainee during questioning or movement." Category III techniques were even more extreme: "the daily use of 20 hour interrogations; the use of strict isolation without the right of visitation by treating medical professionals or the International Committee of the Red Cross (ICRC); the use of food restrictions for 24 hours once a week; the use of scenarios designed to convince the detainee he might experience a painful or fatal outcome; non-injurious physical consequences; removal of clothing; and exposure to cold weather or water until such time as the detainee began to shiver."[18] Had A5891 been law when Leso authored the memorandum that set out interrogation techniques in categories II and III, he clearly would have been in violation of New York law, and efforts to discipline him for professional misconduct would almost certainly have been easier.

George Annas has noted that efforts at accountability can extend beyond domestic mechanisms. For example, German citizens have sought to have Donald Rumsfeld and other American officials prosecuted for war crimes in a German courtroom. As Annas notes, even if such a trial is unlikely, the effort to bring an indictment represents a time-honored strategy of securing a kind of accountability through "naming and shaming." The fact that this effort was made in Germany, says Annas, itself serves as a reminder that the Nuremberg trials held various professionals responsible for the atrocities perpetrated under the Nazi regime.[19]

Annas also notes that, apart from criminal prosecution—either domestically or internationally—there are other actions that can be taken against physicians, lawyers, and other professionals to ensure accountability. For example, Annas, Michael Grodin, and Leonard Glantz have suggested that an international tribunal could be established that would have the authority to investigate allegations of professional misconduct and condemn professionals found guilty of violating norms of professional responsibility. Even though no criminal sanctions could be imposed, the tribunal's ability to publicly identify wrongdoing might provide "a powerful deterrent to grossly unethical conduct."[20]

What precisely such a tribunal would look like is unclear, but Annas and Grodin, in another essay, have sketched out the basic contours of an international medical tribunal. Such a tribunal would ideally be established with the approval and support of the UN. It would have the power to establish (or recognize as authoritative) an international code of ethics, hear cases, and publicly condemn physicians found to have violated the code. Indeed, Annas and Grodin are quite specific about the makeup and operation of such a tribunal. It should consist of a "large panel of distinguished judges" from numerous countries, and because it must be "authoritative and politically neutral, no single country or political philosophy could be permitted to dominate it, either by having a disproportionate representation on the tribunal or by disproportionately funding it."[21]

One of the most interesting aspects of Annas and Grodin's proposal is that it links the work of such a tribunal to national and state licensing boards. They write:

Steps should be taken at the level of national medical licensure boards (and state boards in countries in which political subdivisions have medical licensing authority) to articulate specific rules denouncing physicians who commit war crimes and crimes against humanity. Those found to have been involved in such crimes would lose their license to practice medicine, or be ineligible to obtain one if they were not yet physicians. Physicians who lost their license to practice medicine for war crimes or crimes against humanity in one jurisdiction would be prohibited from practicing medicine in all jurisdictions. Licensing agencies themselves could enter into a compact or agreement to adopt and enforce these rules and goals.[22]

Notice that Annas and Grodin's proposal anticipates lawyers and physicians working together to put in place mechanisms of oversight and discipline to ensure that professionals abide by the norms of practice set out in established codes. In this way, their work recognizes the flip side of the collaboration between medicine and law, documented earlier in this study, which enabled abusive interrogations in the first place. Ideally, professions are self-policing, but a public interest model of professional licensure recognizes that the relationship between the public interest and the work of professionals is mediated by the state and the instrumentality of law.

Earlier in this chapter, I suggested that, as important as the efforts to establish clear norms of professional conduct are, efforts to enforce norms might be even more important. In terms of the material on which we have focused, this point can be illustrated by saying that the collaborative work between psychologists and attorneys to bring allegations of misconduct by licensed psychologists before state licensing boards is possibly more important than the attempt to prevent the APA from embracing a change in its policy that would allow psychologists to participate in abusive interrogations. Both involve recruiting state power to the purpose of maintaining professional identity and accountability, but the former does this directly while the latter moves indirectly toward this end.

In chapter 3 we discussed Associate Deputy Attorney General David Margolis's decision not to accept the recommendation of the OPR that the DOJ refer John Yoo and Jay Bybee to their respective bars for disciplinary action. As we saw, Margolis's view was that the OPR's findings and his decision were "less important than the public's ability to make its own judgments about these documents and to learn lessons for the future."[23]

In one sense this is true. The investigations of and the complaints against various professionals have generated a small mountain of documentary evidence that provides a much clearer picture of the actions of professionals in the war on terror than we would have had without these efforts at accountability.[24] And we should also note that while it is the actions of psychologists, lawyers, and physicians that have been the focus of worries about professional misconduct, the initiatives to secure accountability have been undertaken by professionals seeking to defend professional integrity, often through collaborations with professionals in other fields. For example, lawyers with the Center for Justice and Accountability worked with psychologists to file the complaint against John Leso. Similarly, lawyers from Harvard's International Human Rights Clinic worked with psychologists to file the complaint in Ohio against Larry James. And these joint efforts provide a detailed picture of the role of psychologists at Guantánamo Bay. Those who take the time to review the documentary evidence generated through these efforts are in a reasonable position to judge for themselves whether there was professional misconduct at Guantánamo Bay.

Nevertheless, while transparency is important, so, too, is actual accountability. At least thus far, no psychologist has been disciplined for participating in abusive interrogations. No lawyer has been sanctioned. No doctor's medical license has been genuinely threatened. And although the DOJ appointed a special prosecutor to investigate the actions of the CIA in destroying videotapes of interrogations, no charges were filed. Although the legal work of Yoo and Bybee was found to be substandard, Yoo is a tenured professor at the University of California at Berkeley and Bybee is a federal judge on the US Court of Appeals for the Ninth Circuit. The fact that no actual findings of misconduct associated with professional sanctions have been forthcoming does not, of course, mean that there has been no actual accountability. Yet the evidence of misconduct is substantial enough to lead us to recall Robert Jay Lifton's observation, quoted in chapter 1, that "if a professional society is unable to take a stand against torture, it is pretty much unable to take a stance against any immoral behavior." Before turning to consider the relationship between professional codes and the habits and attitudes of professionals, we might wonder in the spirit of Lifton whether a profession that is unable to discipline a member for participating in torture is able to discipline its members for any behavior. In the idiom discussed in chapter 5, if doctors are not disciplined for acting like schmoctors, then there will be no difference between doctors and schmoctors and no way to protect the public from doctor/schmoctors.

Notes

1. Pagliero, "What Is the Objective?" 2.

2. I use scare quotes here because only a small percentage of the eight hundred occupations would qualify as professions given the definition that we have relied on in this study. For example, barber, hairdresser, embalmer, real estate broker, plumber, and similar occupations would be included in Pagliero's study of professional licensing. Although these occupations would not count as professions as defined in this volume, the general points made by Pagliero still apply.

3. Pagliero, "What Is the Objective?" 5.

4. Ibid., 2.

5. Ibid., 1.

6. Maurizi, "Occupational Licensing and the Public Interest," 412.

7. Gellhorn, "Abuse of Occupational Licensing," 11–12.

8. Steven Reisner and the Center for Justice and Accountability to the New York Office of the Professions, "Complaint—John Francis Leso, NY License #013492," available on the Courthouse News Service website, accessed August 16, 2011, www.courthousenews.com/2011/04/06/Leso%20complaint.pdf.

9. Leso's presence is noted in the records for November 23 and 27, 2003; the log is available on the *Time* website at www.time.com/time/2006/log/log.pdf.

10. Louis Catone to Kathy Roberts, "Re: John Francis Leso, Psychologist (Complaint of Dr. Steven Reisner," New York State Education Department, July 28, 2010, available on the Center for Justice and Accountability website, www.cja.org/down loads/No.%202.%20NYOP%20Denial%20of%20Jurisdiction.7.28.10.pdf.

11. Quoted in "Complaint—John Francis Leso, NY License #013492," 2.

12. "Rules of the Board of Regents: Part 29, Unprofessional Conduct," October 5, 2011, available on the website of the Office of the Professions, New York State Education Department, www.op.nysed.gov/title8/part29.htm, sec. 29.1.b.1 (italics mine).

13. It is worth noting that the MLA explicitly frames the intent of licensure as to promote the public good. For that reason, the APA recommends that legislation should have a section declaring its intent: "'This section declares that the intent of legislation for state licensure of psychologists is to ensure the practice of psychology in the public interest. The consumer should be assured that psychological services will be provided by licensed and qualified professionals according to the provisions of this act. The public must also be protected from the consequences of unprofessional conduct by persons licensed to practice psychology.'" "Model Act for State Licensure of Psychologists," APA, February 20, 2010, www.apa.org/about/policy/model-act-2010.pdf, 1–2.

14. Michael Reese, Trudy Bond, Colin Bossen, and Josephine Setzler to Ronald Ross, "Complaint Form—Larry C. James, License No. 6492," July 7, 2010, available

on the Harvard Law School Human Rights Program website, www.law.harvard
.edu/programs/hrp/documents/Larry_James_6492.pdf; Jim L. H. Cox, "Complaint Form—James Elmer Mitchell, License No. 23564," June 16, 2010, available on
the True/Slant website, www.trueslant.com/toddessig/files/2010/06/MIT-FINL
.pdf. Mitchell helped design the interrogation of Abu Zubaydah.

15. "Senate Joint Resolution No. 19—Relative to Health Professionals, August
14, 2008," available on the Official California Legislative Information website,
http://leginfo.ca.gov/pub/07-08/bill/sen/sb_0001-0050/sjr_19_bill_20080818
_chaptered.pdf.

16. A5891, 2011–12 Ass., Reg. Sess. (N.Y. 2011), available at http://open.ny
senate.gov/legislation/bill/A5891-2011.

17. Ibid., sec. 5(D).

18. Reisner to Office of the Professions, 7.

19. Annas, "Human Rights Outlaws."

20. Grodin, Annas, and Glantz, "Medicine and Human Rights," 463.

21. Annas and Grodin, "Medicine and Human Rights," 16.

22. Ibid., 17.

23. David Margolis, associate deputy attorney general, to the attorney general,
memorandum, January 5, 2010, available on the US House of Representatives
Committee on the Judiciary website, http://judiciary.house.gov/hearings/pdf/
DAGMargolisMemo100105.pdf, 67–68.

24. A report by Human Rights Watch claims that there are over 100,000 pages of
government documents on the mistreatment of detainees: Human Rights Watch,
Getting Away with Torture, 8.

Seven

Professional Responsibility and the Virtuous Professional

> To say that an agent has a regulative ideal is to say that they have internalised a certain conception of correctness or excellence, in such a way that they are able to adjust their motivation and conduct so that it conforms—or at least does not conflict—with that standard.
>
> —Justin Oakley and Dean Cocking,
> *Virtue Ethics and Professional Roles*, 25

Thus far we have examined how codes of ethics and professional responsibility have structured debates among professionals about appropriate conduct in assisting the government in the war on terror. We have also examined an account of how such codes function normatively in regulating behavior. This exploration has taken us a long way toward the goal of understanding how some of our fellow citizens are reasoning in deciding how to act morally in the war on terror. Recall Jeffrey Stout's view that democracy is a tradition in which reason giving is central. The fact that professionals have reasoned by appeal to norms of professional codes of conduct is important. But it is also important to note a second point highlighted by Stout's account of democratic practices; namely, that such practices are sustained by dispositions, virtues, and habits of thought that must be cultivated and continually renewed if democratic practice is to flourish.[1] Up to this point we have focused primarily on the rule-governed character of professional engagement in the war on terror. It is now time to turn to the relationship between role responsibilities, character, and democratic virtues.

To this end, I want to draw on an account of the relationship between role responsibilities and virtues that understands professional responsibility in terms of a general theory of virtue ethics. There are other ways to understand the role responsibilities of professionals, and as we saw when we examined Applbaum's practice positivism, one need not draw on a general moral theory to account for professional ethics. Still, understanding professional responsibility in terms of virtue ethics is one way to explain the importance of the professions to the formation of character and of habits of mind and heart that support democratic practice.

Professional Responsibility and Virtue

The best account I know of the theory of virtue ethics as it applies to professional responsibility is that offered by Justin Oakley and Dean Cocking in their book *Virtue Ethics and Professional Roles*. Oakley and Cocking rely on an Aristotelian conception of virtue in an attempt to show that professional responsibility is best understood by accounting for how professions give rise to particular virtues. Determining whether a particular course of action is a violation of professional responsibility is thus often a matter of asking what a virtuous professional would or would not do in a particular situation. But because they offer an Aristotelian account of virtue, asking about what a virtuous person would do should be understood to include an inquiry into not just the acts that a virtuous person would undertake but the dispositions and motives that would accompany the action.[2]

The criterion of right action offered by virtue ethics can thus be framed in terms of what Oakley and Cocking call a regulative ideal, which is an internalized conception of excellence. As they put the point, a regulative ideal is "an internalised normative disposition to direct one's action and alter one's motivation in certain ways."[3] As the language of internalizing a standard of excellence suggests, Oakley and Cocking's understanding of professional responsibility is a teleological account, according to which the standards of role responsibility are determined by how well one's conduct in a role serves the goals of the profession. For this reason, in order to develop an ethics for a profession, one must specify "what the appropriate orientation and essential guiding concerns of the particular profession ought to be."[4]

In exploring the usefulness of Oakley and Cocking's account for our project, we are aided by the fact that they offer a description of what the guiding concerns of two of the professions we have taken up ought to be. Consider, for example, their account of the goals of medicine.

According to Oakley and Cocking, a good doctor is in fact guided by a conception of the practice of medicine that understands health to be a good that is central to any plausible account of human flourishing. Moreover, the regulative ideal of medicine includes the awareness that disease and illness are particularly threatening to a patient's sense of self-identity. "A particular sensitivity central to the regulative ideal of good doctoring, therefore, is an awareness of a patient's vulnerability to the loss of control and self-direction which disease brings to their lives."[5]

This regulative ideal of medicine would, of course, need to be filled out, but already we can begin to see how a regulative ideal functions in guiding a professional's sense of responsible professional activity. Consider an analogy with the regulative ideal governing one plausible understanding of a good teacher.[6] This analogy can be explored by reviewing the debate in higher education in recent years over the "commodification of education." Any number of studies about the growing commodification of education might be cited here. What they all have in common is a focus on the way universities have increasingly come to understand themselves in market terms. One of the best of these studies is Derek Bok's book *Universities in the Marketplace: The Commercialization of Higher Education.* Bok, a former president of Harvard University, begins his book by describing a commencement address he imagines giving at Harvard that is structured around a series of dreams that Bok tells the assembled crowd he had in the weeks leading up to the address.

Although the address is fictitious, Bok describes how in his dreams an extremely wealthy alumnus approached him with a variety of schemes for easing the constant pressure to raise money for the university. The alum's advice was to let the market work for Harvard in the same way it had worked for him. Among the revenue-generating possibilities was a plan for turning Harvard's football program into a big-time college bowl contender, auctioning off the last hundred spaces in every entering class to the highest bidder, and selling advertising space in Harvard syllabi and classrooms and on the university website.[7] Let us consider this last proposal in some detail.

Almost every academic professional with whom I have discussed the possibility of selling advertising space in a syllabus has been adamantly opposed to the idea. But why? Arguably, selling advertising space might benefit all parties involved. The university would increase revenues, faculty members might receive increased remuneration, tuition might be lowered, and advertisers would reach a target audience in new ways. Why, then, do faculty appear to be so opposed to the idea? The answer, I believe, is clear if we consider the idea of the regulative ideal governing the profession of education.

Particularly if we focus on the ideals governing traditional liberal arts education, we see a commitment to the transfer of knowledge from previous to later generations with the assumption that the search for knowledge can be personally transformative. The regulative ideal of a professor in the liberal arts is that of a mentor and role model for students whose relation to the students is neither that of a parent nor a friend, but closer to that of a guide. If this is the regulative ideal governing teachers in higher education, then selling advertising space in a syllabus is something a virtuous educator simply would not do. Selling advertising space might not violate any provisions in a faculty handbook or contradict one's contractual obligations to a university, but doing so is incompatible with the regulative ideal of higher education.

The logic of the marketplace that would put a price on access to students in the classroom is corrosive of the ideal of a faculty-student relationship. I do not mean to deny that universities are a business or that, in one sense, classes are commodities for sale in the marketplace. Neither do I want to romanticize faculty-student interactions. There are certainly times when teachers and students interact in fairly calculating ways. Still, most faculty members do not take a merely calculative interest in their students, and most understand their work of generating, preserving, and transmitting knowledge as part of a social commitment to shape habits of mind that are crucial to securing the common good. The idea of selling advertising space in a syllabus—with its accompanying vision of faculty-student interactions on the model of seller-buyer—is profoundly at odds with the regulative ideal of a professor concerned about students as individuals whose future is importantly shaped by the disinterested pursuit of knowledge, including the pursuit of self-knowledge.

If we return to the profession of medicine with this analogous regulative ideal drawn from education in mind, we see why Oakley and Cocking suggest that the regulative ideal in medicine rules out certain motives, dispositions, and actions in medical professionals. For example, if a physician's overriding guiding aim or goal in practicing medicine is to make money, he has betrayed the profession of medicine. This is not to say that the goal of making money is incompatible with the ethical practice of medicine. It is to say that a physician whose primary goal is making money is not a virtuous physician, and not merely because his greed is likely to lead to actions that violate codes of professional conduct. He has simply not internalized the regulative ideal of medicine and thus is likely to betray those ideals in a variety of ways.

The example Oakley and Cocking offer here is interesting because it resonates with the example of a professor selling advertising space in his or her syllabus. They cite an advertisement placed in an Australian newspaper by a cosmetic surgery practice. The ad reads as follows: "World leading cosmetic surgery clinic [invites applications for a] Patient Advisor: Working closely with the principal surgeon and other team members, you will develop long term relationships with patients *to insure repeat business.*"[8] Oakley and Cocking are not condemning cosmetic surgery as a field of medicine; their point is that, by making repeat business the focus of this cosmetic surgery practice, the physicians associated with this practice violate the regulative ideal of medicine.

Here it may seem that Oakley and Cocking adopt a position at odds with Arthur Applbaum's practice positivism, for someone might well ask why cosmetic surgeons cannot make soliciting return business the overriding goal of their practice. The practice of cosmetic surgery is just what it is, whether we like it or not. Oakley and Cocking are aware of this tension with Applbaum and in fact respond to Applbaum helpfully and persuasively. They argue that "medicine has characteristic ends that define and set limits on what sorts of actions it is coherent to describe as practising 'medicine.'"[9] In other words, the fact that the goals of medicine are conventional, that they are not rooted in the "nature of things," does not mean that we are free to define medicine any way we please. Oakley and Cocking insist that "the proper application of the label 'doctor' cannot be resolved by mere stipulation, or by appeals to tradition alone." Rather, the issue is to some degree a matter of consistency. Can one profess to serve both goal X and not-X simultaneously? For example, in the case involving the advertisement of the cosmetic surgery clinic, we may reasonably ask whether individuals who profess to be guided by the regulative ideal of health for their patients can make repeat business a fundamental part of their own job description.[10]

Oakley and Cocking make two very important points at this juncture. First, the fact that roles are socially constructed as Applbaum suggests does not mean that the regulative ideals of particular roles are open to wholesale revision, either by an individual practitioner or by the profession as a whole. It is not the case that one can shrug one's shoulders and say, "There really is no difference, but call us schmoctors, if you prefer to refer to us as schmoctors rather than doctors." Second, the conventional nature of roles does nothing to lessen the importance of social expectations created by the recognition of particular roles in a society. When those roles are also connected to goods central to human flourishing, those expectations are especially compelling. As Oakley and Cocking put this point: "Some roles serve worthier goals than others—so it would become a particular cause for concern if a large group of individuals (and very socially powerful and influential individuals) who professed to have an overriding commitment to very worthy goals decided to abandon those goals and pursue ends that are entirely different."[11]

In the previous two chapters we explored both the normative force of role responsibility and the importance of professional accountability when role responsibilities have been neglected or violated. We can now see more clearly why exploring the role responsibilities of psychologists, lawyers, and doctors who were called on to participate in or defend coercive interrogations is so important. Physical health, mental health, justice, and the rule of law are centrally important to individual and group flourishing. If influential members of the professions in which securing these goods is a constitutive ideal abandoned that goal in pursuing the war on terror, then the public trust in these professions will have been violated and the professions themselves called into question.

Medicine and the Public Trust

Were the goals and ideals of psychology, law, and medicine abandoned? Answering that question would require a book in itself, but exploring the question in relation to medicine, if only partially, may help us to see more fully the complexity of professional responsibility and the importance of the teleological account of the virtuous professional that we have explored in this chapter. The first thing to notice as we attempt to answer this question is that this effort will not be as straightforward as

it might seem. In chapter 5, we catalogued some of the codes of medical ethics that prohibit physician involvement with torture. Recall the
UN Principles of Medical Ethics, principles 3 and 4 of which read as
follows:

> Principle 3: It is a contravention of medical ethics for health personnel,
> particularly physicians, to be involved in any professional relationship with
> prisoners or detainees the purpose of which is not solely to evaluate, pro-
> tect or improve their physical and mental health.
>
> Principle 4: It is a contravention of medical ethics for health personnel,
> particularly physicians: (a) To apply their knowledge and skills in order to
> assist in the interrogation of prisoners and detainees in a manner that may
> adversely affect the physical or mental health or condition of such prisoners
> or detainees and which is not in accordance with the relevant international
> instruments; (b) To certify, or to participate in the certification of, the fit-
> ness of prisoners or detainees for any form of treatment or punishment
> that may adversely affect their physical or mental health and which is not in
> accordance with the relevant international instruments, or to participate in
> any way in the infliction of any such treatment or punishment which is not
> in accordance with the relevant international instruments.

Now it might seem that the best way to answer the question of whether
the guiding ideals of the profession of medicine have been abandoned
is to ask, for example, whether principles 3 and 4 or similar provisions
of other codes of ethics have been violated. This has largely been the
tack taken by Steven Miles in his extraordinarily important work *Oath
Betrayed.* Such an examination of the application of codes to actual
practices is important, but it is not enough.

In suggesting that Miles has focused perhaps too narrowly on the
standard provisions of human rights documents and relevant codes of
professional ethics, I do not mean to disparage his work. The profession of medicine is deeply indebted to Miles for his prophetic call for
moral accountability of the physicians who may have violated codes of
professional conduct. Instead, I seek to draw attention to what Miles
himself at times articulates eloquently; namely, that international human rights conventions and the codes of medical ethics that support
those conventions embody and seek to specify ideals that are central
to human flourishing. "The international standards and medical ethics

pertaining to the treatment of prisoners," he writes, "are not dry spec-
ifications such as those constituting the bulk of ordinary federal and
state laws. They are not finicky in a way that can be evaded or undermined with obfuscations. They are breathing statements of worldwide
moral aspirations."[12]

Despite this recognition that provisions of medical codes of ethics
embody profound moral ideals, Miles's treatment of medical complicity in torture is largely confined to how the actions of particular
physicians violated codes of conduct rather than whether the policy
of medical involvement with coercive interrogations was incompatible with the regulative ideal of medicine. Miles notes that physician
involvement with torture typically takes one or another of six forms:
certifying prisoners as fit for harsh treatment, monitoring persons
during torture or interrogation, concealing evidence of abusive interrogation or torture, conducting research on prisoners, overseeing the
systematic deprivation of prisoners' basic needs, and failing to report
abuse.[13] The chapters in *Oath Betrayed* are largely devoted to demonstrating examples of how US physicians were complicit with torture in
these six ways.

Again, this task of documenting physician involvement in the war
on terror is extremely important, but it is also important to ask, for
example, whether examining prisoners to insure that they can withstand harsh interrogation or monitoring prisoners during interrogation
is necessarily incompatible with medicine's regulative ideal of promoting health. The tighter the connection between physician involvement
and coercive interrogation is, the harder it will be to make the case that
screening or monitoring is compatible with the goals of health. This is
why the OMS guidelines put in place by the CIA and the requirement
of physician involvement set out in the "Techniques" and "Combined
Techniques" memoranda issued by the OLC in 2005 are so problematic. Physician involvement is the necessary precondition of abuse.

Paradoxically, the issue of whether screening and monitoring are
compatible with the regulative ideal of medicine may help explain the
puzzling claims of the report of the Office of the Surgeon General of
the Army that we noted in chapter 5. Recall, for example, the apparent
contradiction between the report's claims that medical personnel were
not present at and did not participate in interrogations and the fact that
we know that physicians were present. We saw that the report accounts

for this apparent contradiction by claiming that a physician's presence at an interrogation does not count as participation if he or she is there to ensure the health and welfare of the detainee being interrogated. It is of course possible that the best explanation for why the investigative team chose to define participation narrowly was to protect their own, but it is also plausible to believe that they rejected the tight connection that the OLC sought to secure between the presence of a physician and a green light for EITs. In other words, it is plausible to suppose that some physicians saw screening and monitoring of detainees as consistent with a commitment to the ideals of the profession of medicine, because the detainees were going to be harshly interrogated whether or not physicians monitored their physical and emotional conditions. If detainees would be interrogated with or without physician involvement, better, the reasoning might go, that physicians be present to monitor them.

This is essentially the position we saw articulated in chapter 5 by Fritz Allhoff, who argues that physicians actually have a duty to monitor interrogations. We saw that Allhoff also argues that physicians can choose not to act as doctors, in which case they serve as medically trained interrogators. There is obviously a tension between the position that physicians must help detainees by screening and monitoring them and the position that physicians can choose not to act as physicians and therefore can use their medical knowledge to help break down detainees, but the tension helps us to see that a robust understanding of professional responsibility might lead a physician who has thoroughly internalized the regulative ideal of medicine to feel compelled to screen and monitor detainees.

The tension between the view that physicians can essentially take their doctor hat off and the view that they have a professional responsibility to treat, even in a circumstance where treatment may be a condition of continued abuse, is particularly acute in the case of dealing with hunger strikers. If a physician may not simply step out of his role as a doctor in dealing with detainees, then a conscientious physician will be confronted with a particularly vexing moral dilemma when he or she is asked to force-feed a hunger-striking detainee. Suppose, for example, a physician at Guantánamo Bay has requested and received permission to have no involvement with BSCTs; he has scrupulously avoided medical monitoring of detainees during interrogation but has treated them after interrogation; and he has consistently worked to improve the living conditions of detainees. Conditions have improved, but a number of detainees have started a hunger strike. The physician is now ordered to force-feed the strikers. Is complying with this order an abandonment of the regulative ideal of medicine? Is force-feeding the detainees an abandonment of his responsibilities as a physician? We saw in chapter 5 that numerous codes of medical ethics prohibit force-feeding. This is why prominent medical ethicists have condemned the force-feeding of prisoners at Guantánamo Bay. Yet even opponents of force-feeding acknowledge that this is a difficult case. George Annas and Michael Grodin, for example, point to the lack of consensus on force-feeding:

> For physicians, some of the most difficult situations involve individuals in the custody of the state, usually in prisons or other detention centers. In this context there have been deaths, most notably of 10 Irish hunger strikers in Maze Prison in Northern Ireland in 1981. Hunger strikes present two primary ethical questions for doctors: when is it ethical to force-feed a competent adult hunger striker, and when is it ethical to artificially provide nutrition to a hunger striker who has become incompetent or unconscious? Medical groups have offered conflicting ethical advice on the first issue, and virtually no guidance on the second. Thus, actual practice is mostly based on the personal beliefs of individual physicians rather than on professionally agreed upon ethical principles.[14]

In the face of this situation, our hypothetical physician might appropriately consult the Declaration of Tokyo or a similar ethics code and conclude that he should not force-feed detainees. But he might also appropriately ask whether, in a situation where his government has treated detainees in ways that lead them to prefer death to continued existence, he might reasonably act to keep detainees alive in the hope that they may be released.

I am not claiming that physicians were in fact acting out of a commitment to the best ideals of medicine when they force-fed detainees at Guantánamo Bay. In fact, at least some of the evidence suggests that force-feeding was punitive and was undertaken entirely too early in the strikes to be motivated solely by concern for the medical well-being of the detainee. My point is that it is plausible to suppose that a physician who had internalized the best ideals of medical practice might reach a conclusion that professional responsibility required force-feeding. My point can be illustrated by Oakley and Cocking's discussion of physician-assisted suicide. Many supporters of assisted suicide note that a patient's autonomous request for help in dying ought to be honored by physicians because death may be preferable to continued existence in, say, unremitting pain. Yet Oakley and Cocking claim that physicians may decline to assist a suicide precisely because they see assisting a suicide as incompatible with the substantive goals of medicine to which they are committed as physicians. As Oakley and Cocking put the point, "a substantial number of doctors feel that they cannot, *qua doctors*, act on a patient's autonomous request to be killed," even when the request is well founded. Doctors may simply "feel that to kill such a patient at their autonomous request is to betray the goal of serving health which fundamentally defines their profession of medicine."[15]

A similar point can be made about a physician confronting a decision whether to force-feed a detainee at Guantánamo Bay. Just as a physician whose help in dying has been requested may decide that he cannot, as a physician, assist a suicide, so too may a physician decide that, as a physician, he must not let a detainee die who is driven to a life-threatening hunger strike by actions the physician believes are immoral. In both cases, patient autonomy is important, but in both cases professional integrity may lead the physician to override that autonomy.[16]

It may appear that I am now contradicting positions and arguments I endorsed earlier. I have suggested that codes of professional responsibility are enormously important both for stabilizing the expectations that citizens may reasonably bring to their interactions with professionals and for (thereby) justifying the special treatment professionals are accorded because they serve the common good. It may now seem that I am recommending violating professional codes in the name of professional integrity. This apparent contradiction is reconciled in the fact that the account of professional responsibility on which I am relying is teleological in kind. Codes ought to serve the substantive goods toward which professions strive, and the truly virtuous professionals are those who have internalized the goods and goals of professional life beyond simply knowing what a code of professional ethics requires.

The Importance of Regulative Ideals

Recall that the very notion of a regulative ideal is defined as a conception of correctness or excellence that is internalized by a professional in such a way that he conforms his motivations and conduct to that standard. Codes of ethics help delineate the standard of excellence, and they reflect an effort to specify in practical terms what excellence might require, but they do not exhaust or trump the standard. Ideally, a code helps shape the character of the professional who seeks to embody a standard of excellence, but, in the end, the code is judged by whether it promotes the ends that the profession is expected to serve.

Once again the example of Alberto Mora is deeply instructive. We saw in chapter 3 that Mora was opposed to the enhanced interrogation policy implemented at Guantánamo Bay. He took quick and aggressive action in an effort to change the policy once he discovered it, even though it was clear that his superiors wanted the policy to remain in place. He articulated the reasons why he believed that the enhanced interrogations were both unlawful and unwise practically, but what is striking in the memorandum setting out his concerns is his conviction that coercive interrogations undermine American and military values. This is Mora's description of the meeting at which NCIS Director David Brant and chief NCIS psychologist Michael Gelles briefed Mora and his colleagues about alleged abuses at Guantánamo Bay: "The general mood in the room was dismay. I was of the opinion that the interrogation activities described would be unlawful and unworthy of the military services, an opinion that the others shared."[17] Mora is even clearer about his opposition later in the memorandum: "Even if one wanted to authorize the U.S. military to conduct coercive interrogations, as was the case in Guantánamo, how could one do so without profoundly altering its core values and character? Societal education and military training inculcated in our soldiers American values adverse to mistreatment. Would we now have the military abandon these values altogether? Or would we create detachments of special guards and interrogators who would be trained and kept separate from the other soldiers, to administer these practices?"[18]

There is further evidence that Mora's reaction to the attempts by lawyers to justify enhanced interrogations was rooted in his vision of the law and the fundamental human goods it serves. Jane Mayer's profile of Mora in the *New Yorker* is clear on this point. When Mayer asked Mora about the supposed distinction between torture and cruel or degrading treatment, he responded:

> To my mind, there's no moral or practical distinction. . . . If cruelty is no longer declared unlawful, but instead is applied as a matter of policy, it alters the fundamental relationship of man to government. It destroys the whole notion of individual rights. The Constitution recognizes that man has an inherent right, not bestowed by the state or laws, to personal dignity, including the right to be free of cruelty. It applies to all human beings, not just in America—even those designated as "unlawful enemy combatants." If you make this exception, the whole Constitution crumbles. It's a transformative issue.[19]

If we recall David Luban's work, discussed in chapter 4, we might characterize Mora's repugnance toward abusive interrogation as the response of a virtuous professional who has internalized a view of the legal system as a bulwark against tyranny. As Luban puts the point, torture—and, Mora would add, cruelty—is a form of tyranny and is incompatible with dignity.

We are not accustomed to thinking of lawyers, or, for that matter, doctors or psychologists, as virtuous—at least not in the sense of individuals who display a set of dispositions or habits of mind and heart that support the common good. Yet if we adopt a virtue-ethics approach to professional responsibility, we need to recover a sense of how professional education and training can be a school of virtue. One profession in which the connection between professional responsibility and virtue is still central is the military, and it is to that connection that I next turn.

Notes

1. Stout, *Democracy and Tradition*. See esp. chap. 9.

2. For a different account of virtue and professional responsibility, particularly as regards military professionals, see Sherman, "Torturers and the Tortured."

3. Oakley and Cocking, *Virtue Ethics*, 25.

4. Ibid., 75.

5. Ibid., 113.

6. Oakley and Cocking suggest the analogy with teaching, but I do not use their example here. Instead, I offer my own.

7. Bok, *Universities in the Marketplace*, viii–ix.

8. Oakley and Cocking, *Virtue Ethics*, 87.

9. Ibid., 86.

10. Ibid., 89.

11. Ibid., 90.

12. Miles, *Oath Betrayed*, 93–95.

13. Ibid.

14. Annas and Grodin, "Medicine and Human Rights," 13.

15. Oakley and Cocking, *Virtue Ethics*, 83.

16. In both cases there may also be serious questions about the detainee's capacity to make a competent decision.

17. Alberto Mora to inspector general, memorandum, Department of the Navy, July 7, 2004, available at the Center for Constitutional Rights website, www.ccrjus tice.org/files/Mora%20memo.pdf, 5.

18. Ibid., 11.

19. Jane Mayer, "The Memo," *New Yorker*, February 27, 2006, www.newyorker .com/archive/2006/02/27/060227fa_fact.

Eight

The Day They Enter
Active Service
The Military Conscience

All Armies are expressions of the societies from which they arise. The purposes for which armies fight and the ways in which they do so reflect the values of the societies which send them to war in the first place.

—Joel Rosenthal, "Today's Officer Corps," 104

To some extent, the officer's behavior toward the state is guided by an explicit code expressed in law and comparable to the canons of professional ethics of the physician and the lawyer. To a larger extent, the officer's code is expressed in custom, tradition, and the continuing spirit of the profession.

—Samuel Huntington, *The Soldier and the State*, 16

At several points in this study I have drawn attention to Alberto Mora's opposition to the EITs that were authorized for use with detainees at Guantánamo Bay. I have cited Mora's actions in part because his opposition is well documented and for that reason is better known than the actions of many other critics of the use of enhanced techniques. But I have also noted Mora's opposition because it appears to be rooted in a military mindset that understands professional life inescapably to involve service to American and military values. Mora never served in the military, but his work as general counsel to the navy draws attention to the way the military responded to proposals to use abusive techniques on detainees. We have looked at the responses of psychologists, lawyers, and doctors to abusive interrogations; we turn in this chapter to consider the response of military professionals.

We can begin by looking at the responses of the judge advocates general (TJAGs) to the enhanced interrogations authorized by the OLC. To understand the role of the TJAGs, we need to appreciate the complicated structure of military legal authority. The position of army TJAG is the oldest of the military legal establishment, but today it is complemented by positions of general counsel both to the civilian leadership of the services and to the DOD. In addition, the Office of the Chairman of the Joint Chiefs of Staff has a legal counsel who is a JAG officer.[1] Although the DOD general counsel is the chief legal officer within the DOD, and his or her opinions have primacy when there is conflicting legal opinion within the department, the general counsel does not exercise control over the JAG Corps or the legal counsel for the Office of the Chairman of the Joint Chiefs. As Lisa Turner says, "Together, they support the constitutional framework that assigns responsibilities to both the President and Congress."[2]

It was within this complex legal framework that debates about enhanced interrogation took place among military lawyers. We have seen that Mora, the general counsel for the navy, clashed with William Haynes, the general counsel of the DOD, over the wisdom and legality of using EITs. Where did the JAG Corps stand on the issue? The short answer is that it stood with Mora in opposition to the use of EITs. We know this because Mora brought his concerns to the navy judge advocate general, who then also raised concerns with Haynes, as did the other TJAGs with whom he consulted.

When Haynes set up the working group to review the proposal for using enhanced techniques, it included staff members of the TJAGs, and when the working group prepared a draft report, it sought input from the TJAGs on the draft report. Turner's account of what happened at that point is notable.

> TJAGs and Mora lodged their deep concerns about the working group legal analysis and absence of balanced policy considerations orally and by email to Walker [the chair of the working group]. When that approach failed, TJAGs followed up with memos to Walker. They then met with DOD/GC [Haynes] to express their concerns.
>
> TJAGs and/or their staffs then met with their Service chiefs. The Joint Chiefs met on the issue in a Pentagon conference room called "the Tank." Around this time, DOD/GC met with Secretary Rumsfeld and provided

him with the final working group report. On April 16, 2003, the Secretary authorized some of the interrogation techniques and instructed that further requests for expansion should come to him. TJAGs were not given the final working group report or an opportunity to formally concur or nonconcur. Haynes told at least one TJAG that Secretary Rumsfeld had seen TJAG comments, the report would go no further, and DOD would return to standard techniques. Until the report became public 14 months later, TJAGs and Navy GC believed the working group report had never been finalized. TJAGs did not know about later Secretary-approved requests for expanded techniques.[3]

It is perhaps not surprising that the TJAGs were not asked to concur or nonconcur with the final report of the working group, for it seems clear that they would have rejected the recommendation of the group that EITs be used on detainees.

We do not know for sure what their position would have been on the final report, but we do know their responses to the draft report, and they were not positive. The memoranda cited by Turner are unanimously and unequivocally opposed to the recommendation that EITs be used on detainees. The comments of the deputy JAG for the air force, Major General Jack Rives, capture the sentiment of the other TJAGs. Rives writes: "Several of the more extreme interrogation techniques, on their face, amount to violations of domestic criminal law and the UCMJ [Uniform Code of Military Justice] (e.g., assault). Applying the more extreme techniques during the interrogation of detainees places the interrogators and the chain of command at risk of criminal accusation domestically." Furthermore, Rives argues, US military forces are trained from "the day they enter active duty" to abide by the UCMJ and the Geneva conventions, and to give legal sanction to the EITs completely undermines the moral core of military training and ethics.[4]

Although Rives and the other JAG officers made it clear that they acknowledged the DOD general counsel's authority to render a legal judgment about DOD policy on enhanced interrogation, they also made it clear that they are responsible for legal judgments about the standards to which soldiers will be held under the UCMJ. For example, in his memorandum to the chair of the working group detailing his reservations about the draft report, Rear Admiral Michael Lohr advocated for a remarkable addition to one section of the report. In effect, he suggested that the report make clear that soldiers would be held accountable to the UCMJ, whatever the secretary of defense authorized. He proposed the following addition to the draft report: "Rewrite 3rd to last and penultimate sentences [of p. 75] to read 'The working group believes use of technique 36 would constitute torture under international and U.S. law and, accordingly, should not be utilized. In the event SECDEF decides to authorize this technique, the working group believes armed forces personnel should not participate as interrogators as they are subject to UCMJ jurisdiction at all times.'"[5]

Without a feel for the role responsibilities of TJAGs, this recommendation might suggest a kind of insubordination. After all, Lohr's suggestion is only a slightly veiled recommendation that military personnel not follow orders that might be given by the secretary of defense. But I believe this interpretation misconstrues the responsibilities of TJAGs and the JAG Corps more generally. TJAGs "are general and flag officers who have served for decades in uniform as judge advocates at many levels of command."[6] They have fundamental responsibility for the development of military law and for the application of the UCMJ in particular cases. For that reason, one of their central obligations is to interpret and apply the law of war, even when doing so involves providing unwelcome advice to military commanders. Obviously, the independence of TJAGs is of utmost importance. Indeed, Congress was sufficiently concerned about the independence of the TJAGs and the JAG Corps that their independence is mandated by statute. Section 3037(e) of title 10 of the *United States Code* reads, "No officer or employee of the Department of Defense may interfere with—(1) the ability of the Judge Advocate General to give independent legal advice to the Secretary of the Army or the Chief of Staff of the Army; or (2) the ability of judge advocates of the Army assigned or attached to, or performing duty with, military units to give independent legal advice to commanders."

Military Professionalism and Civilian Authority

Although mandated by federal law to provide independent oversight of military units and to provide Congress with independent advice on military law, the JAG Corps has been accused of overstepping its authority and usurping civilian control of the military. Interestingly, John Yoo is one scholar who has advanced this position. The article in which Yoo develops this argument is written with Glen Sulmasy, a judge advocate with the US Coast Guard.[7] Although I will focus on their comments regarding the JAG Corps and the war on terror, it is important to note that they articulate a position about civilian-military relations more generally.[8] For example, they are concerned about the role of officers, and not just JAG officers, in publicly opposing the policy of civilian leaders. Among other examples, they cite the call from retired officers for the resignation of Secretary of Defense Donald Rumsfeld, the testimony of General Eric Shinseki before Congress that troop strength in Iraq was insufficient, and an on-the-record interview with General Colin Powell in which he opposed military intervention in Bosnia. Nevertheless, the focus of their concern is the role of military lawyers in the war on terror.

In developing an account of civilian-military relations, Sulmasy and Yoo draw on rational choice theory and offer what they describe as a "principal-agent" model. According to this model, the best way to understand the interaction among various constituencies in military affairs is to think of the interaction between a principal actor and those designated to serve as agents of the principal. The problem, say Sulmasy and Yoo, is that "the relationship is strategic—each actor makes decisions to maximize its own interests, taking into account its understanding of the interests and likely responses of the other."[9] The trouble is thus that designated agents will pursue their own interests and not those of the principal.

When this model is applied in the context of civilian-military relations, we find numerous points at which the interests of the agents—namely, the military—may conflict with those of the principal—that is, the president or Congress. Disagreements about "when or how to use force, force structure, strategy, tactics, and the rules governing the military," not to mention a desire for increased autonomy, may lead the agents to seek their preferred position at the expense of the principal.[10] In effect, the theory posits a strictly calculative model of principal-agent interaction that reduces military decision making to narrow self-interest.

The language Sulmasy and Yoo use here is striking. "We would expect the military to follow civilian policy," they write, "when the payoff to do so is greater than the payoff from following its own preferences, minus the expected cost of the discovery of its shirking."[11] The model is thus also predictive. Military resistance to civilian preferences will increase when (1) the differences between civilian and military preferences increase, (2) resistance is unlikely to be discovered, and (3) the likelihood of significant punishment is small.

With this theory in place, Sulmasy and Yoo attempt to explain the actions of JAG officers in the war on terror. They suggest, for example, that one response of agents who disagree with principals is to attempt to exploit divisions within the principal. The fact that JAG attorneys went to Congress to raise concerns about the establishment of military commissions is, they say, a classic manifestation of principal-agent conflict. Similarly, Sulmasy and Yoo reduce JAG Corps concerns about international law to a calculated strategy of weakening the principal. As they see it, the appeal to international law by JAG officers was another way military officers sought allies in opposing civilian authority. They adopted an internationalist perspective on the status of enemy combatants "because this would allow them more autonomy."[12]

No one familiar with civilian-military relations would deny that the bureaucratic infighting for power and resources in the military can be intense. Nor can the prospect of the military making a calculated effort to press its own priorities be easily dismissed. Nevertheless, the suggestion that JAG officers are concerned about violations of international law and the UCMJ simply as a means to greater power and autonomy is particularly cynical.

Sulmasy and Yoo present their principal-agent model as an alternative to Samuel Huntington's theory of civilian-military relations set out in *The Soldier and the State*. They argue that Huntington's analysis of civilian-military relations in terms of the level of external threat in combination with the political-ideological and constitutional nature of a given society is inadequate to explain civilian-military relations in the United States, both during and after the Cold War. Whether or not they are right about the explanatory force of Huntington's model, they miss entirely the centrality of Huntington's insistence on the professional nature of the officer corps. Huntington could scarcely be called a utopian thinker, but he avoided the cynicism of Sulmasy and Yoo by attending to the professionalization of the officer corps. His account of military professionalism thus offers an alternative to the cynicism of the principal-agent model of civilian-military relations; it also offers a far better explanation of the actions of the JAG Corps.

Huntington begins his classic work with a chapter titled "Officership as a Profession." According to Huntington, under any standard definition of a profession, military officers would count as professionals. They possess specialized knowledge and skill; they pursue central social goods for reasons connected to professional goals rather than monetary rewards; and they have a sense of corporate self-identity as separate from laymen.[13] Like other professionals, military officers have a professional code of conduct that is recognized by the state. Indeed, says Huntington, "to some extent the officer's behavior toward the state is guided by an explicit code expressed in law and comparable to the canons of professional ethics of the physician or the lawyer."[14]

Not only do we see the inculcation of a code in the education of an officer, we see the formation of a military mindset. Huntington's account of this mindset is compelling. The first thing to notice about this mindset is that it is organically connected to the goals of a military professional. In Huntington's words, "The military mind consists of the values, attitudes, and perspectives which inhere in the performance of the professional military function and which are deducible from the nature of the function."[15] For our purposes, the teleological nature of this account is more important than Huntington's view that the military mindset includes a fundamental pessimism about human nature, an anti-individualist ethos of service, or a conviction that the state is the basic unit of political organization.[16] The real significance of Huntington's account of the professionalization of the officer corps is the recognition that an officer serves the state by serving values set out in the law and in codes of military conduct.

Military Professionals Take a Stand

If we return to the actions of JAG officers with Huntington's account of military professionalism in mind, we see an alternative explanation that is far more positive than that offered by Sulmasy and Yoo. Rather than a crass play for greater power and autonomy, the actions of the officers in opposing the working group report assembled by the civilian lawyers at the DOD and based on Yoo's legal analysis appear to have been an effort to maintain professional integrity in the face of actions that would erode fundamental military values. A commitment to military professionalism and the state such professionalism serves thus mandated vigorous opposition to the use of EITs.

Ironically, in one sense, Sulmasy and Yoo succumb to what Huntington thought of as a liberal mistake—what he referred to as the fusionist theory of civilian-military relations. According to fusionist theory, with the post–World War II commitment to a large standing army, it became impossible to distinguish between political and military functions at the highest levels of government. Fusionist theory was attractive to liberals who were suspicious of military power, says Huntington, because if functional military expertise could be downplayed, military power in decision making could be muted.

We see very much the same sort of fusionist approach from Sulmasy and Yoo when they set out to explain why civilian and military leaders disagreed so vehemently about the use of EITs. If postwar liberals sought to reduce the power of the military by requiring its leaders to frame their decisions in terms of civilian concerns of social and economic policy, Sulmasy and Yoo attempt to diminish military power by arguing that in a post-9/11 context civilian leaders must reframe traditional military law. The laws of war, they reason, "were drafted primarily to deal with two types of armed conflict—wars between nation-states, and internal civil wars." But terrorist attacks by nonstate actors introduce "a different type of armed conflict, one between a nation-state and an international terrorist organization with international reach and the ability to inflict levels of destruction previously only in the hands of states." The upshot is that traditional military expertise is not particularly relevant to addressing the new situation. "Deciding what rules to apply to a new type of armed conflict," they conclude, "inherently calls for judgments that are based far more on policy preferences and balancing of costs and benefits [than on traditional military expertise]."[17]

In suggesting that Sulmasy and Yoo deploy a fusionist strategy in an effort to cut out military professionals from decisions about how to fight the war on terror, I do not mean to suggest that they are wrong that nonstate terrorist groups require us to rethink the laws of war and counterterrorism tactics.[18] Instead, I wish to draw attention to the fact that the deliberations about the use of EITs intentionally bypassed the military professionals whose expertise and core value commitments would have greatly enriched the decision-making process. More importantly, however, it is necessary to highlight how the principal-agent model obscures the professionalism of the officer corps.

This is, in fact, precisely what Huntington's account would suggest, because fusionist theories in his view effectively erode the professionalism of the military. On this view, if JAG officers sought to prevent civilian leaders from redefining the laws of war, the reason for their actions had more to do with commitments to the regulative ideal of their profession than with a calculative grab for power.

Let us return to the process by which the EITs were approved. As we saw in chapter 3, when the initial interrogations of high-value detainees did not yield immediate intelligence, both the CIA and army commanders at Guantánamo Bay sought approval to use EITs. The memoranda we discussed at length in chapter 3 focused on the request by the CIA for guidance on the legality of coercive interrogations, but the OLC memoranda ultimately served as the basis for DOD approval of the use of EITs by military interrogators. The Yoo memorandum that the working group used to develop its position was essentially a repackaging of the Bybee memoranda. The final DOD working group report, for example, contained much of the analysis found in the interrogation memoranda, including reliance on the notion of specific intent and appeals to presidential powers and a necessity defense, if charges were ever to be brought against interrogators. And it reached essentially the same conclusions.

The problem in both instances is that the legal analysis was prepared with virtually no consultation with anyone having expertise in international or military law. As we saw, the top military lawyers were cut out of the process of consultation when the final report was being prepared. And, as Jane Mayer documents in her book *The Dark Side*, this was a consistent pattern in the aftermath of 9/11. For example, as the Bush administration deliberated about how to handle captured terrorist suspects legally, there was little in the way of consultation. An interagency process was established to address the legal issues, but the interagency group played almost no role in the actual development of administration policy. Mayer points out that the process of policy formation with regard to detainees was highly unusual and cloaked in secrecy. It excluded the most experienced military lawyers and was orchestrated by Vice President Dick Cheney and his legal counsel David

Addington, neither of whom were either veterans or experts on military or international law.[19]

As evidence that key figures were cut out of the deliberations, Mayer notes that neither Condoleezza Rice nor Colin Powell knew that the administration planned to create military commissions to try the terrorists before the decision had already effectively been made. Neither did the TJAGs. Attorney General Ashcroft learned of the plan only two days before it was announced. Although John Yoo, then with the OLC, had written a confidential memorandum on military commissions for the administration, he had done so without informing Ashcroft. Indeed, according to Mayer, Addington had been emphatic about not using the interagency process. "Fuck the interagency process," one White House colleague recalled him saying. To another colleague he said, "Don't bring the TJAGs into the process. They aren't reliable."[20]

Once the TJAGs learned of the administration's plans, they argued for reversing course. In Mayer's words, the "uniformed military lawyers were galvanized by the order into taking the first steps in what would become a remarkable role as defenders of America's honor and its rule of law against what they saw as illegitimate and ruinous incursions by the Bush Administration's political appointees."[21]

What Sulmasy and Yoo see as a power grab by military lawyers, Mayer views as a principled effort to safeguard the values to which military professionals must be committed. Sulmasy and Yoo complain that the JAG Corps encouraged challenges to military commissions by civilian lawyers and that, when the administration sought congressional grounding for military commissions after the Supreme Court ruled in *Hamdan v. Rumsfeld* that the administration's version of the commissions was incompatible with congressional authorization of the UCMJ, the TJAGs and other JAG officers testified against the administration's proposal.

Obviously, the actions of the JAG Corps are open to competing interpretations, but it is worth noting in assessing alternative explanations that there was a clear effort to bypass the usual consultation process by which military professionals would have been able to raise any concerns they might have about EITs or military commissions. Moreover, as Turner points out, "prior to confirmation, Congress requires TJAGs and three- and four-star nominees to take an oath swearing to provide Congress their personal opinions on military matters when asked, even those opposing administration policy."[22] Given these facts, Sulmasy and Yoo's interpretation of the actions of the TJAGs appears strained.

Their position might be stronger if the concerns raised by the TJAGs and JAG Corps generally were trivial or unfounded, but that does not appear to have been the case. Consider, for example, JAG opposition to the use of military commissions. As we saw, when President Bush originally created the commissions by executive order, the TJAGs were not consulted in advance, and when they learned of the commissions they were opposed to them. For the most part, JAG Corps reservations had to do with the way the commissions departed from the procedures and rules of evidence that are in place for military courts-martial. In doing so, the commissions compromised the integrity of military justice to which the JAG Corps were, as professionals, committed. And these were precisely the concerns raised by the US Supreme Court when it struck down the original commissions in *Hamdan v. Rumsfeld*.

> The Government's objection that requiring compliance with the court-martial rules imposes an undue burden both ignores the plain meaning of Article 36(b) and misunderstands the purpose and the history of military commissions. The military commission was not born of a desire to dispense a more summary form of justice than is afforded by courts-martial; it developed, rather, as a tribunal of necessity to be employed when courts-martial lacked jurisdiction over either the accused or the subject matter. Exigency lent the commission its legitimacy, but did not further justify the wholesale jettisoning of procedural protections. That history explains why the military commission's procedures typically have been the ones used by courts-martial. That the jurisdiction of the two tribunals today may sometimes overlap does not detract from the force of this history; Article 21 did not transform the military commission from a tribunal of true exigency into a more convenient adjudicatory tool. Article 36, confirming as much, strikes a careful balance between uniform procedure and the need to accommodate exigencies that may sometimes arise in a theater of war. That Article not having been complied with here, the rules specified for Hamdan's trial are illegal.[23]

After the Supreme Court struck down the original version of the commissions, President Bush sought and received congressional authorization for revised military commissions, about which the JAG Corps also raised concerns. The Supreme Court's worry that the commissions would serve as a vehicle for a more summary form of justice appears to have been prescient, for when detainees were finally brought to trial under this framework, the result was deeply troubling.

Consider the case of Mohammed Jawad. We know the details of this case because both the JAG Corps officer who defended him and the original chief prosecutor of Jawad have written about it.[24] Their accounts document a system that was flawed in precisely the way the military professionals had predicted. Jawad was arrested in Afghanistan when he was fourteen or fifteen years old. He was accused of throwing a grenade into a jeep, an attack that injured two US servicemen and their interpreter. He was arrested and interrogated by Afghan police, who apparently threatened to kill him or members of his family if he did not confess. He signed a confession with his thumbprint, even though he was illiterate and did not speak the language in which the confession was written. When he was turned over to US personnel, he was again subjected to harsh interrogations and again confessed, though the details of the two confessions were markedly different. About two months after his arrest, in February 2003, he was transferred to Guantánamo Bay.

The logs of detainee interrogations indicate that he was subjected to abusive treatment, including sleep-deprivation techniques, euphemistically referred to as the "frequent flyer" program. We know from the records that were kept of his treatment that between May 7 and May 20, 2004, Jawad was moved from one cell to another 112 times, "an average of one relocation every two hours and fifty minutes for two weeks."[25] Although he was arrested in December 2002, he did not go before a combatant status review tribunal until October 2004. Jawad was not allowed legal counsel at that hearing, and he did not have access to a lawyer until 2007, five years after he was arrested. In January 2008, the case was referred to trial by military commission.

Within months of his being assigned a lawyer, the case against Jawad was in shambles. "By November 2008," David Frakt, Jawad's defense counsel, writes, "the case against Jawad had disintegrated: the lead prosecutor had resigned, and the military judge had suppressed the government's primary evidence and rejected its entire theory of the crime."[26] When Jawad later petitioned for habeas corpus, the former prosecutor in the case, Darrel Vandeveld, provided a declaration of support for Jawad. Vandeveld wrote:

> I offer this declaration in support of Mohammed Jawad's petition for habeas corpus. I was the lead prosecutor assigned to the Military Commissions case against Mr. Jawad until my resignation in September 2008. It is my opinion, based on my extensive knowledge of the case, that there is no credible evidence or legal basis to justify Mr. Jawad's detention in U.S. custody or his prosecution by military commission. There is, however, reliable evidence that he was badly mistreated by U.S. authorities both in Afghanistan and at Guantanamo, and he has suffered, and continues to suffer, great psychological harm. Holding Mr. Jawad's [sic] for over six years, with no resolution of his case and with no terminus in sight, is something beyond a travesty.[27]

Vandeveld is not alone in concluding that the legal situation of detainees has been badly handled. Six other military commission prosecutors have resigned. In each case, issues of professional integrity appear to have been the reason for stepping aside.

I have suggested that the JAG officer corps was opposed to the use of EITs and the prosecution of detainees in military commissions because they saw both as a threat to military values and the rule of law, which they were professionally committed to upholding. At least with respect to the use of military commissions, however, my account of JAG actions must also take note of the fact that military lawyers served as prosecutors and judges in these cases. After all, not every military lawyer resigned or asked to be transferred, and these tribunals were military commissions. To be sure, military lawyers were involved in all aspects of the commissions, but it should also be pointed out that the commissions were decidedly unmilitary. Scott Horton puts the point trenchantly. "They had the appearance of being 'military,'" Horton writes, "because the courtroom scene on which all the cameras focused were [sic] filled with men and women in uniform." Nevertheless, behind the scenes, "the puppet masters were pulling the strings. And the puppet masters were suspiciously partisan political figures."[28]

Horton cites two pieces of evidence to support his claim that the system was set up to serve political ends and not the administration of justice. First, the convening authority for the military commissions, Susan Crawford, was not a military officer but a political appointee favored by Vice President Cheney's office. Second, the reporting structure put in place by the secretary of defense had all parties reporting to William Haynes, the civilian general counsel at the DOD. Horton's conclusion is, once again, provocatively but not unreasonably put:

> The cumulative effect of these changes masterminded by Haynes is plain enough: the already very obvious threads attached to the commission participants were replaced with some crude hemp rope. It was obvious to all observers who was calling the shots. And it was plainly illegal and unethical. Professional rules require the defense counsel, prosecutor, and judges to exercise independent professional judgment. Moreover, the Military Commissions Act of 2006 guarantees the professional independence of these actors in the process. The command structure crafted by Haynes was plainly designed to achieve the political subordination of the JAGs, defying the MCA's guarantee of independence.[29]

Arguably, it was a concern about an independent and fair military justice system that led JAG officers to oppose both EITs and a system of military commissions. The fact that the military commissions system allowed self-incriminating evidence obtained through coercive interrogation to be introduced at trial perhaps captures the core worry of military lawyers. Sulmasy and Yoo are not wrong that there was a significant power struggle in play as the JAG Corps fought what they saw as civilian efforts to undermine a long and honorable tradition of military justice. Yet, in depicting this struggle in terms of rational choice theory, with each side calculating its own self-interest, Sulmasy and Yoo miss entirely the way in which JAG opposition was rooted in a professional ethos profoundly at odds with the whole notion of individual self-interest.

Huntington's account of the military professional's code of ethics rooted in custom, tradition, and the spirit of military service captures the motivation for military opposition to EITs far better than the theory of rational self-interest offered by Sulmasy and Yoo. As Horton has written, "Even most critics concede the professionalism and integrity of the military lawyers who [were] assigned to the military commissions system as judges, prosecutors and defense counsel. Their professionalism and integrity are not an issue."[30]

In the end, the view of David Frakt, Jawad's defense counsel, seems closest to the truth when he notes the moral paradox that was

Guantánamo Bay. Despite the fact that the majority of the 774 detainees at Guantánamo were wrongly imprisoned and mistreated, military professionals took a principled stand against this treatment. As Frakt puts it, "The Jawad case epitomizes the worst excesses of the war on terrorism—the wrongful imprisonment and torture of an innocent teenager in a legal black hole, followed by his attempted prosecution for an invented war crime using coerced confessions. But the case also represents what is best about America. The Pentagon assigned, at taxpayer expense, three military officers to defend him, and then promoted two of us, despite our vigorous and outspoken criticism of the government's actions."[31]

In the introduction I suggested that examining how professionals responded to the war on terror provides one barometer of how democratic traditions are faring in the war on terror. If David Frakt is correct, the answer is somewhat mixed. We turn in the next chapter to examine this question in more detail.

Notes

1. This account of the military legal structure is taken from Turner, "Detainee Interrogation Debate."

2. Ibid., 41.

3. Ibid., 45.

4. Jack L. Rives to secretary of the air force general counsel, memorandum, February 5, 2003, available on the Washington Research Library Consortium Aladin Research Commons website, http://dspace.wrlc.org/doc/bitstream/2041/70978/00601_030205_001display.pdf.

5. Rear Admiral Michael F. Lohr, judge advocate general, "Working Group Recommendations Relating to Interrogation of Detainees," memorandum, February 6, 2003, in "JAG Memos—Introduced into Congressional Record by Sen. Lindsey Graham (R-SC) on July 25, 2005," available at ImpeachforPeace.org, http://impeachforpeace.org/evidence/data/jag-memos.pdf.

6. Turner, "Detainee Interrogation Debate," 41.

7. Sulmasy and Yoo, "Challenges to Civilian Control."

8. For a critique of Sulmasy and Yoo's position that highlights their view of presidential powers, see Hansen, "Understanding the Role of Military Lawyers in the War on Terror."

9. Sulmasy and Yoo, "Challenges to Civilian Control," 12.

10. Ibid., 14.

11. Ibid., 16.

12. Ibid., 19–20.

13. Huntington's account of professions is clearly what I have defined as a social-trustee model.

14. Huntington, *Soldier and the State*, 16.

15. Ibid., 61.

16. I do not mean to suggest that I disagree with Huntington's characterization of the substance of this mindset. In fact, it seems to me roughly on target.

17. Sulmasy and Yoo, "Challenges to Civilian Control," 22.

18. One such effort can be found in Cook, "Ethical Issues in Counterterrorism 'War.'"

19. Mayer, *Dark Side*, 80.

20. Ibid., 80, 88.

21. Ibid., 88.

22. Turner, "Detainee Interrogation Debate," 42.

23. Hamdan v. Rumsfeld, 548 U.S. 557, 625 (2006).

24. I rely here on the account provided by David Frakt, Jawad's defense counsel from the Office of Military Commissions. Frakt was a US Air Force JAG officer. See Frakt, "Mohammed Jawad and the Military Commissions of Guantánamo." The account of the chief prosecutor in the case, who in fact resigned because of his concerns, can be found in his declaration in support of dismissing the case against Jawad. See "Declaration of Lieutenant Colonel Darrel J. Vandeveld, September 22, 2008" available on the website of the Center for the Study of Human Rights in the Americas, University of California at Davis, http://humanrights.ucdavis.edu/projects/the-guantanamo-testimonials-project/testimonies/testimonies-of-prosecution-lawyers/declaration-of-lieutenant-colonel-darrel-vandeveld-september-22-2008. Vandeveld also executed a declaration in support of Jawad's habeas corpus petition. I cite this declaration below.

25. Frakt, "Mohammed Jawad," 1397.

26. Ibid., 1371.

27. Declaration of Lieutenant Colonel Darrel J. Vandeveld in support of Mohammed Jawad's habeas corpus petition, January 12, 2009, available on the website of the American Civil Liberties Union, www.aclu.org/pdfs/safefree/veveld_declaration.pdf.

28. Horton, "Great Guantánamo Puppet Theater."

29. Ibid.

30. Ibid.

31. Frakt, "Mohammed Jawad," 1409.

Nine

Lessons Learned
Dignity and the Rule of Law

How we interrogate "post-9/11" detainees is the fundamental question in balancing the inherent tension of national security considerations against individual civil and political rights. More significantly, the interrogation measures we adopt define who we are as a society.
—Amos Guiora, *Constitutional Limits on Coercive Interrogation*, ix

Americans, believing themselves to stand proudly for the rule of law and human rights, have become for the rest of the world a symbol of something quite opposite: a society in which lawbreaking, approved by its highest elected officials, goes unpunished.
—Mark Danner, "After September 11: Our State of Exception,"
New York Review of Books, October 13, 2011

I began this study by noting the threat that terrorism poses to democratic institutions and by asking how the United States has fared in responding to that threat. The concrete example for approaching these matters has been the issue of coercive interrogations, for as Amos Guiora suggests, how a society handles interrogation in the face of terrorist threats tells us a lot about the moral compass of that society. When suspected terrorists are in custody, at least two values may be deeply at odds. We have a moral responsibility to safeguard the lives of innocent civilians by maintaining national security, and we have an obligation not to reduce fellow human beings to nonhuman status, even if we would describe what they have done as inhuman. If the question of how a democratic society handles issues of interrogation is a barometer of its success in responding to terrorism, how is the United States doing?

I believe the answer to this question is that the US response has been decidedly mixed. To explain why I draw this conclusion it is useful to have a schema of interrogation techniques. Following Guiora, I suggest that harsh interrogation techniques can be divided into three kinds: coercive, abusive, and torturous.[1] The point of distinguishing three categories of interrogation is, of course, to provide an answer to the question of how to balance human rights and national security when interrogating suspected terrorists. In my view, coercive interrogation is a morally and legally acceptable form of interrogation; abusive interrogation and interrogation that involves torture are not.

Here it is useful to be concrete. Suppose we turn to the techniques set out in *Army Field Manual (FM) 34-52*, the 1992 army document that spells out guidelines for "intelligence interrogation," and to the ten EITs that the classified Bybee memorandum addressed in August 2002. How should these various techniques be categorized? We can begin with *FM 34-52*. The manual covers interrogation in great detail, with chapters on everything from the general mission of military intelligence units and the structure of such units to the handling of documents produced through intelligence operations, including interrogation. Chapter 3 of the manual covers the actual techniques of interrogation. It identifies roughly a dozen general interrogation strategies, with some variations within each category. The categories are direct, incentive, emotional, fear, pride and ego, futility, we know all, file and dossier, establish your identity, repetition, rapid fire, silence, and change of scene.

The coercive nature of all interrogation can be seen in the fact that even in the most innocuous of these techniques—namely, a direct approach in which the interrogator simply asks for the information he wants—the subject being interrogated is powerless and vulnerable. The detainee does not necessarily know where he is; he does not know what will happen if he refuses to answer; and even if he answers questions truthfully, he may not be believed. Nevertheless, not all techniques are the same. Asking a detainee a direct question is very different from what the manual refers to as a "Fear-Up (Harsh)" approach. According to the manual, "in this approach, the interrogator behaves in an overpowering manner with a loud and threatening voice. The interrogator may even feel the need to throw objects across the room to heighten the source's implanted feelings of fear. . . . This technique is to convince the source he does indeed have something to fear; that he has no option but to cooperate."[2]

The fact that questioning a detainee is coercive and may be harsh, however, does not mean it is morally or legally prohibited. Indeed, all the techniques set out in *FM 34-52* are approved by the military in part because they do not violate the Geneva conventions or the UMCJ. The preface to the manual is clear about the necessity of restraint. "These principles and techniques of interrogation," the manual reads, "are to be used within the constraints established by the following":

- The Uniform Code of Military Justice (UCMJ)
- Geneva Convention for the Amelioration of the Wounded and Sick in Armed Forces in the Field of August 12, 1949, hereinafter referred to as GWS
- Geneva Convention Relative to the Treatment of Prisoners of War of August 12, 1949, hereinafter referred to as GPW
- Geneva Convention Relative to the Protection of Civilian Persons in Time of War of August 12, 1949, hereinafter referred to as GC.[3]

Article 3, which is common to all three of these conventions, provides an indication of the basis upon which interrogations are to be judged. It reads:

(1) Persons taking no active part in the hostilities, including members of armed forces who have laid down their arms and those placed "hors de combat" by sickness, wounds, detention, or any other cause, shall in all circumstances be treated humanely, without any adverse distinction founded on race, colour, religion or faith, sex, birth or wealth, or any other similar criteria. To this end, the following acts are and shall remain prohibited at any time and in any place whatsoever with respect to the above-mentioned persons: (a) violence to life and person, in particular murder of all kinds, mutilation, cruel treatment and torture; (b) taking of hostages; (c) outrages upon personal dignity, in particular humiliating and degrading treatment; (d) the passing of sentences and the carrying out of executions without previous judgment pronounced by a regularly constituted court, affording all the judicial guarantees which are recognized as indispensable by civilized peoples.[4]

From this and other articles in the conventions, it is clear that the standard that is to guide the treatment of prisoners is one that safeguards the dignity and humanity of prisoners. Prisoners should not be degraded; they should not be treated cruelly; and they should not be physically or emotionally abused.

If we return to the techniques approved for use by *FM 34-52*, we see why they are acceptable. They do not fundamentally compromise the humanity of the prisoners interrogated. Prisoners may be manipulated; their emotional vulnerabilities may be exploited; they may even be generally intimidated. Nevertheless, their dignity as persons remains intact.[5]

Dignity as a Standard

If respecting the basic dignity of persons is to be a useful standard, we need at least briefly to explore the idea of dignity. This idea is of course notoriously difficult to define, but we can begin by distinguishing between comparative and noncomparative conceptions of dignity.[6] The former is generally what is meant when advocates of the right to die speak of wanting a dignified death. The idea behind the notion of a dignified death is that one can lose the very capabilities that give life meaning. In such a case, the argument goes, the quality of one's life has been so compromised compared to a life of optimal quality that one might reasonably conclude that life is not worth living. Unbearable pain, dementia, and a permanent vegetative state are all conditions that have been said to be dehumanizing and thus undignified.

Although there are various ways to understand this comparative account of dignity, it is most typically understood in relation to the value of autonomy, at least in an American context. The ability to make one's own decisions, to be able to set goals and then work toward those goals, is so prized that when illness or injury strips us of the ability to make autonomous choices, many conclude that some fundamental human characteristic has been lost. The problem with an account of dignity that rests on the importance of autonomy is that dignity is not always correlated with autonomy. Young children have dignity without having (full) autonomy. The elderly have dignity despite diminished autonomy. We even believe that corpses should be treated with dignity, when the possibility of autonomy is completely gone. A comparative account of autonomy is thus often supplemented by a noncomparative account.

A noncomparative account of dignity embraces the idea that humans have an intrinsic dignity that cannot be lost because it does not rest on any set of capabilities or functions that might themselves be lost. Noncomparative views are often religiously rooted, and at least some writers argue that a religious grounding is the only plausible basis for a noncomparative account of dignity. Gilbert Meilaender, for example, has made this point explicitly. He writes, "It may be that we cannot make good sense of an egalitarian and non-comparative understanding of human dignity, to which our civilization has in many ways been committed, if we abstract it entirely from the context of the religious beliefs that formed it." He continues, "I doubt, in fact, that there is any way to derive a belief in the equal worth of every human being from the ordinary distinctions in merit and excellence that we all use in some spheres of life; it is grounded, rather, not in our relation to each other but in our relation to God, from whom—to use a mathematical metaphor—we are equidistant."[7]

I do not wish to explore the foundations of a noncomparative account of dignity, because even those who insist on the irreducible dignity of humanity acknowledge that one can violate the dignity of a person, despite the fact that the inherent dignity of the person is never lost. In other words, it is the comparative conception of dignity that is relevant to an assessment of interrogation techniques. And the idea that is key here is that there is a threshold of respectful treatment of a human being below which we may not go, if we are to respect the dignity of the person being interrogated.

Let us acknowledge that an account of comparative dignity that grounds dignity in autonomy does not exhaust everything we wish to say about human dignity. Nevertheless, does it provide material for a useful standard by which to evaluate interrogation techniques? I believe it does. If we understand human dignity to reside at least partly in the cognitive capacities associated with the ability to make informed choices and to reason prudentially in relation to those choices, then actions that intentionally strip humans of those capacities can be said to violate basic human dignity. The classical locus for this notion of dignity is found in Kant's conception of human beings as end setters.

Kant's famous statement that we must never treat rational agents as mere means to an end, but always as beings who have their own ends or goals, nicely captures this view of dignity.[8]

Notice that this conception of dignity is in some ways counterintuitive, at least when applied to interrogation techniques. We are inclined, for example, to treat techniques that cause pain more seriously than those that are relatively painless. This is probably why many writers appear to have little concern about the use of truth serum during interrogations. However, on an autonomy-based account of dignity, it is a mistake to equate pain with mistreatment, and the use of truth serum is deeply problematic. Indeed, the use of drugs to elicit information may be a prime example of abusive interrogation, precisely because it is designed to overcome or bypass the will of the detainee completely.

Perhaps I can now be more precise. I said above that prisoners should not be degraded, treated cruelly, or physically or emotionally abused, and the reason has to do with the fact that such actions tend to reduce a person to a mere means. Similarly, the reason that the techniques set out in *FM 34-52* are acceptable is that they do not reduce a detainee to a mere means or strip the detainee of rational choice.

Can we say the same thing about the EITs authorized by the classified Bybee memorandum of August 2002? Ten techniques were considered in that document: (1) attention grasp, (2) walling, (3) facial hold, (4) facial slap (insult slap), (5) cramped confinement, (6) wall standing, (7) stress positions, (8) sleep deprivation, (9) insects placed in a confinement box, and (10) the waterboard. Once again, we see a spectrum. All are coercive, most are harsh, but are any abusive or effectively torture? If the standard were respecting an autonomy-based account of the dignity and humanity of the detainee, I would argue that, with reasonable oversight, (1)–(6) could be used in ways consistent with this standard. The use of stress positions or a confinement box with insects will frequently, if not always, be abusive, and extensive sleep deprivation will always be abusive and can rise to the level of torture. Waterboarding falls into the category of torture. Effectively, the test suggested by the Geneva norms can be formulated in terms of a question: Does the technique strip the person of the basic dignity accorded to persons as rational agents? Or with a more specific focus: Does the technique target the physical or psychological integrity of the detainee in a way intended to break his or her will?[9]

The reason that techniques 1–6 are arguably acceptable is that none of them fundamentally threatens a person's basic dignity. No one desires to be shoved against a wall, slapped, confined, or forced to stand against a wall, but none of these things is intrinsically degrading or humiliating, nor do they threaten physical or psychological integrity. By contrast, the remaining techniques are all designed to compromise the individuality and lucidity of a rational agent. They represent a potential assault on personal identity that is intended to reduce the detainee to raw animality.

Consider the role of sleep deprivation at Guantánamo Bay. As we have seen, sleep deprivation was used so frequently with detainees, it was jokingly referred to as the "frequent flier" program. It was used, for instance, on Mohamadou Walid Slahi. A Senate Armed Services Committee report on the treatment of detainees issued in 2008 describes the interrogation plan for Slahi. Sleep deprivation was clearly part of an overall plan targeting Slahi's physical and psychological integrity.

The January 16, 2003 memo also described techniques directed at breaking down Slahi's ego, including ridiculing him, making him wear a mask and signs labeling him a "liar," a "coward," or a "dog." The memo stated that interrogators would also instruct Slahi to bark and perform dog tricks "to reduce the detainee's ego and establish control." . . .

The January 16, 2003 memo described shaving Slahi's head and beard, making him wear a burka, and subjecting him to strip search "to reduce [his] ego by assaulting his modesty." . . .

The memo stated that Slahi would be denied the opportunity to pray and described techniques to exploit "religious taboos," such as using a female interrogator in "close physical contact." The memo also stated that interrogators would play music to "stress [Slahi] because he believes music is forbidden" and that light in Slahi's interrogation booth would be filtered "with red plastic to produce a stressful environment."

The January 16, 2003 memo indicated that JTF-GTMO [Joint Task Force-Guantánamo Bay] interrogators planned to make use of a completely white room during Slahi's interrogation "to reduce outside stimuli and present an austere environment," that interrogators would use a strobe light in his interrogation booth to "disorient [Slahi] and add to [his] stress level," and that a hood would be placed on Slahi in the booth "to isolate him and increase feelings of futility."[10]

All of these techniques were combined with sleep deprivation in an effort to compromise Slahi's sense of identity through a systematic attack on his connection with reality. That this regime succeeded in its goal is evidenced by the fact that many who underwent this kind of interrogation became psychotic.

In suggesting that sleep deprivation is abusive and not just coercive, I part company with others who have called for moral and legal constraints on any interrogation regime. Guiora, for example, has provided a closely argued rationale for striking a balance between the need for information that might protect national security and the protection of human rights. He thus defends a regime of coercive interrogation that is subject to strict oversight. Under Guiora's system, the director of national intelligence would have the power to approve specific interrogation plans, but the director would be "subject to legislative oversight, active judicial review, and strict scrutiny by authorized members of the executive branch."[11]

While such a system of oversight would have been decidedly preferable to the system at Guantánamo Bay, I disagree with Guiora about the kinds of coercive techniques that may be used. For example, Guiora would allow sleep deprivation, modulation of room temperature, stress positions, the use of hooding, and the playing of loud, cacophonous music.[12] Any of these might possibly be justified as a one-time technique designed to persuade a recalcitrant detainee to cooperate. The problem is that, used as part of an interrogation regime, they are likely to be used in combination (and more than once), and they target physical and psychological integrity. Like solitary confinement, sensory deprivation and sensory bombardment threaten personal integrity by breaking a person's will.[13]

If I am correct that sleep deprivation, stress positions, waterboarding, and other techniques used at Guantánamo Bay are not just coercive but also abusive and, in some cases, forms of torture, then one would have to conclude that, at best, the US response to terrorism is checkered. The techniques were not just used; they were approved for use. And professionals of various sorts actively participated in the process by which abusive techniques were authorized and implemented. This fact is deeply disturbing. Even more troubling, however, is the way in which these techniques were adopted. As we saw in our analysis of the work of the OLC and of the opposition of military professionals to the approval of these techniques, typical processes of analysis and review were short-circuited. In that respect, a very small number of leaders managed to gain extraordinary power and arguably circumvented US and international law.

On the other hand, there is a sense in which the fight over EITs is encouraging. At a time when the professions are often understood in terms of a model of experts for hire, we have seen professionals in numerous fields fight the use of EITs from within their professions and in terms of the fundamental values to which they are committed in their chosen professions. In opposing abusive interrogation techniques, these professionals understood their actions as a form of service to the common good. In this respect, the social-trustee model appears to be alive and well, even if it is widely disparaged.

Drawing Lessons from Guantánamo Bay

The insistence of professionals that moral constraints be placed on the means of fighting the war on terror and their efforts to implement such constraints are important for another reason. They point to the value of open deliberation in formulating policy and consultation where transparency is not possible for reasons of security. While I disagree with Alan Dershowitz's recommendation that the United States set up a system of judicial review that could authorize torture warrants, he is surely right that one of the core democratic values at stake in responding to terrorism is democratic openness and accountability. The term "transparency" is overused, but one thing professional opposition to abusive interrogation demonstrates is the danger of a lack of transparency.[14]

Recall that one of the fundamental complaints, which we examined in chapter 8, that Sulmasy and Yoo make about military officers is that they have offered their expert professional opinion to Congress as Congress has sought to formulate policy about the war on terror. They complain, for example, that during congressional hearings on the Military Commissions Act, JAG Corps officers testified before Congress against commission rules that would not allow defense counsel to see the evidence against their clients. They argue that because the Bush administration favored such commission rules, the actions of the JAG officers undermined civilian control of the military.

On the contrary, I believe that one of the lessons that can be drawn from our examination of the role of professionals in the war on terror is that secrecy and lack of consultation resulted in the implementation of deeply flawed policy. As we saw, the original OLC interrogation memoranda were not widely circulated, at least not beyond a group of administration officials who had already decided that abusive interrogation was necessary. Yet the near universal rejection of the reasoning of the memoranda when they became public, even by those lawyers who supported EITs, suggests that secrecy and lack of consultation did not serve the Bush administration well.

The same can be said about the original plans for the establishment of military commissions. Almost no one outside a very small circle of administration officials was consulted about the plan, not even the attorney general or the TJAGs. That the Supreme Court struck down the original military commissions is thus not surprising. When Congress authorized a revamped military commission system, it suffered from the fact that even prosecutors were reluctant to work within a system that relied on evidence obtained through abusive interrogations and where decisions about prosecutions and plea bargains had more to do with politics than with justice.

Problems with secrecy and lack of consultation also plagued the APA's initial efforts to respond to coercive interrogation. The presidential task force met in closed session and did not consult widely in deliberating about the role of psychologists in interrogation. When APA members responded critically to the PENS report and sought to change APA policy, the APA leadership resisted through the use of the relatively closed bureaucratic structure of the organization.

The problem with the lack of transparency and consultation is not just that a range of viewpoints and perspectives were neglected, but that those engaged in practices that were arguably problematic did not have to defend their actions publicly. We saw in chapter 6, for example, that some writers have called for following a strategy of "naming and shaming" in the absence of general mechanisms of accountability. Whether or not one finds such a strategy useful, it nevertheless points to the importance of accountability. Those like Dershowitz and Guiora who have called for judicial oversight of interrogations are united in their commitment to accountability, however much they may disagree about what courts should allow.

There are other lessons to be drawn here. One has to do with the importance of following established procedures. As we saw in the chapters on the interrogation memoranda, there is evidence that Yoo and Bybee did not follow the established patterns of OLC analyses and that their work suffered as a result. Even more strikingly, however, we saw that the review of the work of Yoo and Bybee conducted by the OPR was deeply flawed because the OPR did not follow the analytical framework that is supposed to govern the office's reviews. In the case of military commissions, when JAG officers opposed their establishment, at least one reason was that the procedures for the new commissions did not follow the standard procedures of military justice.

Another lesson concerns the dangers of not confronting problems forthrightly and honestly. I have tried to be balanced in claiming that despite the fact that the United States tortured and abused many detainees in the years after September 2001, there is much to praise in the work of professionals of various stripes who were called on by their government to serve in the war on terror. Nevertheless, there is a danger in focusing unduly on the positive. I believe that the effort to highlight the good work of army medical personnel in the army surgeon general's report led the authors of the report to make misleading claims about the involvement of physicians in abusive interrogations. We need to confront failures as well as to acknowledge and praise successes. I rejected Dershowitz's conclusion about the need for torture warrants, but there is real merit in his willingness forthrightly to confront the difficult choices we face. There is also merit in acknowledging when we make mistakes.

The lessons we might draw about the importance of openness, procedural regularity, accountability, and consultation might lead us to formulate more explicit rules of professional responsibility, and this would certainly be a welcome outcome. We saw, for example, that after the lack of consultation and procedural irregularities in the promulgation of the interrogation memoranda, the OLC implemented a useful set of practice guidelines for OLC attorneys. Similarly, to address questions raised by the evolution of APA policy on coercive interrogation, the Ethics Committee of the APA is working on a document that contains twenty-five interrogation vignettes with accompanying analysis in relation to APA policy statements on interrogation.[15] Although this Ethics Committee document does not set out practice guidelines, it does offer explicit discussion of scenarios that military psychologists are likely to face.

We have seen that, in formulating guidelines for addressing novel situations and applying ethical norms, professional organizations can play an important, if contested, role. But we have also seen that membership in a profession may help to shape virtues and character in important ways. One reason military professionals responded so negatively to the prospect of using coercive interrogation was certainly that their professional codes explicitly prohibited such interrogation. But there was also an almost palpable, visceral response from some military professionals to the idea that the US military would, for example, sexually humiliate detainees as part of a regime of interrogation or that a prosecution of a detainee in a military commission would use evidence gathered through the use of torture.

Arguably, the rule of law was threatened by the efforts to justify and use EITs that were, according to the schema I have defended in this volume, abusive or torturous. Yet the aversion to the lack of accountability, to excessive executive-branch power, to the lack of procedural safeguards insuring fair and just treatment of detainees, was widespread and fueled a vigorous defense of the rule of law. If, as I believe, the arguments of Jeremy Waldron and David Luban that we examined in chapter 4 are correct, the spirit of American law is incompatible with the kind of brutality evident in some of the practices that emerged in the aftermath of the attacks of September 11, 2001. The hopeful side of the recognition of this fact is that a commitment to the rule of law provides something of an inoculation against tyranny and brutality. However misguided or depressing the actions of some professionals have been in the war on terror, we have also seen how the dispositions shaped by the rule of law mobilized professionals to respond to the perceived threat to justice and fairness.

Has that response been successful? Certainly some of the worst violations of the rule of law have been corrected, but it is hard to conclude that a fundamental commitment to human rights has been restored in the United States and will withstand another successful terrorist attack of any significant magnitude. In worrying about the possibility of long-term erosion of America's commitment to human rights, I follow Mark Danner. Danner notes that in the aftermath of 9/11 there emerged what might be described as a "constitutional dictatorship."[16]

Even better, he says, is the idea that what emerged after September 11 was a "state of exception." As an umbrella term, state of exception "gathers beneath it those emergency categories ["constitutional dictatorship," "9/11 constitution," "emergency constitution"] while emphasizing that this state has as its defining characteristic that it transcends the borders of the strictly legal—that it occupies, in the words of the philosopher Giorgio Agamben, 'a position at the limit between politics and law . . . an ambiguous, uncertain, borderline fringe, at the intersection of the legal and the political.'"[17]

The notion of a state of exception, or perhaps better, a State of exception, includes the idea that we live in a fundamentally different reality than we did before terrorists targeted the United States. There is a pre-9/11 reality and a post-9/11 reality, and the post-9/11 reality does not include all the rights and freedoms once taken for granted in the United States. The problem, says Danner, is that the state of exception has continued for ten years and shows no signs of abating. Where torturing would once have been unthinkable, it is now a policy choice. President Obama repudiated torture, but it is no longer unimaginable. More troubling is the fact that there is little apparent regret among Americans that the United States chose torture as a policy option for counterterrorism in the war on terror. Nor is there any enthusiam for accepting responsibility for the mistreatment of prisoners in US custody. While the Bush administration was in office, there was no possibility of accountability, for, as Scott Horton noted at the time, "the criminal investigative and prosecutorial functions are currently [in 2005] controlled by individuals who are involved in the conspiracy to commit war crimes."[18] Yet little changed when Obama came into office, at least in terms of accountability. President Obama's attorney general, Eric Holder, began an investigation of possible violations of US law, but ultimately chose not to file any charges.

The upshot of the failure to hold policymakers accountable is that the good work of professionals who opposed abusive interrogation and eventually stopped the worst of the practices—some thereby risking or ending their careers—is precarious and fragile. As Danner puts the point, we are left in a state of moral limbo:

> As we look back today at these ghostly figures [of the detainees], at the policymakers sitting in their offices who ordered these techniques, and the

lawyers who deemed them legal, and the interrogators who practiced them on men chained naked in cold sunless rooms, we can have the sense, haunting as it is, that they are all looking forward at us, as we stand here today judging what they did. If we know anything, it is that they knew this moment would come. They were determined to prepare for it, and in a sense they succeeded brilliantly. The legal memos, however grotesque in their reasoning and however widely denounced, have in effect held sway, and imposed a painful unremitting moral limbo on all of us.[19]

This is the great tragedy of living in a state of exception. As long as we exempt our leaders from the norms of international law and a commitment to human rights, not to mention US law, we remain morally compromised. We can no longer serve a leadership role in the promotion of human rights and the rule of law around the world, because we have placed ourselves above the law and have not honored the norms of human rights that we helped forge. This, at any rate, is Danner's view of America's current situation. I turn in the final chapter to offer my own assessment of where we stand nearly eleven years after 9/11 and why the evaluation of counterterrorism policies and practices grounded in professional codes and cultures is crucial going forward.

Notes

1. Guiora divides interrogations into three categories: interrogations, coercive interrogations, and torture. I believe that all interrogations are coercive, but only some are abusive and fewer still rise to the level of torture. I have thus introduced the category of abusive interrogations to describe interrogations that are unacceptable, but do not rise to the level of torture.

2. Department of the Army, *FM 34-52*, 3-16.

3. Ibid., iv–v.

4. "Convention (III) Relative to the Treatment of Prisoners of War, Geneva, 12 August 1949," available on the website of the International Committee of the Red Cross, www.icrc.org/ihl.nsf/WebART/375-590006.

5. *FM 34-52* repeatedly urges caution when a particular technique comes close to violating concerns articulated in the Geneva conventions about prisoner dignity and integrity.

6. The following account is indebted to Gilbert Meilaender's discussion in "Human Dignity."

7. Ibid., 262, 263.

8. Kant, *Groundwork of the Metaphysics of Morals*, 50–51.

9. Note that psychological integrity does not yield a standard that can be applied without some knowledge of particular prisoners. For that reason, there may some disagreement about whether particular techniques threaten psychological integrity. It is also important to note that in speaking of breaking a detainee's will, I mean to highlight the brokenness of the will and not merely the fact that a detainee is pressured into doing something other than he might prefer.

10. "Inquiry into the Treatment of Detainees in U.S. Custody," Committee on Armed Services, US Senate, November 20, 2008, http://armed-services.senate .gov/Publications/Detainee%20Report%20Final_April%2022%202009.pdf, 135–36.

11. Guiora, *Constitutional Limits*, 85.

12. For a discussion of how these techniques have been used as forms of torture, see Rejali, *Torture and Democracy*.

13. For a discussion of the effects of solitary confinement, see Atul Gawande, "Hellhole," *New Yorker*, March 30, 2009, www.newyorker.com/reporting/2009/03/30/090330fa_fact_gawande; see also McCoy, *Question of Torture*.

14. President Obama's escalation of drone attacks and targeted killings raises ongoing concerns about the lack of transparency. According to most accounts, targeted killing has been approved in an OLC memorandum that is not public. It is hard not to wonder whether this memorandum will someday be leaked and be dubbed "the killing memo."

15. "Responses of the APA Ethics Committee to Questions, Comments, and Vignettes Regarding APA Policy on the Role of Psychologists in National Security–Related Activities," APA, June 2011, www.apa.org/ethics/programs/national -security-comments.pdf.

16. The term is taken from Rossiter, *Constitutional Dictatorship*.

17. Mark Danner, "After September 11: Our State of Exception," *New York Review of Books*, October 13, 2011, www.nybooks.com/articles/archives/2011/oct/13/after-september-11-our-state-exception/?pagination=false.

18. "Expert Report of Scott Horton," January 28, 2005, available on the Center for Constitutional Rights website, http://ccrjustice.org/files/Appendix%20N.%20 5%20-%20Scott%20Horton%27s%20Affidavit.pdf.

19. Danner, "After September 11."

Ten

This We Do Not Do

The Future of Interrogation and the Ethics of Professional Responsibility

> I believe there should be a thoughtful debate about what is necessary and moral for a country to survive.
>
> —Jose Rodriguez Jr., *Hard Measures*, 121

I write this concluding chapter of *The Ethics of Interrogation* a little over ten and a half years after the attacks of September 11, 2001. Two items in the news suggest both why debates about counterterrorism practices are not likely to go away and how we might frame the national discussion our country ought to have about the ethics of interrogation and professional responsibility going forward. The first is the publication of a book, *Hard Measures*, by Jose Rodriguez, the former director of the National Clandestine Service of the CIA. In the book and in various interviews during the promotional tour for the volume, Rodriguez vigorously defends counterterrorism measures used by the CIA in the war on terror, including rendition and EITs.[1] He argues that the enhanced techniques used on Abu Zubaydah and Khalid Sheikh Mohammed resulted in intelligence that was key in the prevention of specific terrorist plots.

The second news item is the conviction of Adis Medunjanin on federal charges of conspiring to use weapons of mass destruction and other terrorist-related activities, as part of a plot to engage in suicide bomb attacks on the subway system of New York City. Medunjanin was brought to trial after authorities discovered the plot and after his accomplices, Najibullah Zazi and Zarein Ahmedzay, agreed to testify against him as part of a plea agreement. At trial, Zazi and Ahmedzay testified that they had traveled with Medunjanin to Pakistan in 2008 to train with al-Qaeda. They returned to the United States with the intent of targeting the New York Stock Exchange, Times Square, or Grand Central Station, before settling on the subway system as the desired target. At the conclusion of the trial, Assistant Attorney General for National Security Lisa Monaco described Medunjanin as "an active and willing participant in one of the most serious terrorist plots against the homeland since 9/11. Were it not for the combined efforts of the law enforcement and intelligence communities, the suicide bomb attacks that he and others planned would have been devastating."[2]

These two stories—one about a book lauding the success of EITs; the other about a terrorist attack narrowly averted—provide a useful frame for concluding our discussion of the ethics of interrogation because they highlight the ongoing threat of terrorism and the need for intelligence about potential attacks in order to prevent them. Those who work in the field of counterterrorism know all too well that a successful terrorist attack is almost inevitable and that the effort to prevent terrorist attacks will require an ongoing calibration of the appropriate moral and legal measures to combat that threat.

Assessing Counterterrorism Practices

Jose Rodriguez raises an important issue that has not been sufficiently discussed. He notes that President Obama's repudiation of EITs and the use of rendition and black sites severely limits his options with suspected terrorists. According to Rodriguez, the Obama administration has adopted a "take no prisoners" approach. Because there are limited options for where to imprison captured terrorists and only the techniques of *FM 34-52* available for interrogating prisoners once they are detained, the administration has apparently adopted a policy that it is better to kill terrorists than to capture them.[3] "An administration that thinks it was 'torture' to interfere with the sleep cycle of a handful of the worst terrorists on the planet," Rodriguez writes, "has no problem with authorizing the firing of Hellfire missiles into a group of thirty or forty suspects gathered around a campfire." While I disagree with Rodriguez's casual dismissal of the significance of sleep deprivation, he raises an important issue. As he trenchantly puts the point, "There is no opportunity to interrogate or learn anything from a suspect who is vaporized by a missile."[4]

Indeed, although I have said very little about targeted killing, I agree with Rodriguez that it is the Obama administration's version of coercive interrogation. It is authorized by a secret memorandum issued by the OLC; it is likely to be enormously controversial when the full details of the program are finally revealed; and it departs dramatically from traditional norms of law and morality. Consider, for example, the killing of Anwar al-Awlaki.

Al-Awlaki was an American-born Muslim cleric who was killed in September 2011 by a Hellfire missile fired from a drone operated by the CIA. By all accounts, al-Awlaki was extremely successful in recruiting jihadists for violent attacks against the United States. For example, Major Nidal Malik Hasan, the army psychiatrist who shot thirteen people in Fort Hood, Texas, had communicated with al-Awlaki, and those convicted of the plot to target the New York City subway system were influenced by al-Awlaki's sermons. Nevertheless, al-Awlaki was an American citizen, and he was executed without a trial, without legal representation, and without any form of judicial review of which we are aware. Moreover, Samir Khan, who edited an al-Qaeda online magazine with al-Awlaki, was also killed in the drone strike. Like al-Awlaki, Khan was an American citizen who was neither tried nor convicted before being executed.

I have focused fairly narrowly on the ethics of interrogation, but I believe the close attention we have paid to issues of professional responsibility can help us address the broader ethical issues raised by counterterrorism. This is not to say that the ethics of interrogation are settled. The Obama administration has ruled out the use of EITs, presumably because it deemed them to be contrary to fundamental American values, but it did so at a time when there was not blood on the ground. Yet both the trial of Adis Medunjanin and Jose Rodriguez's endorsement of EITs as effective counterterrorism tools serve to remind us that terrorist activities are a real and continuing threat and that some counterterrorism experts believe that the use of abusive interrogations is justified. Making predictions is not something scholars like to do, but it is a safe bet that the issue of coercive interrogation will be revisited when there is another successful terrorist attack in the United States.

When that happens, or when the issue of targeted killing is taken up in the way that coercive interrogations have been, it will be important to draw upon the expertise of professionals working in support of these activities. In particular, it will be important to encourage a moral discussion of counterterrorism that includes an engagement with the codes of ethics that prevail in the professional fields called upon to facilitate counterterrorist practices. Jose Rodriguez is surely right when he calls for "a thoughtful debate about what is necessary and moral for a country to survive," as quoted in this chapter's epigraph, but what troubles me about his account of CIA activities in *Hard Measures* is that his call for the use of enhanced interrogation is primarily prudential. There is almost no moral argument to be found in the volume and little in the way of moral tradition to which he might appeal in terms of CIA culture.[5]

If we compare his analysis of enhanced interrogation with that taking place among military professionals, the differences are striking. Consider the work being done on military professional ethics in an age of terrorism in which the character of conflict is rapidly changing. One example of this work is a series of reports jointly sponsored by the army's Center for Excellence for the Professional Military Ethic at West Point and the Strategic Studies Institute of the Army War College. The inaugural report, *The Army's Professional Military Ethic in an Era of Persistent Conflict*, authored by Don Snider, Paul Oh, and Kevin Toner, illustrates why reflecting on the morality of counterterrorism from within a tradition of professional ethics is important.

The authors recognize that the character of conflict in the post-9/11 world is changing and that the army's professional military ethic needs to evolve to address the changing environment. But they are clear that this evolution must not emerge merely as an ad hoc response to the demands of fighting a war on terror, but should flow organically from an established moral tradition embodied in the army's professional culture. As Snider, Oh, and Toner point out, *Army Field Manual 1* makes it clear that professional ethics involves establishing a culture that shapes the identity and character of army officers.

It is against this backdrop that Snider, Oh, and Toner take up the challenges posed to military ethics in an era of persistent conflict. They note that there are three major influences on army culture and ethics, all of them currently in flux. The three categories of influence are (1) the functional imperatives of the profession, (2) American values, beliefs, and social norms, and (3) international laws and treaties to which the United States is party. And we can see how dynamic the situation is by noting that the army has moved aggressively to build competencies in counterinsurgency and nation building; Americans have been willing to sacrifice civil liberties for security; and support for international norms against torture has eroded domestically.

Snider, Oh, and Toner use a diagram showing the three categories of influence exerting pressure on a core ethos of professional culture, but their account actually suggests that the influence is exerted in both directions. The erosion of support for international norms like the Geneva conventions exerts influence on the army culture and ethos, but that culture, with its strong commitment to the Geneva conventions, exerts a countervailing pressure against this erosion. Indeed, both the legal and moral foundations of the army culture resist some of the shifting norms of the surrounding society.

We see this if we examine the legal documents that shape army culture. The officer's oath of commission, the Standards of Exemplary Conduct, the UCMJ, and the Soldier's Rules all provide a bulwark against a precipitous embrace of EITs or other forms of counterterrorism that arguably conflict with these documents.[6] Consider the ten rules of the law of war, known as the Soldier's Rules:

1. Soldiers fight only enemy combatants.
2. Soldiers do not harm enemies who surrender. They disarm them and turn them over to their superior.
3. Soldiers do not kill or torture any personnel in their custody.
4. Soldiers collect and care for the wounded, whether friend or foe.
5. Soldiers do not attack medical personnel, facilities, or equipment.
6. Soldiers destroy no more than the mission requires.
7. Soldiers treat civilians humanely.
8. Soldiers do not steal. Soldiers respect private property and possessions.
9. Soldiers should do their best to prevent violations of the law of war.
10. Soldiers report all violations of the law of war to their superior.[7]

Arguably rules 2, 3, 9, and 10 conflict with the use of EITs, and while Jose Rodriguez and others may be right that we need to adjust these rules given the threat that terrorism poses to national security, to revise these rules implicates an interlocking set of norms that has been constitutive of professional military ethics.

The fact that the erosion of the commitment to norms of international law and the rules of war strikes at the heart of army culture may partly help explain the dissent of military professionals on the use of EITs that we discussed in chapter 8. As we saw, there were many harsh critics of the dissenters, and one of the fundamental criticisms was that the dissenters broke with military tradition. This charge was especially aimed at the retired generals who publicly criticized both the conduct of the war in Iraq and Secretary of Defense Donald Rumsfeld. For our purposes, it is not necessary to evaluate their criticism; it is enough to know that it was situated in a context of expectations generated by military culture and tradition.

Indeed, the dissent itself triggered a reassessment by scholars of professional military ethics of when dissent is appropriate, given the military's commitment to civilian leadership and its insistence that military leaders "show in themselves a good example of virtue, honor, patriotism, and *subordination*" (my italics).[8] Yet, in striking contrast to the analysis of dissent offered by Sulmasy and Yoo that we reviewed in chapter 8, this examination of dissent sought criteria for identifying the appropriate occasions for public disagreement from norms of professional military ethics. Thus, Don Snider places the discussion of appropriate dissent within the context of a social-trustee model of military professionalism where trust is key. There are, he says, three critical moral relationships intrinsic to the military profession that are based on trust—the profession and the American people, the profession and civilian leaders, and, within the profession, senior leadership and junior leaders.[9] There are certainly legal and prudential considerations that affect a judgment about whether dissent is appropriate, but the most fundamental question is what effect dissent will have on these relationships. Will it build or will it erode trust?

Snider offers five criteria that a leader who is considering dissent should consult in making his or her decision. Two have to do with the seriousness of the issue involved and with how qualified the leader is to provide an accurate assessment of what the situation requires. The other three criteria concern the motives for dissenting. The five criteria can be stated as questions: Is the issue of sufficient gravity to risk sacrificing a trusting relationship? Does the dissenter have the expertise to reach an appropriate dissenting view? Does the dissenter bear a risk; is he prepared to sacrifice for his dissenting view? Why dissent now? Is the dissent compatible with a record of loyal career service?

Codes of Professional Ethics and Counterterrorism

If we look back at the various professions' responses to coercive interrogation, we in fact see that professional codes—and the core values of professional life they embody—are important to the moral assessment of counterterrorism. Jose Rodriguez presses the issue of the ethics of counterterrorism forcefully in the passage from which the epigraph of this chapter is taken:

> I believe there should be a thoughtful debate about what is necessary and moral for a country to survive. It had been the policy of the U.S. government since the Clinton administration, fully approved by Congress, to support regime change in Iraq. If Saddam could have been removed with a single bullet, might that not have been preferable to a war that killed hundreds of thousands of Iraqis, cost thousands of American lives, created tens of thousands of amputees, and saddled U.S. taxpayers with estimated direct costs of nearly $1 trillion? . . . Is it less moral to have a leader like Qadhafi succumb to what some euphemistically referred to as "the ultimate brush pass," or to bomb his headquarters, hoping he somehow meets his demise, along with the hundreds or perhaps thousands of others who surely will be collateral damage? The answers to these questions are not easy. . . . I am not arguing for broad-based or promiscuous use of operations, but giving up the option without understanding what is at stake strikes me as exceedingly unwise.[10]

Yet, for all the force with which he presses these questions, Rodriguez's effort to answer them is anemic at best. What constitutes a "promiscuous" use of operations? We are not told. Why is waterboarding not torture? We are told only that it was defined as not being torture by the DOJ. Why might targeted killing be unacceptable? Only because it eliminates the possibility of coercive interrogation.

The fact that Rodriguez offers only pragmatic, consequentialist assessments of counterterrorist practices highlights the importance of having a moral tradition upon which to rely in evaluating interrogation and other forms of counterterrorism. When military professionals asked about whether EITs were acceptable, they reflected on this question from within a culture shaped by long-standing legal and moral codes. The Standards of Exemplary Conduct, the UCMJ, the Seven Army Values, the Warrior Ethos, and other articulations of the values that shape military culture are all resources military professionals may consult in assessing counterterrorism practices.

There are two important points to note at this juncture. The first is that these codes are not simply foundational internally. They structure society's expectations of military professionals and are the basis of the trust average Americans place in the military. As we noted in chapter 7, codes of conduct ideally serve to shape the character of professionals who embrace them, and an evaluation of character is essential to trust. This is why Snider argues that the assessment of dissent must include the evaluation of each of his five criteria in terms of its impact on the trust the American people have in the military. It is also why three of these five criteria, the personal sacrifice incurred in dissenting, the timing of the dissent, and the relation of the dissent to previous career service, have to do with the dissenter's motives and thus with his or her character. In deciding whether to dissent publicly or to revise existing military ethics to allow EITs, military professionals must attend to the impact such decisions will have on external relationships.

In most cases, dissent is likely to erode trust. But not always. As Snider puts it, "If the leader believes that an act of dissent best balances the immediate felt obligation to bring his/her professional military expertise to bear in a public forum with the longer-term obligation to lead and represent the profession as a social trustee, as a faithful servant of the American people," then dissent may be necessary. "On rare occasions," he writes, "true professionals must retain the moral space to 'profess.'"[11]

The second fact of significance here is that the moral traditions of the military evolve over time. No history of just war theory could fail to note the evolution of the theory in response to changing historical circumstances. We can trace just war thinking in the West at least back to Augustine, but to read Augustine on the justified use of force is to enter a pre-Westphalian world where the sovereignty of nation-states is unrecognized. Attending to this evolution reminds us that the moral resources that military professionals consult in arriving at moral judgments about counterterrorism are open to revision, as is the application of professed values to the novel threats posed by contemporary terrorism. Martin Cook has put this point about the changing circumstances of military engagement provocatively. Indeed, he suggests that we may be at an epochal historical turning point that necessitates a fundamental shift in our moral thinking about war. The just war theory that emerged in response to the post-Reformation Westphalian order may no longer be adequate given twenty-first-century terrorist threats to civilization itself.[12]

For example, Cook suggests that the Bush doctrine of preemptive or preventative war might be construed as involving a new understanding of terrorism such that the fight against terrorism would be immune from some traditional just war restraints.

> There might be a multilateral agreement, implicit or explicit, that some threats warrant interventions that might not pass the inherited "just war" tests of recent centuries. In that respect, just war would be returning to its origins: rather than seeing war as a conflict among sovereign states in response to aggression, the international community might see itself once again as defending a "tranquility of order" in the international system against incursions of alien systems and ideologies whose sole purpose is a disruption and displacement of that order. In other words, the globalized civilization grounded in democracy, human rights, free trade, communication, technology and science may be defending its civilization itself against forces that seek its complete destruction.[13]

I believe that such a view of terrorism and the need to adjust the tradition of just war and the law of armed conflict informs much of the literature debating the ethics of targeted killing. As Kenneth Anderson points out, the strategy of both the Bush and Obama administrations was to treat al-Qaeda operatives as combatants for the purposes of justifying the use of drone strikes under international humanitarian law. The claim has essentially been that a state of armed conflict exists between the United States and al-Qaeda and targeted killing is a form of self-defense in that conflict. Yet, as Anderson points out, many, including US allies, find this claim increasingly improbable.

The problem, says Anderson, is that the United States has conceded that targeted killing can only be justified if the targets are treated as combatants in an armed conflict. Yet this paradigm may well be ill suited for conceptualizing terrorist threats posed by nonstate actors. If so, then we may need to adapt the paradigm in order to respond to changing historical circumstances. Critics of such an adaptation will claim that we change the paradigm merely to allow us to do what we want, but that is a cynical and ahistorical approach to the rules of war. The better way to understand such a change would be to see it as an attempt to apply the values embedded in the tradition of just war theory to new realities.

Interestingly, Anderson acknowledges that there are legitimate concerns with targeted killing that might well be framed in terms of just war criteria of discrimination and proportionality. How do we know, for example, that we are targeting a terrorist and not an innocent civilian? How can we rule out excessive collateral damage? If the United States is going to address these concerns, it will need to provide what Anderson calls a "visible domestic standard."[14] This is why Anderson suggests that Congress act to provide a transparent, unambiguous articulation of the government's understanding of its legal position in the fight against terrorism.

"The deeper issue here," Anderson writes, "is not merely a strategic and political one about targeted killing and drones" but concerns "covert uses of force under the doctrines of vital national interest and self-defense." On a range of issues, including interrogation techniques, detention policy, and other matters bearing on counterterrorism, "a general approach of overt legislation [from Congress] that removes ambiguity is to be preferred."[15]

Note that, in one sense, we have circled back to the issues of transparency and accountability, which we took up in chapter 4 when we examined Alan Dershowitz's argument that we should create a system of torture warrants. Indeed, what emerges in our exploration of the ethics of interrogation is that it is not possible to take up the issue of coercive interrogation in the aftermath of 9/11 in isolation from other practices and policies of counterterrorism. We saw in the transition from chapter 1 to chapter 2 that questions about the role of psychologists in interrogations raise much broader questions about whether psychologists should play a central role in counterterrorism generally.

In chapter 3 we examined the role lawyers in the OLC played in laying the groundwork for the use of EITs. Five years later, lawyers within the same office at the DOJ were busy writing memoranda authorizing targeted killing. The work of both groups of lawyers was originally conducted in secret, and both authorized practices that would have been considered unthinkable a decade earlier. Many still argue that both practices are fundamentally incompatible with the rule of law.

The chapters on physicians and military professionals also took us beyond enhanced interrogation. Medical and military professionals were involved in interrogations, but they also had to decide generally how detainees should be treated. Questions about whether hunger-striking detainees should be force-fed or whether military tribunals should be used to adjudicate the legal situation of detainees are not directly related to enhanced interrogations, but they raise important moral issues. I also hope it is now clear that the issues raised by practices and policies of counterterrorism are usefully addressed by drawing upon the codes of professional ethics of those who inevitably will be called upon to implement those policies and practices. In this regard, the military's rich tradition of commitment to values and norms that shape a military culture, which in turn shapes individual character, is a model that other professions might emulate in seeking to wrestle with ethical issues raised by the war on terror. The fact that the army is committed to maintaining a culture that produces soldiers of character means that a lot of institutional resources are devoted to thinking and rethinking how to create and sustain such a culture. It would be a good sign for democratic traditions in America if other professions sought so intentionally to understand how best to respond to the war on terror as professionals of character.

It is often said that the Constitution is not a suicide pact. Although the basic idea behind this saying can be traced back to Thomas Jefferson, its provenance in constitutional law is a dissent by Justice Robert Jackson in the Supreme Court case *Terminiello v. City of Chicago*. The case involved a Chicago city ordinance under which Arthur Terminiello was convicted of a breach of the peace for what today might be called hate speech. The majority opinion held that the Chicago ordinance was a violation of Terminiello's First Amendment free-speech rights. However, Justice Jackson believed that the threat to public order justified a limitation of liberty. "This Court has gone far," he wrote, "toward accepting the doctrine that civil liberty means the removal of all restraints from these crowds and that all local attempts to maintain order are impairments of the liberty of the citizen."[16]

Arguably, Justice Jackson captured the core issue at stake in the ethics of interrogation; namely, the tension between security and rights. His claim of an existential threat to the Constitution from allowing hatemongers like Terminiello to use inflammatory rhetoric to stoke the passions of their followers is overblown, but the logic of his position is sound. Jackson wrote that "the choice is not between order and liberty. It is between liberty with order and anarchy without either."[17] In the context of the ethical issues raised by the practices and policies adopted by the United States in the war on terror, I would recast Justice Jackson's insight as follows: In the fight against terrorism, the choice is not between national security and human rights. It is between national security with an appropriate respect for human rights and tyranny without either.

Jackson's worry, of course, was that a rigid and doctrinaire adherence to liberty rights threatened the order necessary to the meaningful exercise of freedom. The same might be said today. A blind and absolutist adherence to human rights in the face of existential threats to national security may well be suicidal. Yet it seems to me that the greater threat comes from too quickly jettisoning concerns about human rights in the face of the dangers of terrorism. Jackson was right to argue that we do not want to "convert the constitutional Bill of Rights into a suicide pact," and that to protect liberty without any regard to consequences is to enter such a pact.[18] But there is more than one way for a democracy to commit suicide. A commitment to security no matter the cost may also be a kind of suicide pact.

How to balance order and liberty or security and human rights are perennial questions for democratic societies. They are particularly pressing in an age of terror. But the United States is not without resources for addressing these questions. If this volume has been at all successful, it will have shown that the professions may provide exactly the sort of resources we need to wrestle with these questions in a serious and sustained way. To that end, it would be helpful to recover a sense of how professions serve the common good and why the cultivation of professional codes of conduct that may function to shape culture and character is important to that service.

I began this volume by quoting Jeffrey Stout's claim that the ethical inheritance of American democracy consists partly of the activity of intellectuals who attempt to make sense of the way ordinary Americans think and talk about ethical issues by reflecting critically on the conversations that inform everyday moral action. I have tried throughout this study to make sense of the American response to terrorism by looking at how several groups of ordinary Americans, professionals of various sorts, thought and reasoned about how best to address the threat of terrorism in the aftermath of the attacks of September 11, 2001.

I believe that we must set limits to the policies and practices of counterterrorism that a liberal democracy must not transgress. Americans should be able to say, "This we do not do." But if there is any hope of drawing such a line, we will need the help of professionals of character to articulate and defend the limits of counterterrorism.

Notes

1. See, e.g., his combative interview on *60 Minutes*, April 29, 2012, available on the CBS News website, www.cbsnews.com/8301-18560_162-57423533/hard-measures-ex-cia-head-defends-post-9-11-tactics/?tag=strip.

2. Mark Rockwell, "Third Conviction in 2009 New York Subway Attack Plot," *Government Security News*, May 2, 2012, www.gsnmagazine.com/node/26254?c=law_enforcement_first_responders.

3. Kenneth Anderson has also made this point. See his working paper "Targeted Killing in U.S. Counterterrorism Strategy and Law."

4. Rodriguez, *Hard Measures*, 252.

5. I do not mean to suggest that Rodriguez or other CIA officers acted unethically or that there is no moral code that shapes CIA practice. Rodriguez makes clear that loyalty is a central virtue for him and that his commitment to remain loyal to his CIA colleagues was a driving force for many of his actions. The point is that there is not a clearly articulated moral tradition to which Rodriguez, unlike, say, JAG officers, could appeal.

6. Snider, Oh, and Toner, *Army's Professional Military Ethic*, 13.

7. "Army Training and Leader Development," Army Regulation 350-1, Department of the Army, August 4, 2011, www.apd.army.mil/pdffiles/r350_1.pdf.

8. See the "Requirements of Exemplary Conduct" in 10 U.S.C. §§ 3583, 5947, and 8583.

9. Snider, *Dissent and Strategic Leadership*.

10. Rodriguez, *Hard Measures*, 121.

11. Snider, *Dissent and Strategic Leadership*, 30.

12. Cook, *Moral Warrior*, 115.

13. Ibid., 36.

14. Anderson, "Targeted Killing in U.S. Counterterrorism Strategy and Law," 28.

15. Ibid., 32.

16. Terminiello v. City of Chicago, 337 U.S. 1, 37 (1949) (Jackson, R., dissenting).

17. Ibid.

18. Ibid.

Bibliography

Abbott, Andrew. *The System of Professions: An Essay on the Division of Expert Labor.* Chicago: University of Chicago Press, 1988.

Allhoff, Fritz. "Physician Involvement in Hostile Interrogation." *Cambridge Quarterly of Healthcare Ethics* 15, no. 2 (2006): 392–402.

Anderson, Kenneth. "'Targeted Killing in U.S. Counterterrorism Strategy and Law." Counterterrorism and American Statutory Law paper no. 9. Brookings Institution, Georgetown University Law Center, and Hoover Institution, May 11, 2009. www.brookings.edu/papers/2009/0511_counterterrorism_anderson.aspx.

Annas, George. "Human Rights Outlaws: Nuremberg, Geneva, and the Global War on Terror." *Boston University Law Review* 87 (2007): 427–66.

———. "Hunger Strikes at Guantanamo—Medical Ethics and Human Rights in a 'Legal Black Hole.'" *New England Journal of Medicine* 355, no. 13 (2006): 1377–82.

Annas, George J., and Michael A. Grodin. "Medicine and Human Rights: Reflections on the Fiftieth Anniversary of the Doctors' Trial." In *Health and Human Rights*, edited by Jonathan M. Mann et al., 301–11. New York: Routledge, 1999.

APA (American Psychological Association) Presidential Task Force. *Psychological Ethics and National Security.* Washington, DC: APA, June 2005. www.apa.org/pubs/info/reports/pens.pdf.

Applbaum, Arthur. *Ethics for Adversaries: The Morality of Roles in Public and Professional Life.* Princeton, NJ: Princeton University Press, 1999.

Arendt, Hannah. *The Origins of Totalitarianism*, new ed. New York: Harcourt, Brace, Jovanovich, 1973.

Arrigo, Jean Maria. "Psychological Torture—The CIA and the APA." *PsycCritiques* 51 (July 26, 2006). doi: 10.1037/a0003712.

Bok, Derek. *Universities in the Marketplace: The Commercialization of Higher Education.* Princeton, NJ: Princeton University Press, 2003.

Borum, Randy, Robert Fein, Bryan Vossekuil, Michael Gelles, and Scott Shumate. "The Role of Operational Research in Counterterrorism." *International Journal of Intelligence and Counterintelligence* 17, no. 3 (2004): 420–34. Available at http://works.bepress.com/randy_borum/8.

Brint, Steven. *In an Age of Experts.* Princeton, NJ: Princeton University Press, 1994.

Camus, Albert. *The Just Assassins.* In *Caligula and Three Other Plays,* 233–302. New York: Vintage Books, 1958.

Candilis, Philip. "Reply to Schafer: Ethics and State Extremism in Defense of Liberty." *Journal of the American Academy of Psychiatry and the Law* 29 (2001): 452–56.

Cole, David. "The Sacrificial Yoo: Accounting for Torture in the OPR Report." *Journal of National Security Law and Policy* 4 (2010): 455–64.

Cook, Martin L. "Ethical Issues in Counterterrorism 'War.'" Paper presented at the US Army Command and Staff College Ethics Conference, November 16–18, 2009. www.leavenworthethicssymposium.org/resource/resmgr/2009_strate gic _papers/ethicsincounterterrorism.pdf.

———. *The Moral Warrior: Ethics and Service in the U.S. Military.* Albany: State University of New York Press, 2010.

Costanzo, Mark, Ellen Gerrity, and M. Brinton Lykes. "Psychologists and the Use of Torture in Interrogations." *Analyses of Social Issues and Public Policy* 7, no. 1 (2007): 7–20.

Davis, Michael. *Profession, Code, and Ethics.* Aldershot: Ashgate, 2002.

Department of the Army. *FM 34-52: Intelligence Interrogation.* Washington, DC: Department of the Army, September 28, 1992. Available on the website of the Library of Congress, www.loc.gov/rr/frd/Military_Law/pdf/intel_interrroga tion_sept-1992.pdf.

Dershowitz, Alan. "Reply: Torture without Visibility and Accountability Is Worse Than with It." *University of Pennsylvania Journal of Constitutional Law* 6, no. 2 (2003): 326.

———. "Should the Ticking Bomb Terrorist Be Tortured?" In *Why Terrorism Works: Understanding the Threat, Responding to the Challenge,* 132–63. New Haven, CT: Yale University Press, 2002.

———. "Tortured Reasoning." In *Torture: A Collection,* edited by Sanford Levinson, 257–80. New York: Oxford University Press, 2004.

———. "The Torture Warrant." *New York Law School Law Review* 48 (2003): 275–94.

Dzur, Albert. *Democratic Professionalism.* University Park: Pennsylvania State University Press, 2008. Kindle edition.

Ewing, Charles, and Michael Gelles. "Ethical Concerns in Forensic Consultation Regarding National Safety and Security." *Journal of Threat Assessment* 2, no. 3 (2003): 95–107.

Fein, Robert A., and Bryan Vossekuil. "Assassination in the United States: An Operational Study of Recent Assassins, Attackers, and Near-Lethal Approaches." *Journal of Forensic Sciences* 50 (1999): 321–33.

Frakt, David. "Mohammed Jawad and the Military Commissions of Guantánamo." *Duke Law Journal* 60 (2011): 1367–411.

Freidson, Eliot. *Professional Dominance: The Social Structure of Medical Care.* New Brunswick, NJ: Transaction, 1970.

————. *Professionalism: The Third Logic*. Chicago: University of Chicago Press, 2001.

Gellhorn, Walter. "The Abuse of Occupational Licensing." *University of Chicago Law Review* 44, no. 1 (1976): 6–27.

Grodin, Michael A., George J. Annas, and Leonard H. Glantz. "Medicine and Human Rights: A Proposal for International Action." *Hastings Center Report* 23, no. 4 (1993): 8–12.

Guiora, Amos. *Constitutional Limits on Coercive Interrogation*. New York: Oxford University Press, 2008.

Hansen, Victor. "Understanding the Role of Military Lawyers in the War on Terror: A Response to the Perceived Crisis in Civil-Military Relations." *South Texas Law Review* 50 (2009): 617–68.

Human Rights Watch. *Getting Away with Torture: The Bush Administration and Mistreatment of Detainees*. New York: Human Rights Watch, 2011. www.hrw.org/sites/default/files/reports/us0711webwcover.pdf.

Huntington, Samuel. *The Soldier and the State: The Theory and Politics of Civil-Military Relations*. New York: Vintage Books, 1957.

James, Larry. *Fixing Hell: An Army Psychologist Confronts Abu Ghraib*. New York: Hachette Books, 2008.

Kant, Immanuel. *Groundwork of the Metaphysics of Morals*. Translated by Thomas Kingsmill Abbott. Radford, VA: Wilder Publications, 2008.

Koocher, Gerald P. "Ethics and the Invisible Psychologist." *Psychological Services* 6, no. 2 (2009): 97–107.

————. "Speaking against Torture." *Monitor on Psychology* 37, no. 2 (2006): 5.

Larson, Magali. *The Rise of Professionalism: A Sociological Analysis*. Berkeley: University of California Press, 1977.

Lauritzen, Paul. "Torture Warrants and Democratic States: Dirty Hands in an Age of Terror." *Journal of Religious Ethics* 38, no. 1 (2010): 93–112.

Luban, David. "Liberalism, Torture, and the Ticking Bomb." *Virginia Law Review* 91 (2005): 1425–61.

Maurizi, Alex. "Occupational Licensing and the Public Interest." *Journal of Political Economy* 82, no. 2 (1974): 399–413.

May, William F. *Beleaguered Rulers: The Public Obligation of the Professional*. Louisville, KY: Westminster John Knox Press, 2001.

Mayer, Jane. *The Dark Side: The Inside Story of How the War on Terror Turned into a War on American Ideals*. New York: Doubleday, 2008.

McCoy, Alfred. *A Question of Torture*. New York: Metropolis Books, 2006.

Meilaender, Gilbert. "Human Dignity: Exploring and Explicating the Council's Vision." In *Human Dignity and Bioethics: Essays Commissioned by the President's Council on Bioethics*, 253–77. Washington, DC: President's Council on Bioethics, March 2008.

Miles, Steven. *Oath Betrayed: Torture, Medical Complicity, and the War on Terror*. New York: Random House, 2006. Kindle edition.

Milgram, Stanley. *Obedience to Authority.* New York: Harper & Row, 1974.

Mongoven, Ann. "The War on Disease and the War on Terror: A Dangerous Metaphorical Nexus?" *Cambridge Quarterly of Healthcare Ethics* 15, no. 4 (2006): 403–16.

Morgan, Charles A. III, et al. "Symptoms of Dissociation in Humans Experiencing Acute, Uncontrollable Stress: A Prospective Investigation." *American Journal of Psychiatry* 158 (2001): 1239–47.

Oakley, Justin, and Dean Cocking. *Virtue Ethics and Professional Roles.* New York: Cambridge University Press, 2001.

Office of the Surgeon General. *Assessment of Detainee Medical Operations for OEF, GTMO, and OIF.* Falls Church, VA: Office of the Surgeon General, Department of the Army, 2005. Available on the University of Minnesota Human Rights Library website, www1.umn.edu/humanrts/OathBetrayed/Army%20Surgeon%20General%20Report.pdf.

Olson, Brad, and Stephen Soldz. "Positive Illusions and the Necessity of a Bright Line Forbidding Psychologist Involvement in Detainee Interrogations." *Analyses of Social Issues and Public Policy* 7, no. 1 (2007): 45–54.

Olson, Brad, Steven Soldz, and Martha Davis. "The Ethics of Interrogation and the American Psychological Association: A Critique of Policy and Process." *Philosophy, Ethics, and Humanities in Medicine* 3 (January 29, 2008). doi: 10.1186/1747-5341-3-3.

Pagliero, Mario. "What Is the Objective of Professional Licensing? Evidence from the US Market for Lawyers." *International Journal of Industrial Organization* 29, no. 4 (2011): 473–83.

Peltz, Rachel. "Learning from History: An Interview with Robert Jay Lifton." *Psychoanalytic Dialogues* 18 (2008): 710–34.

Physicians for Human Rights. *Experiments in Torture: Evidence of Human Subject Research and Experimentation in the "Enhanced" Interrogation Program.* White paper. June 2010. http://phrtorturepapers.org/?dl_id=9.

Posner, Eric A., and Adrian Vermeule. "Should Coercive Interrogation Be Legal?" *Michigan Law Review* 104 (2006): 671–708.

———. *Terror in the Balance: Security, Liberty, and the Courts.* New York: Oxford University Press, 2007.

Reeder, John P., Jr. "What Kind of Person Could Be a Torturer?" *Journal of Religious Ethics* 38, no. 1 (2010): 67–92.

Rejali, Darius. *Torture and Democracy.* Princeton, NJ: Princeton University Press, 2007.

Rodriguez, Jose, Jr. *Hard Measures.* With Bill Harlow. New York: Simon & Schuster, 2012.

Rosenthal, Joel. "Today's Officer Corps: A Repository of Virtue in an Anarchic World?" *Naval War College Review* 50, no. 4 (1997): 104–11.

Rossiter, Clinton. *Constitutional Dictatorship: Crisis Government in the Modern Democracies.* Princeton, NJ: Princeton University Press, 1948.

Rothchild, Jonathan. "Moral Consensus, the Rule of Law and the Practice of Torture." *Journal of the Society of Christian Ethics* 28, no. 2 (2006): 125–58.

Scarry, Elaine. *The Body in Pain.* New York: Oxford University Press, 1985.

Sherman, Nancy. "Torturers and the Tortured." *South African Journal of Philosophy* 25, no. 1 (2006): 77–88.

———. *The Untold War: Inside the Hearts, Minds, and Souls of Our Soldiers.* New York: W. W. Norton, 2010.

Shue, Henry. "Torture in Dreamland: Disposing of the Ticking Bomb." *Case Western Reserve Journal of International Law* 27, no. 231 (2005): 231–39.

Shumate, Scott, and Randy Borum. "Psychological Support to Defense Counterintelligence Operations." *Military Psychology* 18, no. 4 (2006): 283–96.

Snider, Don. *Dissent and Strategic Leadership of the Military Professions.* Carlisle, PA: Strategic Studies Institute, United States Army War College, February 19, 2008. www.strategicstudiesinstitute.army.mil/pubs/display.cfm?pubID=849.

Snider, Don M., Paul Oh, and Kevin Toner. *The Army's Professional Military Ethic in an Era of Persistent Conflict.* Professional Military Ethics Monograph Series. Carlisle, PA: Strategic Studies Institute, United States Army War College, October 2009. www.strategicstudiesinstitute.army.mil/pubs/display.cfm?pubID=895.

Stout, Jeffrey. *Democracy and Tradition.* Princeton, NJ: Princeton University Press, 2004.

Strawson, P. F. *The Bounds of Sense: An Essay on Immanuel Kant's "Critique of Pure Reason."* London: Methuen, 1966.

Sulmasy, Glenn, and John Yoo. "Challenges to Civilian Control of the Military: A Rational Choice Approach to the War on Terror." *UCLA Law Review* 54, no. 6 (2007): 1–32.

Turner, Lisa. "The Detainee Interrogation Debate and the Legal-Policy Process." *Joint Forces Quarterly* 54 (2009): 40–47.

Waldron, Jeremy. "Torture and Positive Law: Jurisprudence for the White House." *Columbia Law Review* 105, no. 6 (October 2005): 1681–750.

Walzer, Michael. "Political Action: The Problem of Dirty Hands." *Philosophy and Public Affairs* 2, no. 2 (1973): 160–80.

Wilks, Michael. "A Stain on Medical Ethics." *Lancet* 366, no. 9484 (August 6, 2005): 429–31.

Wynia, Matthew K., Stephen R. Latham, Audiey C. Kao, Jessica W. Berg, and Linda L. Emanuel. "Medical Professionalism in Society." *New England Journal of Medicine* 341, no. 21 (November 1999): 1612–16.

Zimbardo, Philip. *The Lucifer Effect.* New York: Random House, 2007.

Index